Good Muslim, Bad Muslim

Good Muslim, Bad Muslim

*America, the Cold War,
and the Roots of Terror*

Mahmood Mamdani

THREE LEAVES PRESS
DOUBLEDAY
New York

THREE
LEAVES
PRESS

PUBLISHED BY DOUBLEDAY
a division of Random House, Inc.

Doubleday is a registered trademark and Three Leaves Press
and colophon are trademarks of Random House, Inc.

Good Muslim, Bad Muslim was originally published in hardcover by
Pantheon Books, a division of Random House, Inc., in 2004. This Three
Leaves Press edition published by special arrangement with Pantheon Books.

Book design by Johanna S. Roebas

The Library of Congress has cataloged the hardcover edition as follows:
Mamdani, Mahmood, [date]
Good Muslim, bad Muslim : America, the cold war, and the roots of terror /
by Mahmood Mamdani.
p.   cm.
Includes index.
ISBN 0-375-42285-4
1. United States—Foreign relations—1945–1989. 2. Cold War.
3. United States—Foreign relations—Afghanistan. 4. Afghanistan—Foreign
relations—United States. 5. United States—Foreign relations—Developing
countries. 6. Developing countries—Foreign relations—United States.
7. Islam and politics—History—20th century. 8. Terrorism—Political
aspects—History—20th century. 9. Drug traffic—Political aspects—
History—20th century. 10. September 11 Terrorist Attacks, 2001—Causes.
I. Title.
E840.M346   2004   320.5'57—dc22   2003063965

ISBN 978-0-385-51537-5

July 2005

First Three Leaves Press Edition

147429898

For

our beloved

Ammy

(1927–2003)

who taught us to love and to stand up for what is right

and

For

Zohran,

and his mates

Nishant, Sahira, Ishaan, Sahil, Shayoni, Delia, Wasim, Muneer,
Evan O, Evan S, Adrian, Justin, Gen, Mike Ezra, Timothy, Tefiro,
Kenneth, Karl, Sundeep, Mongezi, Karan, Liam, Naseef, Abdul,
Nandhi, Nyileti

And all children everywhere
Who will inherit the world we make

Man is a *yes*. . . . *Yes* to life. *Yes* to love. *Yes* to generosity. But man is also a *no*. *No* to scorn of man. *No* to degradation of man. *No* to exploitation of man. *No* to the butchery of what is most human in man: freedom.

Frantz Fanon, *Black Skin, White Masks*

Contents

Acknowledgments xiii

Introduction
Modernity and Violence 3

Chapter One
Culture Talk; or, How Not to Talk About Islam and Politics 17

Chapter Two
The Cold War After Indochina 63

Chapter Three
Afghanistan: The High Point in the Cold War 119

Chapter Four
From Proxy War to Open Aggression 178

Conclusion
Beyond Impunity and Collective Punishment 229

Notes 261
Index 291

Acknowledgments

This book grew out of a talk at Riverside Church on the Upper West Side of New York City in the weeks after 9/11. To bear an identifiably Muslim name then was to be made aware that Islam had become a political identity in post–9/11 America. In the talks that took place—from New York and Chicago in the United States to Kampala and Durban in Africa—I set about trying to understand the modern tendency to politicize culture and, in that context, the forging of political Islam and political terror during the Cold War.

Along that journey, I got invaluable help from three friends, Talal Asad of City University of New York, Tim Mitchell of New York University, and Bob Meister of the University of California at Santa Cruz. If I have made mistakes in spite of their careful guidance, the fault is surely only mine. The same cannot be said of my graduate students who made the journey with me and who

Acknowledgments

sometimes anticipated a discovery, and often joined me in making one: Suren Pillay, Brenda Coughlin, and Yogesh Chandrani gave research assistance beyond the call of duty, even friendship. Finally, many thanks to my editor, Shelley Wanger of Pantheon, for insisting that I leave aside all circumlocutions and face the reader directly.

Without loved ones, writing would surely be too lonely an exercise to bear for long. Mira, as always, continues to nourish with love and inspire by example, teaching how to make things happen, no matter the odds. Ammy, Daddy, and Anis gave Zohran the comfort of home in Kampala and made it possible for me to write for extended stretches.

My mother, Ammy, was an ongoing inspiration for this book. A woman of such strong religious conviction that as a child she went to a Catholic convent school in the mornings and an Islamic *madrassah* in the afternoons; she remained incessantly curious about the world in spite of—maybe because of—the fact that she had no more than four years of formal schooling; she combined two great virtues, to struggle for justice no matter what the odds and to remain fair-minded and full of empathy while doing so. I hope this book will help celebrate Ammy's life and make some of its lessons available to, among others, our son Zohran, and his mates in Kampala and Capetown, New York and New Delhi and Dar-es-Salaam. I close with the comforting thought that, together, they will no doubt remake the world they inherit from us.

New York
December 2003

GOOD MUSLIM,
BAD MUSLIM

Introduction

MODERNITY
AND VIOLENCE

We have just ended a century of violence, one possibly more violent than any other in recorded history: world wars and colonial conquests; civil wars, revolutions, and counterrevolutions. Although the magnitude of this violence is staggering, it does not astound us.

The modern political sensibility sees most political violence as necessary to historical progress. Since the French Revolution, violence has come to be seen as the midwife of history. The French Revolution gave us terror, and it gave us a citizens' army. The real secret behind Napoleon's spectacular battlefield successes was that his army was not made up of mercenaries but patriots, who killed for a cause, inspired by national sentiment—what we have come to recognize as the civic religion of nationalism. Reflecting on the French Revolution, Hegel wrote that man was willing to die for a cause of greater value to him than life itself. Maybe Hegel should have added: man is also willing to *kill* for such a cause. This, I think, is truer of our times than it was in the past.

The modern sensibility is not horrified by pervasive violence. The world wars are proof enough of this. What horrifies our modern sensibility is violence that appears senseless, that cannot be justified by progress.

Such violence gets discussed in two basic ways: in cultural terms for a premodern society and theological terms for a modern society. The cultural explanation always attributes political violence to the absence of modernity. On a world scale, it has been called a clash of civilizations. Locally—that is, when it does not cross the boundary between "the West" and the rest—it is called "communal conflict," as in South Asia, or "ethnic conflict," as in Africa.

Political violence in modern society that does not fit the story of progress tends to get discussed in theological terms. The violence of the Holocaust, for example, is explained as simply the result of evil. Like premodern culture, evil too is understood outside of historical time. There is huge resistance, both moral and political, to exploring the historical causes of the Nazi genocide. By seeing the perpetrators of violence as either cultural renegades or moral perverts, we are unable to think through the link between modernity and political violence.

The Modern State and Political Violence

The year 1492 was the onset of the European Renaissance and the birth of political modernity. It is also the year Christopher Columbus set sail for the New World and the year the armies of King Ferdinand and Queen Isabella conquered the city-state of Granada, then seen as the last Muslim stronghold in western Christendom.

Modernity and Violence

Thus, 1492 stands as a gateway to two related endeavors: one the unification of the nation, the other the conquest of the world.

The unification of the nation led to the birth of the nation-state. Today, political modernity is equated with the beginning of democracy, but nineteenth-century political theorists—notably Max Weber—recognized that political modernity depended upon the centralized state monopolizing violence. The nation-state centralized the formerly dispersed means of violence into a single fist, capable of delivering an awesome blow to all enemies of the nation, internal and external. It was also the political prerequisite for a civil society.

Europe on the threshold of political modernity thought of the nation in terms of culture and race. In the Spain of Ferdinand and Isabella, the nation was first and foremost Christian. The unification of Spain began with an act of ethnic cleansing: 1492 was also the year Ferdinand and Isabella signed the Edict of Expulsion, designed to rid Spain of its Jews. The unified Spanish state gave its Jews a stark choice: baptism or deportation. It is estimated that about seventy thousand Spanish Jews converted to Christianity and remained in Spain, only to be plagued by the Inquisition, which accused them of insincerity. Of the remaining 130,000, an estimated 50,000 fled to the North African and Balkan provinces of the Ottoman empire—where they were warmly welcomed—and about 80,000 crossed the border into Portugal. The expulsion from Spain came at the close of a century that had witnessed the expulsion of Jews from one part of Europe after another. In 1499, seven years after the Edict of Expulsion, the Spanish state gave its Muslims the same choice: convert or leave.

So the history of the modern state can also be read as the history of race, bringing together the stories of two kinds of victims of European political modernity: the internal victims of state building and the external victims of imperial expansion. Hannah Arendt noted this in her monumental study on the Holocaust, which stands apart for one reason: rather than talk about the uniqueness of the Holocaust, Arendt sited it in the imperial history of genocide. The history she sketched was that of European settlers killing off native populations. Arendt understood the history of imperialism through the workings of racism and bureaucracy, institutions forged in the course of European expansion into the non-European world: "Of the two main political devices of imperialist rule, race was discovered in South Africa, and bureaucracy in Algeria, Egypt and India." Hannah Arendt's blind spot was the New World. Both racism and genocide had occurred in the American colonies earlier than in South Africa. The near decimation of Native Americans through a combination of slaughter, disease, and dislocation was, after all, the first recorded genocide in modern history.

The idea that "imperialism had served civilization by clearing inferior races off the earth" found widespread expression in nineteenth-century European thought, from natural sciences and philosophy to anthropology and politics. When Lord Salisbury, the British prime minister, claimed in his famous Albert Hall speech on May 4, 1898, that "one can roughly divide the nations of the world into the living and the dying," Hitler was but nine years old, and the European air was "soaked in the conviction that imperialism is a biologically necessary process which, according to the laws of nature, leads to the inevitable destruction of lower races." Its paradigmatic example was in Tasmania, an island the size of Ireland where European colonists arrived in 1803, the first massacre of natives occurred in 1804, and the last original inhabitant died in 1869. Similar fates awaited, among others, the Maoris of New Zealand and the Herero of German South West Africa.

Modernity and Violence

By the beginning of the twentieth century, it was a European habit to distinguish between civilized wars and colonial wars. The laws of war applied to wars among the civilized nation-states, but laws of nature were said to apply to colonial wars, and the extermination of the lower races was seen as a biological necessity. In *A History of Bombing,* Sven Lindqvist writes that bombing originated as a method of war considered fit for use only against uncivilized adversaries. The first bomb ever dropped from an airplane was Italian, and it exploded on November 1, 1911, in an oasis outside Tripoli in North Africa. The first systematic aerial bombing was carried out by the British Royal Air Force against the Somalis in 1920. In the Second World War, Germany observed the laws of war against the western powers but not against Russia. As opposed to 3.5 percent of English and American prisoners of war who died in German captivity, 57 percent of Soviet prisoners—3.3 million in all—lost their lives. The gassings of Russians by Germans preceded the gassings at Auschwitz—the first mass gassings were of Russian prisoners of war in the southern Ukraine. Russian intellectuals and Communists were the first to be gassed in Auschwitz. The Nazi plan, writes Sven Lindqvist, was to weed out some 10 million Russians, with the remainder kept alive as a slave-labor force under German occupation. When the mass murder of European Jews began, the great Jewish populations were not in Germany but in Poland and Russia, where they made up 10 percent of the total population and up to 40 percent of the urban population "in just those areas Hitler was after." The Holocaust was born at the meeting point of two traditions that marked modern Western civilization: "the anti-Semitic tradition and the tradition of genocide of colonized peoples." The difference in the fate of the Jewish people was that they were to be exterminated as a whole. In that, they were unique—*but only in Europe.*

This historical fact was not lost on intellectuals from the colonies. In his *Discourse on Colonialism* (1951), Aimé Césaire wrote that a Hitler slumbers within "the very distinguished, very humanistic and very Christian bourgeois of the Twentieth century," and yet the European bourgeois cannot forgive Hitler for "the fact that he applied to Europe the colonial practices that had previously been applied only to the Arabs of Algeria, the coolies of India and the Negroes of Africa." "Not so long ago," recalled Frantz Fanon in *The Wretched of the Earth* (1961), "Nazism turned the whole of Europe into a veritable colony."

The first genocide of the twentieth century was the German annihilation of the Herero people in South West Africa in 1904. The German geneticist Eugen Fischer's first medical experiments focused on a "science" of race mixing in concentration camps for the Herero. His subjects were both Herero and the offspring of Herero women and German men. Fischer argued that "mulattoes," Herero-Germans born of mixed parentage, were physically and mentally inferior to their German parents. Hitler read Fischer's book *The Principle of Human Heredity and Race Hygiene* (1921) while he was in prison and later made him rector of the University of Berlin, where Fischer taught medicine. One of Fischer's prominent students was Josef Mengele, who conducted notorious medical experiments at Auschwitz.

The Native's Violence

The link between the genocide of the Herero and the Holocaust was race branding, which was used not only to set a group apart as an enemy but also to annihilate it with an easy conscience. Historians of genocide traditionally have sketched only half a history: the annihilation of the native by the settler. The revolutionary theorist Frantz Fanon has written how such attempts could then trigger the native annihilating the settler. Fanon has come to be regarded as a prophet of violence, following Hannah Arendt's claim that his influence was mainly responsible for growing violence on American campuses in the 1960s. And yet those who came to pay homage to Fanon at his burial hailed him as a humanist. Fanon's critics know him by a single sentence from *The Wretched of the Earth:* "The colonized man liberates himself in and through violence." This was a *description* of the violence of the colonial system, of the fact that violence was central to producing and sustaining the relationship between the settler and the native. It was a *claim* that anticolonial violence is not an irrational manifestation but belongs to the script of modernity and progress, that it is indeed a midwife of history. And last and most important, it was a *warning* that, more than celebrate this turning of the tables, we need to think through the full implications of victims becoming killers.

We find in Fanon the premonition of the native turned perpetrator, of the native who kills not just to extinguish the humanity of the other but to defend his or her own, and of the moral ambivalence this must provoke in other human beings like us. No one understood the genocidal impulse better than this Martinique-born psychiatrist and Algerian freedom fighter. Native violence, Fanon insisted, was the violence of yesterday's victims, the violence of those who had cast aside their victimhood to become masters of their own lives. He wrote:

> He of whom they have never stopped saying that the only language he understands is that of force, decides to give utterance by force. . . . The argument the native chooses has been furnished by the settler, and by an ironic turning

of the tables it is the native who now affirms that the colonialist understands nothing but force.

For Fanon, the proof of the native's humanity consisted not in the willingness to kill settlers but in the willingness to risk his or her own life.

To read Fanon is to understand not only the injury that fuels the violence of the native but also the fear that fuels the violence of the settler. Anyone familiar with the history of apartheid in South Africa would surely recognize that it could not have been simply greed—the wish to hold on to the fruits of conquest—but also fear, the specter of genocide, that stiffened white South African resolve against the winds of change blowing across the African continent. That same specter seemingly also haunts the survivors of the Holocaust in Israel, yesterday's victims turned today's perpetrators.

Before 9/11, I thought that tragedy had the potential to connect us with humanity in ways that prosperity does not. I thought that if prosperity tends to isolate, tragedy must connect. Now I realize that this is not always the case. One unfortunate response to tragedy is a self-righteousness about one's own condition, a seeking proof of one's special place in the world, even in victimhood. One afternoon, I shared these thoughts with a new colleague, the Israeli vice chancellor of the Budapest-based Central European University. When he told me that he was a survivor of Auschwitz, I asked him what lesson he had drawn from this great crime. He explained that, like all victims of Auschwitz, he, too, had said, "Never again." In time, though, he had come to realize that this phrase lent itself to two markedly different conclusions: one was that never again should this happen to *my* people; the other that it should never again happen to *any* people. Between these two interpretations, I suggest nothing less than our common survival is at stake.

9/11

The lesson of Auschwitz remains at the center of post–9/11 discussions in American society. An outside observer is struck by how much American discourse on terrorism is filtered more through the memory of the Holocaust than through any other event. Post–9/11 America seems determined: "Never again." Despite important differences, genocide and terrorism share one important feature: both target civilian populations. To what extent is the mind-set of the perpetrators revealed by the way they frame their victims culturally? Not surprisingly, the debate on this question turns around the relationship between cultural and political identity and, in the context of 9/11, between religious fundamentalism and political terrorism. I have written this book as a modest contribution to this debate. Rather than offer the results of original research, this interpretive essay seeks to explain political events, above all 9/11, in light of *political* encounters—historically shaped—rather than as the outcome of stubborn cultural legacies.

The book is really divided into two parts. The first part consists of a single chapter: chapter 1 offers a critique of the cultural interpretations of politics—what I call Culture Talk—and suggests a different way of thinking about political Islam. It traces the development of different tendencies, including the recent rise of a terrorist movement. The chapters that follow explain how Islamist terror, a phenomenon hitherto marginal, came to occupy center stage in Islamist politics. As such, it provides an alternative interpretation of 9/11. I argue that rather than illustrating a deep-seated clash of civilizations, 9/11 came out of recent history, that of the late Cold War.

I define the late Cold War as lasting from the end of the American war in Vietnam to the fall of the Soviet Union in 1990, with the era of proxy war stretching to the recent war in Iraq. If the war in Vietnam was the last Cold War engagement in which American ground troops directly participated in large numbers, the war in Iraq marks the first post–Cold War American engagement in which that prohibition was fully lifted. Between the two lies an era of proxy wars.

The late Cold War was an era of proxy wars marked by two developments. Both were distinctive initiatives of the Reagan administration's foreign policy. They also point up important similarities between the Reagan and the current Bush administrations, illuminating the mind-set of the "war on terror" after 9/11.

The changes in foreign policy during the Reagan era were responses to the revolutionary overthrow of pro-American dictatorships. The Reagan administration saw these revolutions, particularly the 1979 Sandinista Revolution in Nicaragua and the Islamist Revolution in Iran, as setting a trend of reversals after Vietnam. It was against this backdrop that the Reagan administration concluded that America had been preparing to fight the wrong war, that against the massing of Soviet troops on the plains of Europe, which was likely never to take place. Reagan called on America to wage the war that was already on: the war against yesterday's guerrillas who had come to power as today's nationalists, from southern Africa to Central America. The Reagan administration portrayed militant nationalists as Soviet proxies. The shift in focus made for a shift in strategy and a new name: low-intensity conflict. This initiative was the first distinctive characteristic that marked the foreign policy of the Reagan administration.

The second initiative was the shift from "containment" to "rollback," which called for the subordination of all means to a single end: the total war against the "evil empire." Even though couched in hypermoral language, this venture began as an amoral "constructive engagement" with the apartheid regime in South Africa. As official America held hands with Pretoria, the latter moved to harness political terror as the most effective way to undermine militant nationalist governments in the newly independent Portuguese colonies of Mozambique and Angola. As the battleground of the Cold War shifted from southern Africa to Central America and central Asia in the late seventies, America's benign attitude toward political terror turned into a brazen embrace: both the contras in Nicaragua and later al-Qaeda (and the Taliban) in Afghanistan were American allies during the Cold War. Supporting them showed a determination to win the Cold War "by all means necessary," a phrase that could refer only to unjust means. The result of an alliance gone sour, 9/11 needs to be understood first and foremost as the unfinished business of the Cold War.

To the extent my point of view is shaped by a place, that place is Africa. I was a young lecturer at the University of Dar es Salaam from 1973 to 1979. As the U.S. defeat in Vietnam in 1975 coincided with the collapse of the Portuguese empire, the last European colonial power in Africa, the center of gravity of the Cold War shifted from Southeast Asia to southern Africa. From 1980 when I returned to Makerere University in my hometown of Kampala, Uganda, right up to the end of a three-year stay at the University of Cape Town in South Africa in the late nineties, I participated in ongoing debates about the political violence raging in independent Africa: what were we to make of movements, like Renamo in Mozambique and, increasingly, the Inkatha Freedom Party in

South Africa, that targeted civilian populations rather than military concentrations and became my generation's first experience of political terror? Wary of press and politicians co-opted by the establishment who characterized this form of violence as an unfortunate cultural manifestation—"tribal" "black-on-black" violence—we looked for explanations in the rapidly changing political landscape. On 9/11 I was in New York City where I had moved from Cape Town in 1999. The more I participated in teach-ins and discussions around 9/11, and encountered those who thought it signaled the onslaught of "Islamic terrorism" on the American heartland, the more I was reminded of those cultural explanations I had heard the decade before in southern Africa.

I have no intention of explaining away either political ethnicity or political Islam as the result of a Cold War American conspiracy. Political Islam, like the thinking that champions "tribalism," is more a domestic product than a foreign import. But neither was bred in isolation; both were produced in the encounter with Western power. Political Islam was born in the colonial period. But it did not give rise to a terrorist movement until the Cold War. What particular circumstances made it possible for terrorism to be transformed from an ideological tendency into a political force? There was a common ground that nurtured both "black-on-black" violence in Africa from the mid-seventies and "Islamic terrorism" globally from the early eighties. That common ground was the late Cold War after Vietnam. Even if crafted from local raw material, both political tendencies crystallized as strategies to win the Cold War.

For those worried that I see 9/11 through lenses crafted in an earlier era—the late Cold War in Africa—I can only hope that this perspective will bring fresh illumination to a subject of common concern, without obscuring the ways in which 9/11 has indeed come to mark a turning point for America and the world.

Good Muslim, Bad Muslim

Listening to the public discussion in America after 9/11, I had the impression of a great power struck by amnesia. Acknowledging the epochal significance of the event should not necessarily mean taking it out of a historical and political context. Unfortunately, official America has encouraged precisely this. After an unguarded reference to pursuing a "crusade," President Bush moved to distinguish between "good Muslims" and "bad Muslims." From this point of view, "bad Muslims" were clearly responsible for terrorism. At the same time, the president seemed to assure Americans that "good Muslims" were anxious to clear their names and consciences of this horrible crime and would undoubtedly support "us" in a war against "them." But this could not hide the central message of such discourse: unless proved to be "good," every Muslim was presumed to be "bad." All Muslims were now under obligation to prove their credentials by joining in a war against "bad Muslims."

Judgments of "good" and "bad" refer to Muslim political identities, not to cultural or religious ones. For those who have difficulty thinking of cultural (and now religious) identity as distinct from political identity, don't forget the predicament faced by earlier conscripts of Western power. Was not the secular Jew, first in Europe and America and then in Nazi Germany, compelled to recognize that Western modernity had turned "the Jew" from just a cultural or religious identity to a political one? Was not historical Zionism the response of secular Jews who were convinced that their political choices were limited by this political identity imposed upon them?

There are no readily available "good" Muslims split off from "bad" Muslims, which would allow for the embrace of the former and the casting off of the latter, just as there are no "good" Christians or Jews split off from "bad" ones. The presumption that there are such categories masks a refusal to address our own failure to make a political analysis of our times. My hope is that this book will contribute to such an analysis as a prelude to framing real choices.

Chapter One

CULTURE TALK; OR, HOW NOT TO TALK ABOUT ISLAM AND POLITICS

This moment in history after the Cold War is referred to as the era of globalization and is marked by the ascendancy and rapid politicizing of a single term: culture. During the Cold War, we discussed socioeconomic or political developments, such as poverty and wealth, democracy and dictatorship, as mainly local events. This new understanding of culture is less social than political, tied less to the realities of particular countries than to global political events like the tearing down of the Berlin Wall or 9/11. Unlike the culture studied by anthropologists—face-to-face, intimate, local, and *lived*—the talk of culture is highly politicized and comes in large geo-packages.

Culture Talk assumes that every culture has a tangible essence that defines it, and it then explains politics as a consequence of that essence. Culture Talk after 9/11, for example, qualified and explained the practice of "terrorism" as "Islamic." "Islamic terrorism" is thus offered as both description and explanation of the events of 9/11. It is no longer the market (capitalism), nor the state (democracy), but culture (modernity) that is said to be the dividing line between those in favor of a peaceful, civic existence and those inclined to terror. It is said that our world is divided between those who are modern and those who are premodern. The moderns make culture and are its masters; the premoderns are said to be but conduits. But if it is true that premodern culture is no more than a rudimentary twitch, then surely premodern peoples may not be held responsible for their actions. This point of view demands that they be restrained, collectively if not individually—if necessary, held captive, even unconditionally—for the good of civilization.

In post–9/11 America, Culture Talk focuses on Islam and Muslims who presumably made culture only at the beginning of creation, as some extraordinary, prophetic act. After that, it seems Muslims just conformed to culture. According to some, our culture seems to have no history, no politics, and no debates, so that *all* Muslims are just plain bad. According to others, there is a history, a politics, even debates, and there *are* good Muslims and bad Muslims. In both versions, history seems to have petrified into a lifeless custom of an antique people who inhabit antique lands. Or could it be that culture here stands for habit, for some kind of instinctive activity with rules that are inscribed in early founding texts, usually religious, and mummified in early artifacts?

We need to distinguish between two contrasting narratives of Culture Talk. One thinks of premodern peoples as those who are not yet modern, who are either lagging behind or have yet to embark on the road to modernity. The other depicts the premodern as also the antimodern. Whereas the former conception encourages relations based on philanthropy, the latter notion is productive of fear and preemptive police or military action.

The difference is clear if we contrast earlier depictions of

Africans with contemporary talk about Muslims. During the Cold War, Africans were stigmatized as the prime example of peoples not capable of modernity. With the end of the Cold War, Islam and the Middle East have displaced Africa as the hard premodern core in a rapidly globalizing world. The difference in the contemporary perception of black Africa and Middle Eastern Islam is this: whereas Africa is seen as *incapable* of modernity, hard-core Islam is seen as not only incapable of but also *resistant* to modernity. Whereas Africans are said to victimize themselves, hard-core Muslims are said to be prone to taking others along to the world beyond. There is an interesting parallel between the pre–9/11 debate on terrorism in Africa and the post–9/11 debate on global terrorism. As in the current global debate, African discussions, too, looked mainly or exclusively for internal explanations for the spread of terror. In a rare but significant example that lumped African "tribalists" and Muslim "fundamentalists" together as the enemy, Aryeh Neier, former president of Human Rights Watch and now president of the George Soros–funded Open Society Institute, argued in an op-ed piece in the *Washington Post* that the problem is larger than Islam: it lies with tribalists and fundamentalists, contemporary counterparts of Nazis, who have identified modernism as their enemy.

Premodern peoples are said to have no creative ability and antimodern fundamentalists are said to have a profound ability to be destructive. The destruction is taken as proof that they have no appreciation for human life, including their own. This is surely why Culture Talk has become the stuff of front-page news stories. Culture is now said to be a matter of life and death. This kind of thinking is deeply reminiscent of tracts from the history of modern colonization. This history stigmatizes those shut out of modernity as antimodern because they resist being shut out. It assumes that people's public behavior, particularly their political behavior, can be read from their habits and customs, whether religious or traditional. But could it be that a person who takes his or her religion literally is a potential terrorist? And that someone who thinks of a religious text as metaphorical or figurative is better suited to civic life and the tolerance it calls for? How, one may ask, does the literal reading of sacred texts translate into hijacking, murder, and terrorism?

Two Versions of Culture Talk

Contemporary Culture Talk dates from the end of the Cold War and comes in two versions. It claims to interpret politics from culture, in the present and throughout history, but neither version of Culture Talk is substantially the work of a historian. If there is a founding father of contemporary Culture Talk, it is Bernard Lewis, the well-known Orientalist at Princeton who has been an adviser to the U.S. policy establishment. The celebrated phrase of contemporary Culture Talk—"a clash of civilizations"—is taken from the title of the closing section of Lewis's 1990 article "The Roots of Muslim Rage." Lewis's text provided the inspiration for a second and cruder version, written by Samuel Huntington, a political scientist at Harvard, whose involvement with the U.S. policy establishment dates from the era of the Vietnam War. Whereas Lewis confined his thesis to historical relations between two civilizations he called "Islamic" and "Judeo-Christian," Huntington's reach was far more ambitious: he broadened Lewis's thesis to cover the entire world.

"It is my hypothesis," Huntington proclaimed in an article titled "The Clash of Civilizations?" (1993) in *Foreign Affairs,*

that the fundamental source of conflict in this new world will not be primarily ideological or primarily economic.

Culture Talk

The great divisions among humankind and the dominating source of conflict will be cultural. Nation-states will remain the most powerful actors in world affairs, but the principal conflicts of global politics will occur between nations and groups of different civilizations. The clash of civilizations will dominate global politics. The fault lines between civilizations will be the battle lines of the future.

Huntington's argument was built around two ideas: that since the end of the Cold War "the iron curtain of ideology" had been replaced by a "velvet curtain of culture," and that the velvet curtain had been drawn across "the bloody borders of Islam." Huntington cast Islam in the role of an enemy civilization. From this point of view, Muslims could be only bad.

Huntington was not alone. Several others joined in translating his point of view into a vision broadly shared in hawkish circles of the policy and intellectual establishment. The thrust of the new vision was that the ideological war we have come to know as the Cold War was but a parochial curtain-raiser for a truly global conflict for which "the West" will need to marshal the entire range of its cultural resources. For William Lind, the Cold War was the last in a series of "Western civil wars" that started in seventeenth-century Europe; with the end of the Cold War, he argued, the lines of global conflict become cast in cultural terms. Régis Debray, himself an active participant in the ideological struggles of the Cold War, saw the new era as sharply defined by a "Green Peril"—the color green presumably standing for Islam—far more dangerous than the red scares of yesteryears because it lacks rational self-restraint: "Broadly speaking, green has replaced red as the rising force. . . . The nuclear and rational North deters the nuclear and rational North, not the conventional and mystical South."

The idea of a clash of civilizations, with civilizations marching through history like armed battalions—with neither significant internal debates nor significant exchanges—has been widely discredited. Edward W. Said, the late Palestinian literary scholar who was University Professor at Columbia, forcefully argued for a more historical and less parochial reading of culture, one informed by the idea that the clash is more *inside* civilizations than *between* them: "To Huntington, what he calls 'civilizational identity' is a stable and undisturbed thing, like a room full of furniture in the back of your house."

It is Bernard Lewis who has provided the more durable version of Culture Talk. Lewis both gestures toward history and acknowledges a clash within civilizations. Rather than claim an ahistorical global vision of a coming Armageddon, Lewis thinks of history as the movement of large cultural blocs called civilizations. But Lewis writes of Islamic civilization as if it were a veneer with its essence an unchanging doctrine in which Muslims are said to take refuge in times of crisis. "There is something in the religious culture of Islam," Lewis noted in "The Roots of Muslim Rage,"

> which inspired, in even the humblest peasant or peddler, a dignity and a courtesy toward others never exceeded and rarely equaled in other civilizations. And yet, in moments of upheaval and disruption, when the deeper passions are stirred, this dignity and courtesy toward others can give way to an explosive mixture of rage and hatred which impels even the government of an ancient and civilized country—even the spokesman of a great and ethical religion—to espouse kidnapping and assassination, and try to find, in the life of their Prophet, approval and indeed precedent for such actions.

Lewis elaborated his notion of the doctrinal core of Islam in a book that "was already in page proofs" by 9/11 but was published soon after, provocatively titled *What Went Wrong?* Paraphrasing Hegel's old claim that freedom is the distinctive attribute of Western civilization, Lewis wrote: "To a Western observer, schooled in the theory and practice of Western freedom, it is precisely the lack of freedom . . . that underlies so many of the troubles of the Muslim world." To this, he added the absence of secularism as the second explanation for the yawning gap between contemporary Islam and modernity: until the influence of French revolutionary ideas began percolating into the Middle East in the nineteenth century, Lewis argued, "the notion of a non-religious society as something desirable or even permissible was totally alien to Islam."

It is Bernard Lewis, not Samuel Huntington, who provides the intellectual support for the notion that there are "good" as opposed to "bad" Muslims, an idea that has become the driving force of American foreign policy. Keen to draw an unambiguous conclusion for the policy establishment, Lewis begins by recognizing that "fundamentalism is not the only Islamic tradition" and that "there are others" and that "before this issue is decided there will be a hard struggle." Warning the policy establishment that in this struggle "we of the West can do little or nothing . . . for these are issues that Muslims must decide among themselves," he counsels that "in the meantime"—that is, while Muslims settle their internal accounts—the West needs "to avoid the danger of a new era of religious wars." Whereas Huntington had issued a clarion call for the West to get ready for a clash of civilizations, Lewis has a different point: the West must remain a bystander while Muslims fight their internal war, pitting good against bad Muslims. In spite of this difference, one cannot help but note that both stand as representatives of the official "West."

If Bernard Lewis provides intellectual support for the Bush administration's post–9/11 policy, the return to a roughshod, Cold War–style focus on "rolling back" history is politically more in line with Huntington. Rather than wait for "good" Muslims to triumph over "bad" Muslims, as Lewis counsels, the Bush administration is determined to hasten such a civil war. If necessary, as in Iraq, it is prepared to invade and bring about a regime change intended to liberate "good" Muslims from the political yoke of "bad" ones.

Culture Talk has also turned religion into a political category. Democracy lags in the *Muslim* world, concludes a Freedom House study of political systems in the non-Western world. As if taking a cue from Bernard Lewis, Stephen Schwartz, director of the Islam and Democracy Project for the Foundation for the Defense of Democracies, claims that the roots of terrorism really lie in a sectarian branch of Islam, the Wahhabi. Even the pages of the *New York Times* now include regular accounts distinguishing good from bad Muslims: good Muslims are modern, secular, and Westernized, but bad Muslims are doctrinal, antimodern, and virulent. The self-appointed leaders of "the West," George W. Bush and British prime minister Tony Blair, have visibly stepped back from a Huntington-style embrace of a war between civilizations to a Lewis-style caution against taking on an entire civilization. After Bush's early public flirtation with the idea of an anti-Muslim crusade, both he and Blair have taken to warning audiences about the need to distinguish "good" Muslims from "bad" Muslims. The implication is unmistakable and undisguised: whether in Afghanistan, Palestine, or Pakistan, Islam must be quarantined and the devil exorcized from it by a Muslim civil war.

Lewis opens *What Went Wrong?* with a reductive discussion of the thirteen hundred years since the birth of Islam in the seventh century: "the first thousand years or so after the advent of Islam" were followed by "the long struggle for the reconquest," which "opened the way to a Christian invasion of Africa and Asia." In the beginning, there was "conquest" and then followed "reconquest." The conquest was Islamic, the reconquest Christian. No period in history fits this model of "Christians" confronting "Muslims" better than the time of the Crusades.

One of the best studies of the Crusades is by the Slovenian historian Tomaž Mastnak, who points out that it was at that moment in history that the Muslim became the enemy. When "Christian society became conscious of itself through mobilization for holy war . . . an essential moment in the articulation of self-awareness of the Christian commonwealth was the construction of the Muslim enemy." Mastnak is careful to point out that this was not true of earlier centuries: "When, with the Arab expansion in the seventh and eighth centuries, the Muslims reached the European peninsula, they became in the Latin Christians' eyes one among those pagan, or infidel, barbarians. Among the host of Christian enemies, they were assigned no privileged place."

Militant Christian animosity was initially aimed at all non-Christians; only later did it become focused on Muslims: "It was with the crusade that Palestine ceased to be the Promised Land (*terra repromissionis*) of the Old Testament and became the Holy Land, *terra sancta*." Only with the Crusades did Christendom define a universal enemy and declare a "state of permanent war against the heathen." No longer just another earthly enemy, the Crusades demonized the Muslim as evil incarnate, "the personification of the very religion of the Antichrist." This is why the point of the Crusades was not to convert Muslims but to exterminate them: "The Muslims, the infidels, did not have freedom of choice; they could not choose between conversion and death because they were seen as inconvertible." Their extermination "was preached by the Popes" and also by St. Bernard, who "declared that to kill an infidel was not homicide but 'malicide,' annihilation of evil, and that a pagan's death was a Christian's glory because, in it, Christ was glorified."

Bernard Lewis treats what is actually a series of different historical encounters—the Crusades, 1492, European colonization—as if they were hallmarks of a single clash of civilizations over fourteen hundred years. Rather than recognize that each encounter was fueled by a specific political project—the making of a political entity called "Christendom," the Castilian monarchy's desire to build a nation-state called Spain following its conquest of neighboring territories, modern European imperial expansion, and so on—Lewis claims that these "clashes" were driven by incompatible civilizations. And he assumes that the clashes take place between fixed territorial units that represent discrete civilizations over the fourteen-hundred-year history. To understand the political agenda that drives such civilizational histories, we should question the presumed identity between cultural and political history.

To avoid Lewis's distortions, one needs more details at key historical turning points. Can one, for example, speak of Judeo-Christian civilization over two millennia as does Bernard Lewis? The Israeli cultural historian Gil Anidjar reminds us that Jewish culture in Spain is better thought of as "Arab Jewish"—rather than Judeo-Christian—and that the separation of "Jews from Arabs" did not occur until 1492. Moses Maimonides (1135–1204) wrote *The Guide of the Perplexed*, "the most important work of Jewish philosophy ever written," a text "possibly written in Hebrew script, but 'speaking' to us in Arabic and/or Judeo-Arabic" in al-Andalus. And it was the loss of al-Andalus in 1492 that produced the major text of Jewish mysticism, the *Zohar* and also marked the beginning of the second Jewish diaspora.

It does not make sense to think of culture in political—and therefore territorial—terms. States are territorial; culture is not. Does it make sense to write political histories of Islam that read like histories of places like the Middle East? Or to write political histories of states in the Middle East as if these were no more than political histories of Islam there? We need to think of culture in terms that are both historical and nonterritorial. Otherwise, one is harnessing cultural resources for very specific national and imperial political projects.

Modernity and the Politicization of Culture

Culture Talk does not spring from the tradition of history writing but rather from that of the policy sciences that regularly service political establishments: Bernard Lewis is an Orientalist, and Samuel Huntington a political scientist. Orientalist histories of Islam and the Middle East have been consistently challenged since the 1960s by a diverse group of such intellectuals as Marshall Hodgson and Edward Said, Cheikh Anta Diop and Martin Bernal, Samir Amin and Abdallah Laroui. These thinkers came out of the ranks of the antiwar and anti-imperialist movements of the 1960s, and they were followed by a whole generation of historians. But even if discredited as an intellectual anachronism by two generations of scholarship, the Orientalist histories have managed to rebound.

The key reason lies in the relation between history writing and forms of power, and there are two broad forms of history writing: nationalist and metanationalist. If nationalist history writing has been mainly about giving the nation—a very modern and contemporary political subject—an identifiable and often glorious past,

metanationalist writings have given us equally glorified civilizational histories, locating the nation in a global context.

When the sixteenth-century Italian missionary Matteo Ricci
brought a European map of the world—showing the new discov-
eries in America—to China, he was surprised to find that the Chinese were offended by it. The map put Europe in the center of
the world and split the Pacific, which meant that China appeared
at the right-hand edge of the map. But the Chinese had always
thought of China as literally the "Middle Kingdom," which obvi-
ously should have been in the center of the map. To please his
hosts, Ricci produced another map, one that split the Atlantic,
making China seem more central. In China, maps are still drawn
that way, but Europe has clung to the first type of map. The most
commonly used map in North America shows the United States at
the center of the world, sometimes even splitting the Asian continent in two. Today, the most widely used world map has western
Europe at its center. Based on the Mercator projection, it systematically distorts our image of the world: even though Europe has
approximately the same area as each of the other two peninsulas
of Asia—prepartition India and Southeast Asia—Europe is called
a continent, whereas India is but a subcontinent, and Southeast
Asia is not even accorded that status; at the same time, the area
most drastically reduced in the Mercator projection is Africa.

The civilizational history of "the West" came to a triumphant
climax in the nineteenth century, along with European imperialism. Written from the vantage point of a modern power that had
exploded into global dominance in the centuries following the Renaissance, civilizational history gave "the West" an identity that
marched through time unscathed. From this point of view, "the
West" occupied the center of the global stage, and "the Orient"
was its periphery. Not surprisingly, initial criticism of Eurocentric
history came from scholars whose main focus was the "non-West."

Culture Talk

In the traditional story, as recounted by the University of Chicago historian Marshall Hodgson, "history began in the 'East,'" and "the torch was then passed successively to Greece and Rome and finally to Christians of northwestern Europe, where medieval and modern life developed."

Hodgson should have added that the division of the world into "the West" and "the East," "Europe and Asia" left out a third part—in the words of the Yale historian Christopher Miller, "a blank darkness"—that was said to lack history or civilization because it lacked either great texts or great monuments. This blank darkness comprised Africa, the pre-Columbian Americas, and the lands of the Pacific, excepting, of course, Egypt and Ethiopia—which for this purpose were classified as belonging to Asia. In other words, the notion of "the West" went alongside two peripheries: whereas "the Orient" was visible, Africa and the others were simply blanked out into a historical darkness.

Marshall Hodgson made it a lifelong project to counter the West-centered studies of Islam. He began his classic three-volume study, *The Venture of Islam,* by showing how, throughout history, the notion of "the West" had changed at least three times. "The West" referred "originally and properly to the western or Latin-using half of the Roman empire; that is, to the *west Mediterranean lands.*" After the first change, the term came to refer to "the west European lands generally." But this was not a simple extension, for it excluded "those west Mediterranean lands which turned Muslim." The second shift was from West European lands to peoples, thus incorporating their overseas settlements. Then, there was the third shift as the definition of "the West" was further stretched to include *"all European Christendom."* Whereas the second shift referred to a global western Europe, the third extension referred to a global Europe, western *and* eastern. Thus did the notion of "the West" develop from a geographical location to a racialized notion referring to all peoples of European origin, no matter where they lived and for how long.

Can there be a self-contained history of Western civilization? Historians have been chipping away at this claim in a number of fields, ranging from the development of science to that of society. Hodgson had earlier remarked that the equation of "the West" with "science" had given rise to an absurdity whereby it was presumed that Arabic-writing scientists in the classical age of Islam were simply marking time. Rather than making any original contribution to science, they were presumed simply to be holding up the torch for centuries—until it could be passed on to "the West." The notion that the main role of Arabic-writing scientists was to preserve classical Greek science and pass it on to Renaissance Europe was fortified by Thomas Kuhn's claim that Renaissance science represented a paradigmatic break with medieval science and a reconnection with the science of antiquity. Whereas Kuhn associated the paradigmatic break with the work of Copernicus, recent works in the history of science challenge this presumption. With the advantage of accumulated findings, Otto Neugebauer and Noel Swerdlow, two distinguished historians of science, explored the influence of "astronomers associated with the observatory of Marāgha in northwestern Iran," whose works, written in Arabic, "reached Europe, Italy in particular, in the fifteenth century through Byzantine Greek intermediaries." They concluded in their now-classic 1984 work on the mathematical astronomy of Copernicus: "In a very real sense, Copernicus can be looked upon as, if not the last, surely the most noted follower of the 'Marāgha School.'" The contemporary history of science shows similar rethinkings in other fields, such as anatomy (the pulmonary circulation of blood) and mathematics (decimal fractions). The lacuna in the history of science points to a larger historical gap: the place of

Andalusia—Arabic-writing Spain—in the historical study of the Renaissance.

We have seen that Eurocentric history constructed two peripheries: one visible, the other invisible. Part of the invisible periphery was Africa. The same political project that produced a self-standing history of the West also produced a self-standing history of Africa. Like the notion of "the West," that of Africa was also turned into a racialized object. The difference was that Africa was debased rather than exalted, redefined as the land south of the Sahara, coterminous with that part of the continent ravaged during the slave trade. The scholars who questioned the racialized degradation of Africa at the same time further eroded the production of Eurocentric history.

The reconsideration of African history began with the Senegalese savant, Cheikh Anta Diop, who wrote his major work, *The African Origin of Civilization,* in the 1960s. Diop questioned the racist tendency to dislocate the history of pharaonic Egypt—in which roughly one quarter of the African population of the time lived—from its surroundings, particularly Nubia to the south, thereby denying the African historical identity of ancient Egypt. Diop targeted the cherished heart of the Eurocentric tradition, the classics, which not only cast Greece and Rome as eternal components of "the West" but also stripped Egypt of its historical identity. In the study of classics, Egypt faced a double loss: its connection with Greece in ancient times was reduced to being external and incidental, and its location in Africa was denied historical significance.

Diop's work provided the foundation on which the British scholar Martin Bernal based his monumental two-volume work, *Black Athena: Afroasiatic Roots of Classical Civilization.* Bernal showed the ways in which the main tradition of Egyptology had been shaped by a metanationalist Western way of thinking rooted in the nineteenth-century imperial, particularly, German, imagination. Bernal contrasted this imperial imagination with what Greeks had to say about themselves, particularly about their great historical and civilizational debt to pharaonic Egypt. In particular, he showed how the Greeks' image of themselves as the product of an invasion from Egypt in the south was reversed in the European imperial imagination to portray classical Greece as the product of an Aryan invasion from the north. Bernal also made it clear that Greece, originally a colony of Egypt, was an amalgam of diverse influences, initially African, Phoenician, and Jewish, later northern European. If early classical Egypt is better thought of as an African civilization, classical Greece is better thought of as a Mediterranean—rather than European—civilization.

Edward Said summed up "the principal dogmas of Orientalism" in his majesterial study of the same name. The first dogma is that the same Orientalist histories that portray "the West" as "rational, developed, humane [and] superior," caricature "the Orient" as "aberrant, undeveloped [and] inferior." Another dogma is that "the Orient" lives according to set rules inscribed in sacred texts, not in response to the changing demands of life. The third dogma prescribes "that the Orient is eternal, uniform, and incapable of defining itself; therefore it is assumed that a highly generalized and systematic vocabulary for describing the Orient from a Western standpoint is inevitable and scientifically 'objective.'" And the final dogma is "that the Orient is at the bottom something either to be feared (the Yellow Peril, the Mongol hordes, the brown dominions) or to be controlled (by pacification, research and development, outright occupation whenever possible)."

There is reason to be hugely skeptical of claims that describe civilizations discretely and identify civilizational histories with particular geographies and polities. One has to distinguish between civilization and power. The very notion of an uninterrupted "Western civilization" across linear time is an idea that only arises from the vantage point of the power we know as the West. This power has both a geography and a history: that history stretches from 1492 through the centuries of the slave trade and colonization to the Cold War and after.

Like the history of Western civilization, the history of Arabs is linked to particular political agendas. At times, such a history doubles as a history of "Islam," just as the history of "the West" often doubles as the history of "Christianity." Here, too, the tendency is for cultural identities to get politicized and to take on identities defined by the law.

In its North African colonies, France drew a legal distinction between "Berber" and "Arab." By governing "Berbers" with a "customary law" (*dahir*) and "Arabs" with a religious law, they turned "Berber" and "Arab" into mutually exclusive identities, first legal, then political. The nationalist response was in reality a backlash that reified the identity "Arab," so much so that simply "to acknowledge any distinction between Arabs and Berbers was to risk associating oneself with the French colonial attempt to divide the nation into ethnic enclaves." This response turned the politically charged world of Orientalist culture upside down but failed to change it.

Not surprisingly, who is a Berber and who is not—and what percent of Morocco's population is Berber today—is now a profoundly political question. How else are we to understand wildly differing estimates of Berbers in the Moroccan population, from the BBC's claim of "more than 60%" to estimates of "less than 45%" by Berber scholar Fatima Sadiqi and "about 40%" by

activist-scholar Salem Chaker? One problem with equating political identities and cultural ones is that everything becomes too one-
dimensional. Cultural developments that are amalgams are given
one identity, Arab, as if springing from a single fountainhead. Arabic-
speaking North African Berbers thus become "Arabs" and so the
conquest of Spain by mainly Berber dynasties from Senegambia,
becomes an "Arab" conquest.

Conventional Arab civilizational history has been most effectively questioned by Africans themselves. In 1972, the Sudanese
civil war—already the longest civil war in the history of postcolonial Africa—was the subject of a negotiated settlement in Addis
Ababa. All those involved in the civil war—the power in the north,
the rebels in the south, and the range of foreign states and interests
that lined up behind either side—agreed that the civil war had pit-
ted "Arabs" in the north against "Africans" in the south. The presumption that the political adversaries represented two distinct
cultural identitites, "Arab" and "African," was challenged by a
group of northern and southern Sudanese intellectuals who came
to control the Ministry of Foreign Affairs when a coalition government came to power. In a book written in 1973 and presented
to the Organization of African Unity (OAU) at its tenth anniversary, they put forth a radically different perspective on the history
of Sudan, one that distinguished its cultural from its political history. The fact that the power that came to rule Sudan after the fifteenth century defined itself as "Arab" was no reason to identify
the culture of the period as "Arab." Those who did so assumed
that the Sudanese culture was a result of a one-sided assimilation
and deracination of native Sudanese to foreign Arab. Instead, the
authors argued that the complexity of this culture could best be
understood as the outcome of a many-sided "integration" of its
multiple and different ingredients:

Afro-Arab integration in the North tended to be referred to as Arabization. To the extent that Arab symbols of identification, especially their language and religion, have been highlighted over and above their African equivalents, this characterization may be justified, but the process involved more give-and-take than the term "Arabization" would adequately reflect. A significant degree of African-ization of the Arab element also took place.

The point is that even if political identities are singular, cultural identities tend to be cumulative.

Identities shift and histories get rewritten as a result of chang-ing political agendas. The aftermath of civil conflicts often pre-sents us with conflicting histories, each representing the point of view of a contending power in an unstable political context. Wherever adversaries resolve to live together in a single political community—as did Arab and African in 1972 Sudan, Hutu and Tutsi in postgenocide Rwanda, or black and white in postapartheid South Africa—an acute need for a new history is felt. Not surpris-ingly, none of these places has such a readily available history.

The history of "the West" also underwent a fundamental revi-sion in the aftermath of the Holocaust. In post-Holocaust history Judaism has been recast and the Jewish people have gone from being a prominent other who lived inside Europe to being an in-tegral part of Europe. Contrast the post-Holocaust notion of "Judeo-Christian" civilization with pre-Holocaust notions, equally entrenched, about a Christian civilization that had excluded Euro-pean Jews. This, for example, is how the nineteenth-century French philologist Ernest Renan distinguished Semites from Caucasians:

> One sees that in all things the Semitic race appears to us to be an incomplete race, by virtue of its simplicity. This

race—if I dare use the analogy—is to the Indo-European family what a pencil sketch is to painting; it lacks that variety, that amplitude, that abundance of life which is the condition of perfectibility. Like those individuals who possess so little fecundity that, after a gracious childhood, they attain only the most mediocre virility, the Semitic nations experienced their fullest flowering in their first age and have never been able to achieve true maturity.

The shift of perspective after the Second World War that relocated Judaism and Jews to the heart of Western history and Western civilization signifies no less than a sea change in consciousness. The notion of a Judeo-Christian civilization crystallized as a post-Holocaust antidote to anti-Semitism. In the same way, I propose to distinguish between fundamentalism as a religious identity and political identities that use a religious idiom, such as political Christianity and political Islam, which are political identities formed through direct engagement with modern forms of power.

Modernity, Fundamentalism, and Political Islam

"Fundamentalism" is, in fact, a term invented in 1920s Protestant circles in the United States. Like conservatism, fundamentalism is a latecomer on the scene. Just as conservatism was a political response to the French Revolution and not a throwback to premodern times, fundamentalism, too, was a reaction within religion to its changing political circumstances. There is a difference between Christian fundamentalism, which emerged in the 1920s in America, and political Christianity, a phenomenon that arose in America after the Second World War.

To speak of fundamentalist Islam, at least in the case of mainstream Sunni Islam, is misleading. Since mainstream Islam did not develop a religious hierarchy parallel to a secular state hierarchy, as historical Christianity did, it lacks the problem of secularism. "Fundamentalism" can be applied to those forms of Shi'a Islam that have indeed developed a religious hierarchy. When this book focuses on political movements that speak the language of religion, they will be referred to as political Islam and not Islamic fundamentalism.

This book will also question those writers who speak of "religious fundamentalism" as a political category and associate it with "political terrorism." "Fundamentalism" as a religious phenomenon has to be distinguished from those political developments that are best described as political Christianity and political Islam. Religious "fundamentalism" is akin to a countercultural, not a political, movement. The problem with using the term "fundamentalism" to describe all such movements is that it tends to equate movements forged in radically different historical and political contexts, and obscures their doctrinal differences, including the place of violence in religious doctrine. This is why after explaining the historical context in which Christian "fundamentalism" emerged, and distinguishing it from political Christianity, I won't use the term "fundamentalism" to describe countercultural movements inside Islam or other religions. And I question the widespread assumption that every political movement which speaks the language of religion is potentially terrorist.

The clue to the nature of a political movement lies not in it's language but in its agenda. Just as the onset of political Christianity after the Second World War in America produced movements as diverse as the civil-rights and the Christian-right movements, so did the onset of political Islam during the Cold War give rise to movements with diverse, even contradictory, political agendas.

Moderate movements organize and agitate for social reform within the existing political context. Radical movements organize to win state power, having concluded that the existing political situation is the main obstacle to social reform. There are two kinds of radical movements, society-centered and state-centered: whereas society-centered radicals link the problem of democracy in society with the state, state-centered radicals pose the problem of the state at the expense of democracy in society. It is state-centered political Islam that has been the harbinger of Islamist political terror.

Christian Fundamentalism and Political Christianity

The term "fundamentalism" was invented in 1920 by the Rev. Curtis Lee Laws and was immediately taken up as an honorific by his Baptist and Presbyterian colleagues who swore to do "battle royal for the fundamentals of the faith." Karen Armstrong has located this phenomenon in a rapidly growing set of American debates over the validity of biblical literalism then being taken up by the increasingly powerful and entrenched conservative Republicans who supported it. In 1910, the Presbyterians of Princeton defined a set of five dogmas standing for the infallibility of Scripture: (1) the inerrancy of Scripture, (2) the virgin birth of Christ, (3) Christ's atonement for our sins on the cross, (4) his bodily resurrection, and (5) the objective reality of his miracles. Between 1910 and 1915, they issued a series of twelve paperback pamphlets called *The Fundamentals,* dispatching some three million copies to every pastor, professor, and theology student in America. Their next step was to try to expel liberals; the fiercest institutional battles were fought where fundamentalists were the strongest, among Baptists and Presbyterians.

Karen Armstrong concludes her historical discussion of fundamentalism with the observation that fundamentalism is not a throwback to a premodern culture but a response to an *enforced* secular modernity. In other words, there would be no fundamentalism without modernity. Furthermore, fundamentalism emerged as a struggle inside religion, not between religions, as a critique of liberal forms of religion that religious conservatives saw as accommodating an aggressive secular power.

Begun in the late nineteenth century, these debates rapidly turned into contests for power and influence across the institutional landscape of America, in universities and public schools, seminaries and churches, elections and the press, courts and legislatures. The outcome was mixed and unstable: fundamentalists won partial legislative victories in several states. Then they won a full victory in 1925 when the Tennessee legislature passed a law that made it a crime to teach evolution in state-funded schools. A few months later, the law was challenged in court when a young biology teacher, John T. Scopes—having decided to strike a blow for free speech against religious convention—confessed that he had broken the law when substituting for his school principal in a biology class.

Brought to trial in July 1925, Scopes was defended by the great rationalist lawyer Clarence Darrow, sent by the American Civil Liberties Union (ACLU). On the side of the law was the well-known Democratic politician and Presbyterian leader William Jennings Bryan, who had already launched a crusade against the teaching of evolution in schools. The Scopes trial not only invoked important principles of liberal democracy against one another, it also made for a public debate on the dichotomy in modern Western thinking. If Darrow claimed to stand for free speech, Bryan championed "common sense" as understood by ordinary people. If Darrow stood for progress, Bryan contended that there was a link between

Darwinist theories of progress and the German militarism that had surfaced in the carnage of the First World War. Known for the lecture with which he had toured the United States, "The Menace of Darwinism," Bryan argued that the notion that the strong could or should survive had "laid the foundation for the bloodiest war in history." He warned that "the same science that manufactured poisonous gases to suffocate soldiers is preaching that man has a brutal ancestry" and is "eliminating the miraculous and the supernatural from the Bible." In the final analysis, though, the trial provided a public spectacle of a historic "contest between God and Science."

Put on the stand by Darrow, Bryan was forced to concede that a literal interpretation of the Bible—holding, for example, that the world was six thousand years old and created in six days—was not possible. Bryan was ridiculed publicly and died a few days after the trial, and Darrow emerged "the hero of clear rational thought." Even though the fundamentalists won the legal battle, they lost the cultural one. Susan Harding, writing in *The Book of Jerry Falwell: Fundamentalist Language and Politics,* comments on how the triumph of modernism at the same time involved a caricature of "fundamentalism":

> The modern point of view in America emerged in part from its caricature of conservative Protestants as Fundamentalists. They were the "them" who enabled the modern "us". You cannot reason with them. They actually believe the Bible is literally true. They are clinging to traditions. They are reacting against rapid social change. They cannot survive in a modern world. . . . Before the Scopes trial, it was unclear which of the opposed terms, Fundamentalist or Modern, would be the winner and

which the loser, which was superior and which was inferior, which term represented the universal and the future and which the residual, that which was passing away.

Derided as fundamentalists, conservative Protestants were humiliated by the outcome of the Scopes trial, which marked the beginning of their exile from American public life. Leaving their denominations, they founded new organizations. They disavowed social reform, as they did all modern forms of sociability. The fundamentalist counterculture was typified by Bob Jones University, founded in 1927. The founder, Bob Jones, was no intellectual, but an evangelist who wanted a "safe" school, that taught liberal arts alongside "commonsense Christianity"—at least one Bible course a semester, compulsory chapel attendance, strict social rules that banned interracial dating on campus, and a code of conduct that defined disobedience and disloyalty as "unpardonable sins." Bob Jones University decided not to seek academic accreditation, thereby retaining tighter control over admissions, curriculum, and library resources. By their actions, if not by admission, they seemed to accept the secular caricature of religious conservatives as fundamentalists stuck in time, as premodern people unfit for modern cultural and political life in a secular America.

It took three decades for religious conservatives to return to public life, and that return happened in two separate but connected waves. The first wave followed the Second World War and was spearheaded by "evangelicals" who renounced the separatism championed by fundamentalists, arguing that "the duty of saving souls in this rotten civilization demanded some degree of cooperation with other Christians, whatever their beliefs." The founding act of the evangelical movement was the formation in 1942 of the National Association of Evangelicals (NAE), a public lobby on a par with the National Council of Churches, which was affiliated with the Liberal World Council of Churches. With the arrival of television in the 1950s, young "televangelists" such as Billy Graham, Rex Humbard, and Oral Roberts replaced old traveling revivalist preachers and formed their own broadcasting empires and publishing houses. Televangelists started the national "prayer breakfast movement" that "rapidly gathered members of Congress and preachers, and evangelist Billy Graham became the spiritual counselor of choice for the post-war generation of U.S. presidents."

The second wave came on the heels of *Roe v. Wade,* the 1973 Supreme Court decision that affirmed abortion as a woman's right, which religious conservatives saw as a historic defeat. Taking a cue from southern black churches, which had dramatically and successfully entered public life at the helm of the civil-rights movement, fundamentalists resolved to shed the mainstream moderation of evangelicals for an equally bold leadership. Speaking on the "Nebraska tragedy" at a 1982 conference, Jerry Falwell challenged the new Christian right to breach the line of separation between religion and politics and to muster the "kind of backbone to stand up for their freedom that Civil Rights people had."

Their quarantine had lasted nearly half a century. The return of "fundamentalism" to American public life was unabashedly political and was at first associated with mass mobilization of white Protestant Christians. The movement's most visible leaders were national televangelists—Jerry Falwell, Jim and Tammy Faye Bakker—who were also key in forming organizations with an explicitly political agenda: the Moral Majority, the Religious Roundtable, and Christian Voice. When Falwell founded the Moral Majority in 1979, he "rode piggyback on networks of fundamentalist Baptist churches." He called on Christians to change history.

The idea that "religion and politics don't mix," he said, "was invented by the devil to keep Christians from running their own country." As conservative Protestants rushed into the Moral Majority, they "tore up a tacit contract with modern America" not to mix Bible-believing Protestant rhetoric with day-to-day politics. Falwell's Moral Majority sermons were known as jeremiads. Named after Jeremiah, the Old Testament prophet, a jeremiad "laments the moral condition of a people, foresees cataclysmic consequences, and calls for dramatic moral reform and revival." In his jeremiads, Jerry Falwell defined abortion as "the biological holocaust," AIDS as "a judgment of God against America for endorsing immorality," and "God's absolute opposition to abortion and homosexuality" as part of the "litmus tests of Bible truth."

Protestant fundamentalists had several victories in the last decades of the twentieth century. They were able to make sure that Arkansas and Louisiana passed bills to ensure that equal time was given in the school curriculum to the literal teaching of Genesis alongside Darwinian evolution. Their most notable achievement, though, was the blocking of the Equal Rights Amendment. Phyllis Schlafly, a Roman Catholic leader whose "Eagle Forum" often held joint events with the Moral Majority, chastised feminism as a "disease," the cause of the world's illness. Ever since Eve disobeyed God and sought her own liberation, she said, feminism had brought sin into the world and with it "fear, sickness, pain, anger, hatred, danger, violence, and all varieties of ugliness." Though thirty of thirty-two required states had voted for the Equal Rights Amendment by 1973, Christian right activists were able to halt its momentum: Nebraska, Tennessee, Kentucky, Indiana, and South Dakota all reversed their previous votes for the amendment.

As early as the mid-1970s, George Gallup, Jr., had polled Americans about their religious views and found that more than one third—that is, more than fifty million adult Americans—described themselves as "born again," defined as having experienced "a turning point in your life when you committed yourself to Jesus Christ." Jimmy Carter was America's first "born-again" president. Ronald Reagan was the second, and George W. Bush is the third. Presidential candidate Reagan embraced the Christian right publicly when he spoke at the National Religious Broadcasters Convention in 1980, hosted that year by Jerry Falwell's Thomas Road Baptist Church. Later that year, the Christian right organized a march of several hundred thousand born-again Christians on the Washington Mall for a "Washington for Jesus" rally. Three years later, Reagan boldly introduced the language of self-righteousness, of "good" and "evil," to American postwar politics when he told the NAE that the Soviet Union was an "evil empire." By the time of the 1992 Republican national convention in Houston, the religious right showed strong evidence of having consolidated its electoral strength. The party platform included two new planks: one unequivocally opposed abortion under any circumstance, the other denounced the Democrats' support for gay-rights legislation. In his speech on the opening night of the convention, Patrick Buchanan warned of a coming "religious war" that would plague the United States from within: "It is a cultural war, as critical to the kind of nation we shall be as the Cold War itself, for this war is for the soul of America."

Jerry Falwell had been right about the civil-rights movement: it did represent a dramatic and successful reentry of religion into politics. The civil-rights and the Christian-right movements illustrate two different forms of political Christianity in the modern world. The contrast between them also shows that the involvement of religious movements in politics is not *necessarily* reactionary.

Islamic Reformism and Political Islam

Long before political Islam appeared in the twentieth century, Islamic reformers had felt that colonialism was the key challenge facing contemporary Muslims. The question was posed squarely by Jamal al-Din al-Afghani (1839–1897), famous as Ernest Renan's protagonist in mid-nineteenth-century Paris. When Renan published a piece on "Islam and Science" in *Journal des Débats* (March 29, 1883), al-Afghani responded in the same journal (May 18, 1883). Renan published a rejoinder the very next day after al-Afghani's response, acknowledging what a great impression al-Afghani had made on him and praising him as a fellow rationalist and infidel. In his lecture, Renan had claimed that "early Islam and the Arabs who professed it were hostile to the scientific and philosophic spirit, and that science and philosophy had only entered the Islamic world from non-Arab sources." Al-Afghani's response was to challenge Renan's racist assumptions—that the Arabs and/or Islam were hostile to science—and in its place argue a surprisingly modern case, that science, as philosophy, develops everywhere over time.

Al-Afghani had traveled widely outside his native Iran, from India in the east to France in the west, before he came to Egypt. His traditional *madrassah* education had included *fiqh* (jurisprudence) alongside *falsafah* (philosophy) and *irfan* (mysticism). His Indian experience both convinced al-Afghani of the future importance of modern science and mathematics and exposed him to Britain's brutal repression of the 1857–58 anticolonial revolt in India. Whereas early-nineteenth-century Islamic thinkers who embraced progress tended to be enamored with Western modernity and saw Britain and France as benign bearers of progress, al-Afghani highlighted modernity's *contradictory* impact. His religious vision came to be informed by a very modern dilemma. On the one hand, Muslims needed modern science, which they would have to learn from Europe. On the other, this very necessity was proof "of our inferiority and decadence," for "we civilize ourselves by imitating the Europeans." Al-Afghani had located the center of this historical dilemma in a society that had been subjected to colonialism: if being modern meant, above all, free rein for human creativity and originality, how could a colonial society modernize by imitation?

This was also a debate about colonialism and independence. Not surprisingly, forward-looking Islamic thinkers looked within Islamic tradition for sources of innovation, renewal, and change. Even if both reformers and radicals spoke the language of Islam, they looked to doctrine and history not just for continuity but also for renewal, and so they provided different answers to the question of how to confront Western modernity and global dominance. The main lines of demarcation in the twentieth century were worked out through debates in three different countries: India, Egypt, and Iran.

This process was completely different from the earlier development of Christian fundamentalism and political Christianity. Unlike Christianity, mainstream Islam has no institutionalized religious hierarchy; it has a religious clergy, but not one organized parallel to the hierarchy of the state. There is a major debate on the significance of this historical difference. Reinhard Schulze has argued that the absence of a conflict between secular and religious hierarchies is why the problem of secularism does not appear in Islam and why Islamic religious movements are not necessarily antisecular. In contrast, Bernard Lewis claims that the absence of a clear line of demarcation between the religious and the secular indicates the absence of secular thought in Islam. However, Schulze points out that modern Islamic discourse is largely secular, concerned more with contemporary political and social issues than with a spiritual concern with salvation or the hereafter, precisely because Islamic societies were able to secularize within Islam, rather than in opposition to it.

Whereas the development of a political Christianity in the United States was mainly the work of a "fundamentalist" religious clergy—such as Jerry Falwell, Pat Robertson, and others—the development of political Islam has been more the work of non-clerical political intellectuals such as Muhammad Iqbal and Mohammed Ali Jinnah in colonial India, and Abul A'la Mawdudi, Sayyid Qutb, and Ali Shariati in postcolonial Pakistan, Egypt, and Iran respectively. The glaring exception was Ayatollah Khomeini. The secular discourse in Iran has tended to resemble that in western Christianity precisely because only in revolutionary Iran has clerical power received constitutional sanction. Whereas fundamentalist clergy were the pioneers of political Christianity, the pioneers of political Islam were not the religious *ulama* (scholars) but political intellectuals with an exclusively worldly concern. This is another reason why it makes more sense to speak of political Islam—the preferred designation in the Arab world for this movement—than of Islamic fundamentalism, the term most often used in post–9/11 America.

The split between religious ulama and political intellectuals was evident as early as the anticolonial movement in India in the first half of the twentieth century. There, religious and political conservatism did not necessarily go hand in hand: the intellectuals, not the ulama, pioneered the development of Islamist political movements, ultimately championing a call for a separate homeland for Indian Muslims, Pakistan. Contrary to what we might expect, the conservative ulama remained inside the secular Indian

National Congress, whereas modernist secular intellectuals called for an Islamic polity, at first autonomous, then independent. Whereas the ulama made clear distinctions between Islam as a cultural and religious identity and various political identities that Muslims may espouse, secular intellectuals came to insist that Islam was not just a religious or cultural identity; it had become a political identity.

The Indian experience reveals that those who called for nationalist politics were not always progressive, and those who championed religious political nationalism were not all reactionary. The two camps were not divided by the line between democracy and authoritarianism. The poet Muhammad Iqbal and the politician Mohammed Ali Jinnah, both spokespersons for the political rights of Muslims, were determinedly secular in orientation. Iqbal, considered the spiritual founder of Pakistan, was among the few Muslim intellectuals who rejoiced in 1922 when Turkey abolished the Ottoman Khilafat, in effect severing any relationship between the state and religion. He called for the institution of *ijtihad* (legal interpretation) to be modernized and democratized: he argued that the law should be interpreted by a body elected by the community of Muslims, the *umma,* and not the ulama. Jinnah, considered the political founder of Pakistan, was similarly determined that independent Pakistan must have a secular constitution, guaranteeing separation between the state and religion and due protection for the rights of minorities.

The shift from a reformist to a radical agenda in political Islam is best understood in the context of the transition from colonialism to postcolonialism, and can be highlighted by the history of a single mass organization, the Society of Muslim Brothers, in Egypt. The society was founded in March 1928 when Hassan al-Banna, a young teacher inspired by the ideas of al-

Afghani, among others, heard a plea for action from workers in the town of Ismailiyyah. Echoing al-Afghani, he argued that Muslims must draw on their own historical and cultural resources instead of imitating other peoples, as if they were "cultural mongrels." The six-point program of action that al-Banna devised focused on creating an extensive welfare organization and disavowed violence.

It was the defeat of Arab armies in 1948 and the subsequent creation of the state of Israel that convinced the society to expend its energies beyond welfare to armed politics: Hassan al-Banna called for the formation of a battalion to fight in Palestine. Said to be a state within a state, with its own "armies, hospitals, schools, factories and enterprises," the society was banned in Egypt on December 6, 1948, and relegalized in 1951. When young army officers led by Gamal Abdel Nasser came to power in 1952, the society gave them full support. But the society soon split with Nasser and sided with those who called on the military to recognize the freedom to form political parties and to hand over power to a civilian government. Nasser moved to arrest those calling for a civilian order; more than one thousand society members were arrested. In Nasser's prisons, some of them abandoned their vision of reform and created a new and potentially violent version of political Islam. If the reform vision was identified with the thought of Hassan al-Banna in the formative period of the society, the extremist turn was inspired by the pen of Sayyid Qutb (1906–1966), writing in prison. The experience of such brutal repression under a secular government was one influence shaping the birth of a radical orientation in Egyptian Islamist thought. The second influence, a more theoretical one, came from Marxism-Leninism, already the most important alternative to political Islam in intellectual debates on how best to confront a repressive secular state that had closed off all possibilities of democratic change.

Sayyid Qutb is the most well known among the intellectual pioneers of radical political Islam, a movement that now stands for a radically reformulated notion of *jihad,* a doctrine shared by all Muslims, and now hotly contested. The debate around radical political Islam is thus increasingly a debate on the meaning of "jihad." Concern for the umma, the Muslim community, is part of the five pillars *(rukn)* of Islam and is binding on every Muslim. The Koran insists that a Muslim's first duty is to create a just and egalitarian society in which poor people are treated with respect. This demands a jihad (literally, effort or struggle) on all fronts: spiritual and social, personal and political. Scholars of Islam distinguish between two broad traditions of jihad: *al-jihad al-akbar* (the greater jihad) and *al-jihad al-asghar* (the lesser jihad). The greater jihad, it is said, is a struggle against weaknesses of self; it is about how to live and attain piety in a contaminated world. Inwardly, it is about the effort of each Muslim to become a better human being. The lesser jihad, in contrast, is about self-preservation and self-defense; directed outwardly, it is the source of Islamic notions of what Christians call "just war," rather than "holy war." Modern Western thought, strongly influenced by Crusades-era ideas of "holy war," has tended to portray jihad as an Islamic war against unbelievers, starting with the conquest of Spain in the eighth century. Tomaž Mastnak has insisted, "Jihad cannot properly be defined as holy war": "Jihad is a doctrine of spiritual effort of which military action is only one possible manifestation; the crusade and jihad are, strictly speaking, not comparable." At the same time, political action is not contradictory to jihad. Islam sanctions rebellion against an unjust ruler, *whether Muslim or not,* and the lesser jihad can involve a mobilization for that social and political struggle.

Historically, the practice of the lesser jihad as central to a "just struggle" has been occasional and isolated, marking points of crisis in Islamic history. After the first centuries of the creation of the Islamic states, there were only four widespread uses of jihad as a mobilizing slogan—until the Afghan jihad of the 1980s. The first was by the Kurdish warrior Saladin in response to the conquest and slaughter of the First Crusade in the eleventh century.

The second widespread use was in the Senegambia region of West Africa in the late seventeenth century. In the second half of the fifteenth century, Senegambia had been the first African region to come into contact with the Atlantic trading system. By the second half of the seventeenth century, the slave trade had become the principal business of European powers on the African coast. One of its main effects was widespread violence in day-to-day life. Among those who sold slaves were Islamic rulers in the region. The crisis was felt most deeply in Berber society, which was caught in a pincer movement between Arab armies closing in from the north and the expanding frontiers of the European slave trade in the south.

Militant Islam began as a movement led by Sufi leaders (*marabout*) intent on unifying the region against the negative effects of the slave trade. The first War of the Marabout began in 1677 in the same area that had given rise to the eleventh-century Al-Moravid movement. The difference was that whereas the Al-Moravids had moved north, ultimately to conquer Spain, the marabout moved south. The second War of the Marabout culminated with the Muslim revolution in the plateau of Futa Jallon in 1690. Among the Berbers of the north and the peoples of the south, militant Islam found popular support for jihad against Muslim aristocracies selling their own subjects to European slave traders. The leaders of the revolution in Futa Jallon set up a federation divided into nine provinces, with the head of each appointed a general in the jihad. When the last of the revolutionary leaders died in 1751, the leadership passed from the religious marabout to commanders in the army. The new military leaders began an aggressive policy targeting neighbors and raiding for slaves—all under the guise of a jihad. The Muslim revolutions that had begun with the first War of the Marabout had come full circle in the space of eighty years: from leading a popular protest against the generalized violence of the slave trade, they founded a new state whose leaders then joined the next round of slave trading.

The third time jihad was widely waged as a "just war" was in the middle of the eighteenth century in the Arabian peninsula, proclaimed by Muhammad Ibn Abdul Wahhab (1703–1792), who gave his name to a contemporary doctrine identified with the House of Saud, Wahhabism. Ibn Wahhab's jihad was declared in a colonial setting, on an Arab peninsula that had been under Ottoman control from the sixteenth century. It was not a jihad against unbelievers. Its enemies included Sunni Muslim Ottoman colonizers and Shi'a "heretics," whereas its beneficiaries were a newly forged alliance between the ambitious House of Saud and the new imperial power on the horizon, Great Britain.

The fourth widespread practice of jihad as an armed struggle was in the Sudan when the anticolonial leader, Muhammad Ahmed (1844–1885), declared himself al-Mahdi (the Messiah) in 1881 and began to rally support against a Turko-Egyptian administration that was rapidly becoming absorbed into an expanding British empire. The battle for a jihad in this context was a battle against a colonial occupation that was both Muslim (Turko-Egyptian) and non-Muslim (British). Al-Mahdi was spectacularly successful as the organizer of the revolt. Armed with no more than spears and swords, the Mahdists (followers of al-Mahdi) won battle after battle, in 1885 reaching the capital, Khartoum, where they killed

Charles Gordon, the British general and hero of the second Opium War with China (1856–1860), who was then governor in the Turko-Egyptian administration. So long as they fought a hated external enemy, the Mahdists won widespread support in all regions. But once the victorious al-Mahdi moved to unite different regions and create a united Sudan under a single rule, the anticolonial coalition disintegrated into warring factions in the north—where Messianic interpretations of Islam fought it out against Sufi (mystical) ones—and a marauding army of northern slavers in the south. As the war of liberation degenerated into slave raids, anarchy, famine, and disease reigned. It is estimated that the population of Sudan fell from around 7 million before the Mahdist revolt to somewhere between 2 and 3 million after the fall of the Mahdist state in 1898. As in Saudi Arabia and West Africa in previous centuries, the experience of Sudan also showed that the same jihad that had begun as the rallying cry of a popular movement could be turned around by those in power—at the expense of its supporters.

Whereas an armed jihad was not known in the nine decades preceding the Afghan jihad of the 1980s, the *call* for one in radical Islamist thought can be traced to two key thinkers at the beginning of the Cold War: the Pakistani journalist and politician Abul A'la Mawdudi, whose work began to be published in Egypt in 1951, and Sayyid Qutb. Mawdudi (1903–1979) appeared at a moment when the ulama, organized as the Jam'iyat-i-Ulama-i-Hind (Society of the Ulama of India), were supporting a multireligious, decentralized yet united India against the demand, led by political intellectuals, for the creation of Pakistan. As we have seen, Muhammad Iqbal had envisioned Muslim political identity not in terms of a nation-state, but as a borderless cultural community, the *umma*. The irony was that though the formation of Pakistan gave its Muslim inhabitants self-determination, this was as residents of a common territory and not as an umma. Instead of being the profound critique of territorial nationalism and the nation-state that Muhammed Iqbal had intended it to be, Pakistan was a territorial nation as banal as any other nation preoccupied with building its own state. Mawdudi seized upon this contradiction in his appeal to postcolonial Islamist intellectuals. Mawdudi claimed that Pakistan ("the land of the pure") was still Na-Pakistan (either "not yet the land of the pure" or "the land of the impure"). For Mawdudi, the Islamic state could not just be a territorial state of Muslims; it had to be an ideological state, an *Islamic* state. To realize that end, he established Jamaat-i-Islami (the Islamic Community) in Karachi in 1941 and had himself confirmed as its emir.

Key to Mawdudi's thought was centralized power and jihad as the ultimate struggle for the seizure of state power. He defined "the ultimate objective of Islam to abolish the lordship of man over man and bring him under the rule of the one God," with jihad as its relentless pursuit: "To stake everything you have—including your lives—to achieve this purpose is called Jihad. . . . So, I say to you: if you really want to root out corruption now so widespread on God's earth, stand up and fight against corrupt rule; take power and use it on God's behalf. *It is useless to think you can change things by preaching alone.*" (italics mine) With both eyes focused on the struggle for power, Mawdudi redefined the meaning of *Din* (religion) in a purely secular way: "Acknowledging that someone is your ruler to whom you must submit means that you have accepted his Din. . . . Din, therefore, actually means the same thing as state and government." He also secularized Islam, equating it not with other religions but with political ideologies that seek the conquest of the state, such as popular sovereignty or monarchy or, above all, Communism: "A total Din, whatever its nature, wants power for itself; the prospect of sharing power is unthinkable. Whether it is popular sovereignty or monarchy, Communism or Islam, or any other Din, it must govern to establish itself. A Din without power to govern is just like a building which exists in the mind only." Mawdudi was the first to stress the imperative of jihad for contemporary Muslims, the first to claim that armed struggle was central to jihad and, unlike any major Muslim thinker before him, the first to call for a universal jihad.

Mawdudi's influence on Sayyid Qutb regarding the necessity of jihad as an armed struggle is widely recognized. Less recognized, though, is the difference between the two. Even if Qutb proclaims the absolute sovereignty of God, he does it in a sense entirely different from Mawdudi: "A Muslim does not believe that another besides the one God can be divine, and he does not believe that another creature but himself is fit to worship him; and he does not believe that 'sovereignty' may apply to any of his servants." Indeed, unlike Mawdudi's preoccupation with the state as the true agent of change in history, Qutb's thought is far more society centered; Reinhard Schulze has noted that "the deputy of divine sovereignty" for Qutb is "man as an individual" and "not the state, as Mawdudi saw it."

Sayyid Qutb began his public career in the service of the Egyptian Ministry of Education after graduating from a prestigious teacher-training college in Cairo in 1933. His first book, *The Task of the Poet in Life,* suggested the promise of a literary career. In 1948, Qutb was sent by the ministry on a study mission to the United States. Though the manuscript had been finished prior to his departure, Qutb's first important book, *Social Justice in Islam,* was published during the time he was in America. Qutb explained his objective in the opening chapter of the book:

> We have only to look to see that our social situation is as
> bad as it can be; it is apparent that our social conditions

have no possible relation to justice; and so we turn our eyes to Europe, America or Russia, and we expect to import from there solutions to our problems . . . we continually cast aside all our own spiritual heritage, all our intellectual endowment, and all the solutions which might well be revealed by a glance at these things; we cast aside our fundamental principles and doctrines, and we bring in those of democracy, or socialism, or communism.

The search for an Islamic road to modernity placed Qutb alongside al-Afghani and al-Banna as predecessors.

Qutb returned from America in 1951, the year the Society of Muslim Brothers was legalized. An active member of the anti-monarchical Wafd Party when he left for America, Qutb began cooperating with the society immediately on his return. After the 1952 revolution, Qutb was appointed cultural adviser to the Revolutionary Council and was the only civilian allowed to attend its meetings. Imprisoned by Nasser in 1954, Qutb had his letters smuggled out by his sisters and distributed widely. Published as *Signposts Along the Road*—also translated as *Milestones*—this collection of letters has achieved the status of a manifesto of contemporary radical political Islam. Released from jail in 1964, Qutb was rearrested and executed in 1966, reportedly at the insistence of Nasser.

Qutb elaborated Mawdudi's thought and took it to a more radical conclusion. He made a distinction between modernity and Westernization, calling for an embrace of modernity but a rejection of Westernization. Qutb also made a sharp distinction between science and ideology, arguing that modernity is made up of two types of sciences, physical and philosophical. The pursuit of material progress and the mastery of practical sciences are a divine command and a "collective obligation" on Muslims. Modernization through the natural sciences was fine but not through the westernizing philosophical sciences.

Qutb's reformulation of jihad resonated with contemporary Marxism-Leninism, both Maoist and Leninist. Echoing the Maoist distinction between ways of handling contradictions among the people and with the enemy, Qutb argued that jihad involves both persuasion and coercion, the former appropriate among friends but the latter suited to enemies. In the final analysis, only physical force will remove the political, social, and economic obstacles to the establishment of the Islamic community. The use of force to realize freedom is not a contradiction for Qutb—as, indeed, it is not for America. Islam has not only the right but also the obligation to exercise force to end slavery and realize human freedom.

> Islam is a declaration of the freedom of every man or woman from servitude to other humans. It seeks to abolish all those systems and governments that are based on the rule of some men over others, or the servitude of some to others. When Islam liberates people from these external pressures and invites them to its spiritual message, it appeals to their reason, and gives them complete freedom to accept or reject it.

Indeed, "Islam does not force people to accept its belief, but it wants to provide a free environment in which they will have the choice to believe."

Here there is more than just a passing resemblance to the dialectics of Marxism-Leninism. Qutb argued that jihad is a process beginning with the organization of a vanguard, followed by a withdrawal that would make possible both study and organization and then a return to struggle. Here, Qutb echoed a key dictum of Leninism: "How to initiate the revival of Islam? A vanguard must set out with this determination and then keep going, marching through the vast ocean of *jahaliyyah* which encompasses the entire world. . . . I have written *Milestones* for this vanguard, which I consider to be a waiting reality about to be materialized."

The Islamist intellectuals did not always win in the struggle against the ulama. In Iran, the ulama won a dramatic victory. The intellectual initiative in Iran is identified with the work of Ali Shariati, who sought to build on and preserve the revolutionary Shi'a identity as the identity of the oppressed, as a project for a humane and just Islamic society. The struggle in revolutionary Iran did not pit just the clergy against non-Islamic intellectuals but also Islamists who were secular against those who were not. Recognizing the threat to the authority of the ulama from an autonomous intellectual reinterpretation of Islam, the nonsecular clergy transformed Shi'ism. In an effort to reorganize the ulama as an institutional hierarchy, Ayatollah Khomeini created an entirely new institution, *vilayat-i-faqih*, government by jurists. Acting as a trustee of the sovereignty of God, this institution was to function in parallel to civil government, accountable only to the ulama, of whom there were almost one hundred thousand in Iran at the time.

In the history of the Society of Muslim Brothers in Egypt, Sayyid Qutb is identified with the ascendancy of radical Islam in contrast to Hassan al-Banna's moderation. The difference between moderate and radical political Islam lay in the following: whereas moderates fought for social reforms within the system, radicals were convinced that no meaningful social reform would be possible without taking over the state. Had fifteen years of hard labor in Nasser's camps convinced Qutb that religious and secular intellectuals could not live at peace in the same society? To what extent was his renunciation of reform through coexistence—and the conviction of the need for a vanguard to wage a fight to the finish—an echo of other contemporary schools of political thought, such as Marxism-Leninism?

In their preoccupation with political identity and political power, Islamist intellectuals were like other intellectuals, whether religious or not. Islamist intellectuals crafted their ideologies through encounters not only with the ulama but also with these secular intellectuals who ignored the Islamic tradition and drew on other intellectual sources, such as Marxism or Western liberalism. Through this double encounter, they developed political Islam in multiple directions, both emancipatory and authoritarian. Just as it is historically inaccurate to equate political Islam with religious fundamentalism, it also makes little sense to equate every shade of political Islam with political terrorism. Of the four Islamist intellectuals written about here—Mohamed Iqbal, Mohamed Ali Jinnah, Abdul A'la Mawdudi, and Sayyid Qutb—only Mawdudi was an unabashed advocate of creating an ideological Islamic state as the true subject of history. In contrast, Qutb's thought was more society centered. Iqbal sought to constitute the Islamic umma beyond the nation-state as a broad, borderless cultural community. Finally, Jinnah was a secular Muslim, for whom Islam had become a political identity in colonial India; he pursued a secular, not an Islamic, state ideal, one that would safeguard the democratic rights of both the Muslim majority and the non-Muslim minorities.

The single conviction that unites radical Islamist intellectuals is the preoccupation with taking power. They are convinced that the historical moment defined by the collapse of Communism is the moment Muslims must seize to advance Islam as a universal ideology of emancipation. This is how Sayyid Qutb opened his 1963 manifesto of radical political Islam, *Milestones:*

Mankind today is on the brink of a precipice, not because of the danger of complete annihilation which is hanging over its head—this being just a symptom and not the real disease—but because humanity is devoid of those vital values for its healthy development and real progress. . . . Democracy in the West has become sterile to such an extent that its intellectuals borrow from the systems of the Eastern bloc, especially in the economic sphere, under the name of socialism. . . . Marxism stands intellectually defeated and it is not an exaggeration to say that in practice not a single nation in the world is truly Marxist. . . . The era dominated by the resurgence of science has also come to an end. . . . All the nationalistic and chauvinistic ideologies that have appeared in modern times, and all the movements and theories derived from them, have also lost their vitality. In short, all man-made theories, both individualistic and collectivist, have proved to be failures. At this crucial and bewildering juncture, the turn of Islam and the Muslim community has arrived because it has the needed values.

The key division among radical Islamist intellectuals concerns the status of *sharia* (Islamic law) and thus of democracy in the state. Ijtihad refers to the institutionalized practice of interpreting the sharia to take into account changing historical circumstances and, therefore, different points of view. It makes for a substantive body of law constantly changing in response to changing conditions. The attitude toward ijtihad is the single most important issue that divides society-centered from state-centered—and progressive from reactionary—Islamists. Whereas society-centered Islamists insist that the practice of ijtihad be central to modern Islamic society, state-centered Islamists are determined that the "gates of ijtihad" remain forever closed. Iqbal called for the modernization and democratization of ijtihad, so the law could be interpreted by a body elected by the community of Muslims, the umma, and not just the religious ulama. The emphasis on ijtihad is also key to the thought of Sayyid Qutb and distinguishes his intellectual legacy from the state-centered thought of Mawdudi. My argument is that the theoretical roots of Islamist political terror lie in the state-centered, not the society-centered, movement.

The question we face today is not just why a radical state-centered train of thought emerged in political Islam but how this thought was able to leap from the word to the deed, thereby moving from the intellectual fringe to the mainstream of politics in large parts of the Islamic world. Culture Talk cannot answer this question, nor can even the best of its cultural critics, such as Karen Armstrong. Culture Talk sees a clash of civilizations as the driving force behind global conflicts; its critics point to the cultural clash inside civilizations as being more important than the clash between them. Culture Talk sees fundamentalism as a resistance to modernity; its critics point out that fundamentalism is as modern as modernity—that it is actually a response to modernity. Both sides, however, seek an explanation of *political* terrorism in culture, whether modern or premodern. Both illustrate different sides of the same culturalist argument, which downplays the *political* encounter that I think is central to understanding political terrorism.

To distinguish cultural from political Islam, I shall place political Islam in the context of the the Cold War. My aim is to question the widely held presumption—even among critics of Culture Talk—that extremist religious tendencies can be equated with political terrorism. Terrorism is not a necessary effect of religious tendencies, whether fundamentalist or secular. Rather, terrorism is born of a *political* encounter. When it harnesses one or another aspect of tradition and culture, terrorism needs to be understood as a modern political movement at the service of a modern power. As such, the genesis of the form of political terrorism responsible for the tragedy of 9/11 can be traced to the late Cold War.

Chapter Two

THE COLD WAR AFTER INDOCHINA

I was a young lecturer at the University of Dar-es-Salaam in Tanzania in 1975. It was a momentous year in the decolonization of the world as we knew it: 1975 was the year of the American defeat in Indochina, and of the collapse of Portuguese rule in the colonies of Mozambique, Angola, and Portuguese Guinea, the last European empire in Africa. In retrospect, it was the year that the focal point of the Cold War shifted from Southeast Asia to southern Africa. The strategic question was this: Who would pick up the pieces of the Portuguese empire in Africa, the United States or the Soviet Union? With a shift in the focal point of the Cold War, there was a corresponding shift in U.S. strategy. Two major influences, each a lesson from the war in Indochina, informed that shift. One was drawn by the president of the United States, the second by Congress. The executive lesson was summed up as the Nixon Doctrine; the legislative lesson was passed as the Clark Amendment.

Two Contrasting Paradigms: Laos and Vietnam

The Nixon Doctrine held that "Asian boys must fight Asian wars." It summed up the lesson of more than a decade of U.S. involvement in Indochina. More specifically, it weighed the Vietnam debacle against the conduct of relatively successful proxy wars in Laos. The contrast could not have been sharper. With a free hand in Vietnam, the United States had decided to wage the war in a more traditional fashion, introducing hundreds of thousands of troops to fight a ground war against local Communist guerrillas. But when it came to Laos, the United States found its hands tied by a 1962 treaty with Moscow, which disallowed the introduction of ground troops in that country, and was forced to improvise.

The Vietnam War began in 1964 when the Johnson administration claimed that two U.S. destroyers had been attacked by North Vietnamese torpedoes in the Gulf of Tonkin. As the media painted a picture of national humiliation and demanded a response, President Johnson launched reprisal bombings against North Vietnam. He called on Congress to pass a resolution that would allow him to send U.S. ground troops to Vietnam. Later, the crews of the destroyers said the attack stories had been fabricated. A joint resolution of both houses of Congress, passed soon after the Tonkin Gulf incident in 1964, gave the president the endorsement needed in Vietnam. Armed with war powers that amounted to a blank check, President Johnson and his advisers took to a rapid "Americanization" of the war. In the course of a year, 1964, the number of U.S. "military advisers" increased from sixteen thousand to twenty-three thousand men. With still no discernible progress, the United States ordered sustained bombing of North Vietnam—Operation Rolling Thunder—in the expectation that the destruction of power plants and industrial facilities would force the north to surrender. When this failed to produce the expected results, Johnson decided to commit enough combat troops to take over the running of the counterinsurgency war from the South Vietnamese. Each failure led to a bolder initiative, which in turn led to a greater failure. The first of these was the strategic-hamlet program, which aimed to herd village populations into government-controlled areas; then followed search-and-destroy operations, each concluding with a public announcement of a grisly "body count" of the number of Vietnamese Communists killed; and then came the pacification program, designed to go beyond targeting one village at a time to controlling the civilian population as a whole. When the pacification program, too, was found wanting, it was supplemented by Operation Phoenix, "a CIA-inspired South Vietnamese campaign aimed at identifying and liquidating the Viet Cong political apparatus in the villages." Each successive failure led to a more ambitious effort, and finally the Tet offensive in 1968. After Tet, the United States tried to bring the lesson of Laos to Vietnam: during the last five years of the war, from 1970 to 1975, "Americanization" gave way to "Vietnamization."

The war in Laos had developed as a consequence of the expanding war in Vietnam. As the Vietnam War intensified, troops and supplies from the north made their way to battlefields in the south, often via the jungles of southern Laos. The American strategic objective was to close this route—dubbed Ho Chi Minh Trail by the U.S. military. Toward this end, the United States cultivated a proxy of local mercenaries and reinforced them with massive airpower. For more than a decade, the CIA led a secret army of thirty thousand Hmong mercenaries against Communist guerrillas in the mountains of northern Laos. As opposition to the Vietnam War mounted back home, the advantages of proxy war became clear: waged in secret, it was at the same time removed from congressional oversight, public scrutiny, and conventional diplomacy. Even at the end of the war, few Americans knew that the U.S. Air Force had fought "the largest air war in military history over Laos, dropping 2.1 million tons of bombs over this small, impoverished nation—the same tonnage that Allied powers dropped on Germany and Japan during World War II." The Laos model combined proxy war on the ground with a fierce and relentless American air war. Whereas proxy war became the order of the day throughout the late Cold War, the air war came into its own only after that war's end.

Financing Proxy Wars

If one advantage of proxy war was that its conduct could be hidden from public scrutiny, the disadvantage was that it was not easy to finance from public funds. This explains why covert wars have often tended to go hand in hand with illicit trade, usually in drugs. There has been a long-established link between the drug trade— whether licit or illicit—and the financing of colonial wars. In the early nineteenth century, the British empire set up an official monopoly for the cultivation of opium seed in its Indian colony and exported the harvest to China. When the Chinese emperor objected, the British claimed he was in violation of freedom of trade. To defend the freedom to trade opium, the empire sent gunboats up the Yangtze River and fought the ignoble Opium War. Similarly, in neighboring Indochina, the French used officially sanctioned opium revenues to pay the cost of their colonial occupation.

In a monumental historical study of the link between the drug trade and counterinsurgency, *The Politics of Heroin*, University of Wisconsin scholar Alfred McCoy has traced the global expansion of drug-production centers—in Burma (Myanmar), Laos, Colombia, and Afghanistan—to the political cover provided by CIA-sponsored covert wars. At the heart of the global drug trade after the Second World War has been trade in opium, the raw material base for the industrial manufacture of high-grade heroin. When the CIA began its alliance with drug lords, the global opium trade was "at its lowest ebb in nearly two centuries." The war had disrupted international shipping, and tight security had blocked heroin smuggling into the United States. The CIA entered into two sets of alliances it considered key to waging the Cold War, both of which boosted the drug trade far beyond prewar levels. The first was with the Mafia in Italy and France, the second was with anti-Communist Chinese forces along the Burma-China border. From 1948 to 1950, the CIA allied "with the Corsican underworld in its struggle against the French Communist Party for control over the strategic Mediterranean port of Marseille." The Corsicans triumphed and "used their control over the Marseille waterfront to dominate the export of heroin to the U.S. market" for "the next quarter century." At the same time, "the CIA ran a series of covert operations along the China border that were instrumental in the creation of the Golden Triangle heroin complex." Beginning in 1950, these operations were aimed at creating an anti-Communist Chinese force to mount an invasion of mainland China. The invasion never happened, but the anti-Communist Chinese (KMT) "succeeded in monopolizing and expanding the Shan states' opium trade." The CIA retained these forces along the Burma-China border, hoping they would function as an advance warning system against an anticipated Chinese invasion of Southeast Asia. Instead, this anti-Communist army "transformed Burma's Shan states into the world's largest opium producer" over the next decade.

The CIA applied these very tactics to Laos from 1960 to 1975 when it created a secret army of thirty thousand Hmong peasants to battle Laotian Communists near the border with North Vietnam. The Hmong's main cash crop was opium, and the CIA readily turned the other way as the Hmong commander, General Vang Pao, used a Corsican charter to export his crop to distant markets. In 1965, when the escalating air war and the political infighting in the Laotian elite "forced the small Corsican charter airlines out of the opium business," General Pao was able "to use the CIA's Air America to collect opium from his scattered highland villages" for delivery to Long Tieng and Vientiane. The Air America operation played a key role in expanding the opium market: "CIA and USAID funds went to the construction of more than 150 short, so-called LIMA landing strips in the mountains near the opium fields, thus opening these remote spots to the export trade." In 1967, the CIA and USAID bought two C-47 planes for General Pao, who then opened his own air-transport company, which he called Xeng Khouang Air and everyone else called Air Opium. Interestingly, when General Pao decided in 1969 to bring in Chinese master chemists from Hong Kong and set up an enormous heroin plant to manufacture fine-grain, high-grade, 80 to 99 percent pure, number 4 heroin—instead of number 3 crude that had long been the stuff of local and regional consumption—and began to supply it to the growing concentration of U.S. troops in Vietnam, the CIA still looked the other way. That Pao was becoming a world-class player in the heroin market became evident on April 25, 1971, when French custom officials opened a suitcase belonging to the newly arrived Laotian ambassador in Paris, Prince Sopsaisana, and found it contained sixty kilos of high-grade Laotian heroin, worth $13.5 million on the streets. It was "one of the biggest heroin seizures in French history." Later reports received by the U.S. Bureau of Narcotics showed that the Laotian ambassador's venture "had been financed by Hmong General Vang Pao, and the heroin itself had been refined in a laboratory at Long Tieng, the CIA's headquarters for clandestine operations in northern Laos."

The Long Tieng laboratory was reputed to be the world's largest heroin-processing plant. When massive American bombing and the ensuing refugee-relocation program reduced the amount of Hmong opium available for the laboratory, Pao's officers turned to northeastern Laos for supplies of Burmese opium. Guaranteed a captive high-income market with the U.S. troops in Vietnam, the Golden Triangle came to grow "about 70% of the world's illicit opium supply" by 1971, and Laos emerged as "the most important processing center of raw opium" there. Its laboratories rivaled those of Marseille and Hong Kong in the quality and quantity of their production.

Alfred McCoy has gone through U.S. intelligence reports to identify the ownership of key heroin-processing facilities in the Golden Triangle. In a classified report leaked to the *New York Times,* the CIA identified twenty-one opium refineries in the area, of which seven were capable of producing 90 to 99 percent pure number 4 heroin. McCoy noted that most of these operated under the protection of key CIA assets: "These intelligence reports indicated a clear pattern: the CIA's covert action assets had become the leading heroin dealers in Laos."

Proxy Wars and the Clark Amendment

Arising out of the contrast between Laos as an example to be emulated and Vietnam as the danger to be avoided, the Nixon Doctrine turned one lesson of Laos—proxy war—into a model for military strategy in Third World theaters. When it was applied to Africa in the period after Vietnam, it was also modeled on an earlier American experience on the African continent, in the Congo, on the eve of African independence in the early sixties. Determined to prevent the ascent of militant nationalism in Africa's prize resource-rich country, Washington did not hesitate to put together a mercenary force of mainly South African and Rhodesian whites. From Washington's point of view, militant nationalism was nothing but a proxy for Soviet expansion into a rapidly decolonizing Africa. The mercenary solution worked, but it left a bitter legacy in independent Africa. When the United States turned to Africa a decade later, this time determined to block the ascent of another militant nationalist movement, the Popular Movement for the Liberation of Angola (MPLA), a renewed attempt to use mercenaries did not work. With hardly an ally in a region impatient to decolonize, Secretary of State Henry Kissinger—speaking for the United States—encouraged apartheid South Africa to intervene. The result was the Angolan debacle. Following close on the heels of defeat in Vietnam, it produced a powerful antiwar response in the American legislature. That response crystallized as the Clark Amendment.

Embracing Mercenaries in Congo

Congo became independent on June 30, 1960. Less than two weeks later, on July 11, its richest province, Katanga, seceded. The armed contingent of secessionists led by Moise Tshombe, who was made president, was supervised and trained by officers from Belgium, the former colonial power there. Katanga's mines were operated by a Belgian company, Union Minière du Haut-Katanga, in which the Rockefellers were soon to acquire a major interest.

Late in the summer of 1960, the Eisenhower administration concluded that Patrice Lumumba, Congo's militantly nationalist prime minister, was "an African Castro" and must be eliminated. Lumumba's crime was that he had requested and received some military aid from the Soviet Union in August 1960, in the face of "considerable Western support for the Katanga secession and UN reluctance to use force to end it." On August 18, following a National Security Council briefing, Eisenhower asked his aides whether "we can't get rid of this guy." True, the 1975–1976 Senate committee headed by Frank Church investigated the role of the CIA in Lumumba's assassination and later absolved the agency of any direct role in it. But subsequent investigation by a Belgian parliamentary committee in 1999, combined with research in the UN archives by a Congolese intellectual, Georges Nzongola-Ntalaja, has brought new facts to light. After Eisenhower's comment of August 18, the CIA began a two-track strategy. Having received a direct order from CIA head Allen Dulles, Sidney Gottlieb, the CIA's chief scientist, already on the lookout for a way to poison Castro's cigars, landed in Leopoldville (Kinshasa) "equipped with a deadly substance made of cobra venom, to be applied on Lumumba's food or toothpaste." The problem was how to deliver the venom to the target. In light of the obstacles faced by a James Bond–type operation, the CIA station chief in Kinshasa proposed a second plan of action: to eliminate Lumumba "politically, and maybe later, physically." It is this plan that the United States followed in collaboration with Belgium. On December 1, Lumumba was captured by soldiers loyal to Congolese chief of staff Joseph Mobutu (also a CIA asset), flown to secessionist Katanga, and killed—as Belgian officers stood watching. With Lumumba out of the way, in December 1962 President Kennedy concurred with the use of UN troops to quash the Katangan rebellion. In May 1963, a grateful Kennedy welcomed Mobutu in the White House: "General, if it hadn't been for you, . . . the Communists would have taken over."

By the end of 1963, anti-Mobutu rebellion broke out in Kwilu, led by Pierre Mulele, a prominent Lumumbist. The rebels were poorly armed, and there was no evidence of outside (i.e., Soviet) involvement. But the CIA did intervene on the government's behalf, hiring several Cuban exile pilots with American green (residency) cards and providing them with a few Italian planes for aerial bombing missions. No sooner was the Kwilu rebellion crushed than another broke out in the eastern province of Kivu. Once again, the rebels were poorly armed, according to the French daily *Le Monde,* with no more than "bows, arrows, and bicycle chains." Led by Lumumba's followers, the rebels were known as the Simba (lions). The U.S. ambassador confirmed that their confused ideology reflected a purely local rebellion: "Despite the revolutionary slogans which its leaders mouthed . . . the rebels have to all intents and purposes no political programme. It's definitely an African and a Congolese movement but all very confused." Yet the revolt spread quickly, and the Congolese army collapsed as the Simba took Stanleyville (Kisangani), Congo's third-largest city, on August 5, 1964. Just two days before, Congress had passed the Tonkin Gulf resolution; anti-Communist hysteria seemed to have gripped Washington. Piero Gleijeses, professor of American foreign policy at Johns Hopkins University, the first scholar to have read through official U.S. archives on the Congo crisis, remarked after looking at the National Security Council debates on Congo: "No one challenged the basic premise" that "the rebels had to be defeated."

On August 5, the day the Simba took Kisangani, a cable from the American embassy in Congo laid out three options for the government of Congo (GOC):

a) GOC can seek direct Belgian military intervention; b) it can attempt to recruit white mercenary brigade[s]; c) it can ask for U.S. troops. . . . If Belgian government refuses to accept risks of intervention . . . mercenary brigade is second best alternative. . . . From U.S. standpoint employment of mercenaries would carry advantage of being done on GOC responsibility and would reduce overt Western [i.e., Belgian or U.S.] involvement. . . . It would place burden of responsibility on GOC and not on ourselves or Belgians.

Already, Washington had tried to convince the Belgians to intervene, but British ambassador Edward Rose reported from Kinshasa that the Belgians were amused at the Americans seeing the Communist specter everywhere. In Brussels, the Belgian foreign minister, Paul-Henri Spaak, told the U.S. ambassador that Belgian industrialists who had the largest investments in Congo felt that they could do business with rebel leaders since those leaders were aware that the Belgian investment and technical know-how were crucial to the economy of Congo. The French agreed that there was no need to be concerned since the revolt had not been stirred up by outside forces. On August 7, after Spaak told Washington "unequivocally that neither Belgium nor any other European country would send troops," Secretary of State Dean Rusk approved a proposal to recruit a mercenary force and pressured Belgium to join in the effort. This is how Gleijesis summed up Rusk's cable to roving ambassador Averell Harriman in Brussels: "Washington and Brussels would supply the money to pay the mercenaries and the weapons to arm them" but "Washington alone would provide the planes to fly them." Gleijesis concludes his reading of the archives thus: "Bowing to U.S. pressure, the Belgians embraced the mercenary option."

By October 1964, the CIA estimated the number of mercenaries in Congo at more than one thousand. There were two hundred Belgians, forty-six Spaniards, and a handful from other European locations. More than half were whites from South Africa and Rhodesia. The CIA noted that many "are actually South African Army regulars placed on leave status for six months." Washington was clear from the outset that there would be no U.S. citizens among the mercenaries. Without American support, however, the mercenaries would have been lame. Four U.S. C-130s with American crews transported mercenaries and their equipment across the west-east span of Congo, roughly the same distance as from Paris to Moscow. When they met resistance, the mercenaries called on the Congolese air force, which did not include a single Congolese but several T-28s and B-26s supplied by the United States and flown by Cuban exiles, as well as a squadron of seven T-6s from Italy, piloted by South African and European mercenaries. The *New York Times* reported in 1966, long after the entire operation was complete: "Guiding them into action were American 'diplomats' and other officials in apparently civilian positions. The sponsor, paymaster and director of all of them, however, was the Central Intelligence Agency." The rebels had neither planes nor antiaircraft guns, and the planes "operated over insurgent territory with impunity," the CIA noted. The Simba responded by taking American and Belgian hostages, the majority in Stanleyville, now the rebel capital, and the mercenaries and their apologists in turn cited this as justification for their own intervention.

The mercenaries signed up for money but also to defend white privilege in a rapidly decolonizing Africa. Many behaved as if they were on a hunting safari, sending photos of their exploits back home. The British weekly *The Observer* printed two of these: "The first showed two almost naked black men, their hands tied behind their backs, ropes around their necks, being led by a white mercenary to their hanging. In the second, 'smiling mercenaries' fought for the privilege of doing the 'stringing up.' " "The pictures," *The Observer* noted, "show how mercenaries not only shoot and hang their prisoners after torturing them, but use them for target practice and gamble over the number of shots needed to kill them." An Italian journalist described their entry into the town of Boende in late October 1964: "Occupying the town meant blowing out the doors with rounds of bazooka fire, going into the shops and taking anything they wanted that was movable. . . . After the looting came the killing. The shooting lasted for three days. Three days of executions, of lynchings, of tortures, of screams, and of terror."

The American press, however, was loathe to report any of this. Piero Gleijeses gives several examples of "the patriotic press." The *Washington Post* said that, led by the "intelligent, poetry-reading colonel Mike Hoare," mercenaries were doing an essential service, saving Congo. The *New York Times,* which provided more intensive coverage of the Congo crisis than any other American paper, devoted a two-part series to a South African mercenary who confided that he had enlisted "because he believed that Premier Moise Tshombe was sincerely trying to establish a multiracial society in the Congo. I thought that if I could help in this creation, the Congo might offer some hope, some symbol in contrast to the segregation in my own country." The *New York Times*'s version of the sensitive mercenary was flatly contradicted by a two-part article in the South African *Cape Times,* in which a returning South African mercenary wrote of the "senseless, coldblooded killings," of never taking a prisoner "except for the odd one for questioning, after which they were executed," and of their thievery; he pleaded with his government "not to allow decent young South Africans" to become "senseless killers."

The crisis in Congo was America's baptism in independent Africa. It was also, in retrospect, America's tentative embrace of terror for reasons of power, and the government, particularly the CIA, seemed aware of this. The U.S. ambassador described the mercenaries as "an uncontrollable lot of toughs . . . who consider looting or safe-cracking within their prerogatives." The CIA listed "robbery, rape, murder and beatings" among their "serious excesses." The Simba rebellion ended with the U.S.-Belgian mercenary drop on Kisangani on November 24, 1965. That same day, Joseph Mobutu seized power in Kinshasa. No longer of use, mercenaries were gradually phased out. Down to 230 from more than 1,000, they rebelled on July 5, 1967, taking about one thousand Congolese troops with them. Mobutu appealed to Washington. "We must keep Mobutu in power because there is no acceptable alternative to him," Undersecretary of State Nicholas Katzenbach told a July 13 National Security Council meeting. Since no one disagreed, Washington returned Cuban exiles to Congo, this time to strafe mercenaries, who withdrew into Rwanda. Mobutu wanted them to be returned to Congo to stand trial. The *New York Times* said the mercenaries had fought for the West against the Simba and, in the process, had saved "innocent lives—mostly white lives." *Le Monde* was more honest: "Western public opinion is more sensitive, one must acknowledge, to the death of one European than to the deaths of twenty blacks." However, as Piero Gleijeses notes, their trial would have offended more than just Western sensibilities; it "could have led to embarrassing revelations about their contacts with the CIA." So Washington adopted a dual solution. Whereas their Congolese auxiliaries were handed back to an understanding ally, Mobutu—who proceeded to slaughter them in spite of a promise of amnesty—the mercenaries were flown to Europe in two planes chartered by the International Red Cross.

The Angolan Disaster

When the American government turned to Africa a decade later, the opposition to the war in Vietnam had radically changed the atmosphere in the States. President Nixon was disgraced in August 1974, and three months later, a Democratic Congress was re-elected. Deeply suspicious of the Cold War legacy of a cloak-and-dagger foreign policy conducted in secret by the executive branch, many antiwar congressmen and -women were eager to establish legislative control over foreign policy. In December 1974, Congress passed the Hughes-Ryan Amendment, requiring the CIA to report the "description and scope" of covert operations "in a timely fashion" to eight congressional committees.

These developments shaped the setting in which the post-Nixon administration, led by Gerald Ford, who had never before been elected to any major public office, set about defining its African options in the face of a rapidly disintegrating Portuguese empire. Washington was determined to block any possibility of the MPLA coming to power, having identified it as a Soviet proxy. In pursuit of this goal, it explored different options, comprehensively documented by Piero Gleijeses.

Washington's preferred option was to give covert support to the two movements that were opposed to MPLA: the Front for National Liberation of Angola (FNLA), which operated more or less as a surrogate of Congo's General Mobutu, and the Union for the Total Independence of Angola (Unita), which had few external contacts apart from fledgling ones with apartheid South Africa. But more funds had to be approved by Congress since the assistance soon used up the CIA Contingency Reserve Fund for 1975. When Ford asked for $28 million for covert support of FNLA and Unita, Congress flatly declined, the Senate by a vote of 54–22, and the House by 323–99. By that time, MPLA was already receiving military aid, matériel, training, and advisers from Cuba, though there was as yet no large-scale entry of Cuban troops. Kissinger devised a second option in this rapidly changing situation: "in response to the arrival of the Cubans, the administration tried to raise a mercenary army, just as Johnson had done in Zaire [Congo] in 1964." But the mercenaries were few, less than 250, mainly English, and many rapidly graying veterans of a decade earlier. The result was a debacle. They were inferior, some "literally lured from London pubs with the offer of easy money and high living," and they were unable to stop the Cubans. Mutual recriminations followed "the execution of 14 of the mercenaries," while forty-five "limped home [to London] on crutches and wheelchairs." Seeing the writing on the wall, Mobutu deported twenty-two who just had arrived from London. Meanwhile, instead of fighting MPLA, FNLA and Unita took to fighting each other. Faced with an ignominious end, Kissinger opted to back a proxy invasion by regular South African forces. Gleijeses has summarized the internal debates between hawks and doves in both Pretoria and Washington and the contacts between the two capitals. In Pretoria, the debate pitted the Foreign Office against hawks in the defense establishment. In Washington, it pitted CIA director William Colby against Kissinger.

One of the sharpest disagreements was recorded in the minutes of the National Security Council meeting of April 9, 1975. Three weeks before the fall of Saigon, Colby warned of the dangers of overreaction:

> Mr. President, there is the question of how these recent events [in Vietnam] may affect the attitudes of other nations towards us. In general, the current debacle is seen

not as a turning point, but as the final step on a particular path that most governments had long seen coming. . . . Adjustments were already being made. . . . Soviet, Chinese and other Communist leaders, for their part, will not automatically conclude that other U.S. commitments are placed in question, unless U.S. public reaction points to a repudiation of other foreign involvement, or internal U.S. recriminations are so divisive as to raise doubts of the U.S. ability to develop any consensus on foreign policy in the near future.

Kissinger disagreed, sharply and immediately:

I want to take issue with the estimate of the Director of Central Intelligence regarding the impact on our worldwide position of a collapse in Vietnam. It was his judgment that the world reaction would be negligible, based on the fact that everybody would be anticipating what would happen. Let me say that . . . no country expected so rapid a collapse. . . . Especially in Asia, this rapid collapse and our impotent reaction will not go unnoticed. I believe that we will see the consequences although they may not come quickly or in any predictable manner. . . . I believe that even in Western Europe, this will have a fallout.

Having failed to defend the line in Vietnam, Kissinger was now determined to draw the line in Angola. South African troops entered Angola in mid-October 1975, and Cuban troops followed in early November.

The irony is that as soon as the South African invasion became public knowledge, it turned into a massive liability for its

U.S. sponsors. Most observers believe that a quid pro quo—a withdrawal of South African troops in exchange for a guarantee of U.S. economic interests in Angola—was agreed to during Kissinger's January 21–24 meeting with Soviet leader Leonid Brezhnev in Moscow. Gulf Oil Cabinda began operations on February 21, and the U.S. diamond-mining monopoly, CFB, continued exploitation without threat of nationalization. In the years that followed, the U.S. ambassador to the United Nations, Andrew Young, would remind his audiences that Moscow may have made inroads into the Angolan state apparatus, but the Angolan economy remained very much in the Western orbit.

On February 10, 1976, the U.S. Congress passed the Clark Amendment, prohibiting any covert aid to any side in the Angolan civil war. The next month, on March 31, the UN Security Council branded South Africa the aggressor and demanded that it compensate Angola for war damages. The vote was 9–0, with the United States, France, Britain, Italy, and Japan abstaining. The die was cast. South Africa was both bruised by the Cubans in combat and cold-shouldered by the West precisely in the hour of its need. "Angola may well be regarded as South Africa's Bay of Pigs," a retired South African general lamented the day South African troops withdrew from Angola. "Next to us they have been the most discredited in Angola," Kissinger told Ford. The events in Angola were to have a far-reaching impact on both sides of the Atlantic. It brought hope to children in the streets of Soweto, who burst on the political scene with a remarkable uprising only a few months after South African troops were disgraced in Angola, and it also lent courage and reason to those in the U.S. Congress determined to curb the excesses of the Cold War.

The Clark Amendment

The Angolan fiasco reinforced the lessons of Vietnam, but those lessons provoked contradictory interpretations by the executive branch and by Congress, each asserting a different influence on post-Vietnam U.S. foreign policy. The Vietnam experience led to a determined executive search for regional proxies, particularly in parts of the world considered strategic to the conduct of the Cold War. It also reinforced popular distrust of a free hand for the executive branch in foreign affairs. Public resistance to Vietnam-type overseas involvement was echoed in Congress with the election of a host of antiwar legislators and led to a number of changes: the draft was abolished; the Pentagon's budget for special operations was cut; the CIA's paramilitary capabilities were reduced and its activities subjected to congressional oversight; and the president was required by the War Powers Act to seek congressional approval before any extended commitment of U.S. troops overseas. "The lesson of Vietnam is that we must throw off the cumbersome mantle of world policeman," said Senator Edward Kennedy, summing up the antiwar mood in Congress. The clearest expression of this surge in antiwar sentiment was the amendment of the Freedom of Information Act and the passage of the Clark Amendment.

The two years and three months between the passage of the 1973 War Powers Act and the 1976 Clark Amendment (and the Tunney Amendment that preceded it) marked the high point of the antiwar movement that swept the United States. The War Powers Act was the first brake on growing executive power, an institutional legacy of the Cold War; it fortified Congress's constitutional role on issues related to war making and treaty making. The Tunney Amendment was attached to the Department of Defense appropriations bill that the U.S. Senate passed on December 20, 1975: it terminated covert assistance to anti-Communist forces in Angola, but only for that fiscal year. Before the fiscal year ended, however, Congress had passed the Clark Amendment, which extended the ban and made it permanent and categorical:

> That, notwithstanding any other provision of law, no security assistance may be furnished, and no assistance may be furnished for military or paramilitary operations, or to provide police training, assistance, or advice, in connection with such operations in, to, or on behalf of Angola or any individual, group, organization, or movement therein, unless such assistance is specifically authorized under the Foreign Assistance Act of 1961.

Not since the start of the Cold War had Congress asserted its control over the intelligence community in such strong terms.

A generational gulf separated the architects of the Tunney and Clark amendments from the framers of the War Powers Act. For Senator Jacob Javits, a key sponsor of the War Powers Act, the objective of the act was to restore a "partnership" between the executive branch of government and Congress. But not so for John Tunney and Dick Clark, who had been elected as junior senators in 1970 and 1972 respectively, riding the crest of a nationwide anti-war wave. Tunney had been in the House of Representatives and had "regularly voted to check executive authority and to back a more reform-minded foreign policy." Questioning the assumptions behind the Cold War consensus, he repeated former senator Robert Taft's earlier warnings against giving "the military adventurists what they wanted," for the policy "has gotten us repressive right-wing dictatorships as allies all over the world." Dick Clark, a former political science professor and congressional staffer who had scored an upset victory on an antiwar platform to win a seat from Iowa in 1972, was known to question "the way things have always been done" from the time he entered the Senate. Clark was convinced that Congress would have to go beyond passing the War Powers Act and fully reevaluate foreign policy "to reassert itself as an equal branch of government." His sentiments were shared by other Democratic freshmen, such as Harold Hughes, Tunney, Thomas Eagleton, and James Abourezk. Soon after Clark became chair of the African Affairs Subcommittee of the powerful Senate Foreign Relations Committee in 1974, he organized public hearings on the brewing Angolan fiasco and then followed with an Angolan tour. On return, Clark announced that the United States needed to atone for not supporting the Angolan people's struggle against colonialism and that the best way to do so was to respect Angola's right to self-determination, an act that would also have the virtue of ending years of neglect in congressional oversight of the CIA. Following the passage of the amendment that bore his name, Clark "outlined an ambitious African agenda for 1976, calling for assistance to the liberation struggles elsewhere in colonial Africa, opposition to South Africa's continued occupation of Namibia, and considerations of economic sanctions against the South African regime." He expected these initiatives to end American "political and military interference in the internal affairs of other countries." If the United States intended to occupy a higher moral ground than its adversaries, it would have to affirm that in the foreign policy of a democracy "openness should be the rule, secretiveness the exception—not the other way around."

Enacted in 1976, the Clark Amendment was repealed in 1985. More than just a return to business as usual, its declining significance mirrored a larger development in the making of American foreign policy: the more the winning of the Cold War became central to the making of foreign policy, the more it dashed hopes of reforming U.S. foreign policy in line with the anticolonial solidarity that had driven the antiwar movement.

Proxy Wars and the Safari Club

The executive branch in Washington also drew a lesson from the Angolan debacle: no matter its military strength and geopolitical importance, apartheid South Africa was confirmed to be a political liability. The recognition only aggravated the search for proxies. Its first success was a regional alliance called the Safari Club, put together with the blessing of Henry Kissinger.

The existence of the club came to light after the 1979 Iranian Revolution when Mohamed Heikal, a highly respected Egyptian journalist and onetime adviser to President Nasser, was given permission by the new Khomeini government to go through the deposed shah's archives. Heikal came upon an agreement setting up a formal association, dated September 1, 1976, and signed by heads of several intelligence agencies, all strategic allies of the United States in the Cold War. The brainchild of Comte Claude Alexandre de Marenches, the head of the French secret service, the emphasis of the Safari Club was Africa; its members—France, Egypt, Iran, Morocco, and Saudi Arabia—had plenty to lose as the focal point of the Cold War moved to Africa. The African focus was clear from the very first sentence of the agreement: "Recent events in Angola and other parts of Africa have demonstrated the continent's role as a theatre for revolutionary wars prompted and conducted by the Soviet Union, which utilizes individuals or organizations sympathetic to, or controlled by, Marxist ideology." To face a common Soviet danger in Africa, they agreed to set up their main center in Cairo, with a secretariat, a planning section, and an operations branch. The chair was to rotate, but France was to be in charge of security and communication.

The Safari Club was responsible for three notable developments in Africa: in Congo, Egypt, and Somalia. Taken together, they underscored both the possibilities and the limits of a club formed by key American Cold War allies with interests of their own in Africa. The club's first success was in Congo. Faced with a rebellion in mineral-rich Katanga (now Shaba) province in April 1977 and a plea for help from French and Belgian mining interests conveyed through their close ally Mobutu, the club combined French air transport with logistical support from diverse sources to bring Moroccan and Egyptian troops to fight the rebellion. The operation was an unqualified success. The club registered an even greater success when it helped bring about the historic rapprochement between two strategic American allies, Egypt and Israel, laying the ground for Anwar al-Sadat's pathbreaking November 1977 visit to Jerusalem. The suggestion for the meeting was first made in a letter from Israeli Prime Minister Yitzhak Rabin to President Sadat, carried by the Moroccan representative in the club. There followed a secret meeting between General Moshe Dayan of Israel and Egypt's Deputy Prime Minister Hassan Tuhamy under the auspices of King Hassan II of Morocco. "When Itzhak Rabin later claimed that the breakthrough with Egypt had started before Mr. Begin came to power he was speaking no more than the truth," Heikal concluded in his examination of the club's papers.

The least successful of the club's initiatives was the Somali operation, which highlighted the limits that a syndicate of regional proxies would have to observe when its interests did not dovetail with those of its superpower patron. The Somali operation followed on the heels of the Ethiopian Revolution in 1974. The crisis of the monarchy and the revolution that ensued signaled historic possibilities for the leadership of both Somalia and the Soviet Union, even if the aspirations of one later contradicted those of the other. For Siad Barre of Somalia, there could be no better opportunity than the Ethiopian Revolution to realize the dream of creating a pan-Somali state by launching a war to incorporate the Ogaden, inhabited by Somalis but claimed by Ethiopia, into Somalia. For the Soviet Union—hitherto a Somali ally against the Ethiopian monarchy—the same revolution presented an opportunity to win over a strategic country in the region as a major ally. The Soviet initiative had disastrous consequences for Somali ambitions: when Somalia invaded the Ogaden in 1977 and its troops advanced over the next few months, the Soviet Union switched sides. As eighteen thousand Cuban troops poured into the Ogaden, the result of an operation "strictly coordinated with and supported by the Soviet Union," Somali forces retreated in disarray.

When the turn left Siad Barre standing high and dry on the battlefield, the Safari Club stepped in: "Members told Siad Barre that if he would get rid of the Russians they would supply the arms he needed." As Barre followed Sadat's example and expelled the Soviets, the shah of Iran pressed the United States to extend to Somalia the support promised Egypt. But the United States was not prepared to do so for a simple reason: Egypt was a strategic ally, and Somalia was not, as the shah was accordingly informed. "I have had three messages from President Carter," wrote the shah, who in turn summoned the Somali ambassador three times in one month. "You Somalis are threatening to upset the balance of world power." Barre had little choice but to conclude that he had been the naïve victim of a superpower deal, in which the Russians had agreed to keep out of Rhodesia's transition from white rule, provided the Americans stayed out of the Ogaden.

"Kissinger," Heikal noted, "was more than happy to see his aims in Africa implemented by proxy": what could be better than "a syndicate over which Congress had no control, and one which, moreover, was prepared to be self-financing"?

Southern Africa

The Safari Club vindicated the essence of the Kissinger perspective: the constraints of democracy at home required that the United States work through proxies in the international arena. In the search for proxies, South Africa continued to have a special place. The lesson of Angola in 1975 was that the place was restricted to covert operations. As U.S. operatives worked around the Clark Amendment, they continued "constructive engagement" with South Africa. The Clark Amendment was formally repealed at the start of Reagan's second term, in 1985, but even its decade-long duration had failed to forestall the Cold Warriors, because they were able to redirect public attention from one global reality, the movement for decolonization, to another, the Cold War. As they looked for ways to bypass legislative restrictions on the freedom of executive action, these ideologues embraced proxy wars enthusiastically and terrorism gradually. CIA chief William J. Casey eventually took the lead in orchestrating support for terrorist and prototerrorist movements around the world—from Renamo in Mozambique to Unita in Angola, and from contras in Nicaragua to the mujahideen in Afghanistan—through third and fourth parties. In a nutshell, after defeat in Vietnam and the Watergate scandal at home, the U.S. government decided to harness and even to cultivate terrorists in the struggle against guerrillas who had come to power and regimes it considered pro-Soviet.

If southern Africa is where the United States provided a protective umbrella for South Africans to practice the art of proxy war, Central America is where it took the lead in applying the lessons it had learned from its own proxies. A more theoretical influence came from counterinsurgency specialists, including General Magnus Malan, chief of the South African Defense Forces and minister of defense from 1980. Interestingly, as the postapartheid Truth and Reconciliation Commission acknowledged in its report, Malan was introduced to the art of counterinsurgency in the United States when he went there for an officer-training course in 1962–1963. Malan's tenure as chief of army (1973–1976) was noted for the application of counterinsurgency warfare to South West Africa. He was well-known for insisting that counterinsurgency specialists study famous texts on guerrilla war, particularly those by Mao Zedong. The mixture of practice and theory resulted in a key tenet of low-intensity conflict: if guerrilla war involved a focus on "soft targets," such as local political representatives of unpopular governments, counterinsurgency must also target political supporters of left-wing governments. The shift from targeting the armed forces of a government to its political representatives and then its civilians blurred the distinction between military and civilian targets. This blurring led to political terror—the targeting of civilians for political purposes—as a sustained strategy in peacetime combat. Practiced consistently, terrorism consciously distinguished between targets and victims. Victims may as well be anonymous, as if their fate had been determined by lottery, for the point was simply to bleed the target in as many ways as available, so as to weaken and expose it for a final showdown. In the language of low-intensity conflict, victims, as distinct from targets, came to be known as "collateral damage."

Renamo: Africa's First Genuine Terrorist Movement

The partnership between the United States and apartheid South Africa bolstered two key movements that practiced a varying mixture of terrorism and politics at different points in their history: Renamo in Mozambique and Unita in Angola. This similarity should in no way blur important differences between Renamo and Unita: whereas Renamo began as no more than a counterinsurgency operation, one that was compelled to learn the art of political organization as a survival strategy, Unita began as a political movement that learned the practice of counterinsurgency along the way.

Renamo was created as a terrorist outfit by the Rhodesian army in the early 1970s and was patronized by the South African Defense Forces after the fall of Rhodesia in 1980, when entire sections of white Rhodesian military and security fled to South Africa and were integrated in its military and intelligence apparatuses. Even if Renamo learned over time to turn the mistakes of the ruling Front for the Liberation of Mozambique (Frelimo) into opportunities for mobilizing political support, it never ceased to use terror with abandon. In contrast, Unita began as a movement with a local political base, though not one strong enough to have survived the beginning of civil war in 1975 without sustained external assistance. The resulting alliance with apartheid South Africa opened it to learning the tactics of terrorism by example. Unita was a contender for power in Angola, even if a weak one, whereas Renamo was not really one in Mozambique. In sharp contrast to its unabashed support for Unita, the U.S. government never openly supported Renamo. But this did not rule out collaboration between the political right in the United States and representatives of Renamo: "Renamo's Washington office shared an address with the Heritage Foundation" and, by 1987, right-wing pressure "brought Senate Minority Leader Robert Dole into the pro-Renamo camp." Because the 1975 debacle in Angola showed that South Africa could not be used as a direct link for U.S. assistance and because the Clark Amendment barred U.S. covert aid in Angola, the CIA took the initiative to find fourth parties through which to fund, train, and support Unita. Congressional testimony documented at least one instance of a $15 million payment to Unita through Morocco in 1983. Undermining democratic accountability was the most important domestic cost of supporting terrorism overseas. In a candid remark to journalists, Jonas Savimbi, the Unita chief, acknowledged the ineffectiveness of the Clark Amendment in the face of an uncooperative executive power: "A great country like the United States has other channels. . . . [T]he Clark Amendment means nothing."

Even before the Clark Amendment was repealed, the United States did understand the high political cost of supporting terrorism openly; it thus continued covert—alongside overt—support to terrorist and prototerrorist movements. An example during Reagan's second term was the provision of $13 million's worth of "humanitarian aid" to Unita, followed by another $15 million in "military assistance." Because South African assistance to Unita dried up following the end of apartheid and the internal Angolan settlement in May 1991—and in spite of the fact that the Cold War was over—the United States stepped up assistance to Unita. The hope was that a combination of terrorism and political organization would deliver a political victory in Angola, as it had in Nicaragua, where the counterrevolutionary coalition had triumphed at the polls. The logic was simple: if only the level of collateral damage could be made unacceptably high, the people would surely vote the terrorists into power as the price of peace.

By any reckoning, the cost of terrorism in southern Africa was high. A State Department consultant who interviewed refugees and displaced persons concluded that Renamo was responsible for 95 percent of the instances of civilian abuse in the war in Mozambique, including the murder of as many as ten thousand civilians. A 1989 United Nations study estimated that Mozambique suffered an economic loss of approximately $15 billion between 1980 and 1988, a figure five and a half times its 1988 GDP. When it came to Angola, Africa Watch researchers documented Unita strategies aimed at starving civilians in government-held areas, through a combination of direct attacks, kidnappings, and planting land mines on paths used by peasants. The extensive use of land mines put Angola—alongside Afghanistan and Cambodia—in the ranks of the most mined countries in the world, with amputees conservatively estimated at more than fifteen thousand. UNICEF calculated that 331,000 civilians died of causes directly or indirectly related to the war. And the UN estimated the total loss to the Angolan economy from 1980 to 1988 at $30 billion, six times the country's 1988 GDP.

Political terror had brought a kind of war never before seen in Africa. The hallmark of the terror was that it targeted civilian life: blowing up infrastructure such as bridges and power stations, destroying health and educational centers, mining paths and fields, and kidnapping civilians—particularly children—to press-gang them into recruits. Terrorism distinguished itself from guerrilla struggle by making civilians its preferred target. If left-wing guerrillas claimed that they were like fish in water, right-wing terrorists were determined to drain the water—that is, civilian life—so as to isolate and eliminate the fish. What is now termed collateral damage was not an unfortunate by-product of the war; it was the very point of terrorism.

"Constructive Engagement"

America's role when it came to perpetuating the reign of terror that Renamo unleashed in Mozambique and that Unita periodically resorted to in Angola was one of political support. We have seen that the United States openly backed Unita but was careful never to associate itself with Renamo. The State Department even documented and denounced acts of terror by Renamo. The United States did, however, warmly support the South African regime, which directly nurtured Renamo, Africa's first genuine terrorist movement, from birth to maturity. The Reagan administration called that embrace "constructive engagement," a term coined by then assistant secretary of state for Africa, Chester Crocker. Without American political support, the South African government could not have continued to prop up a terrorist movement in a newly independent African country for more than a decade and done so with impunity.

The point of constructive engagement was to bring South Africa out of political isolation so as to better tap its military potential in the war against militant—and pro-Soviet—nationalism. The salvage operation began at the government level, with South African being rehabilitated in those multilateral institutions outside the Soviet orbit and under U.S. tutelage. As a curtain-raiser, in 1982 the United States urged the International Monetary Fund (IMF) to grant South Africa $1.1 billion in credit, an amount that William Minter notes happened to be equal to the increase in South African military expenditure from 1980 to 1982. In an effort to bolster public support for constructive engagement, the South African government made numerous soft investments in the U.S. media, which were ultimately exposed; the case came to be known as Muldergate, after the apartheid regime's minister of information, Cornelius Mulder. Muldergate included investigation of assorted South African government investments in 160 to 180 secret media projects, including in the *Washington Times,* owned by the Unification Church; the *Sacramento Union;* UPITN, "the second largest newsfilm producer and distributor in the world . . . jointly owned by United Press International and Independent Television News of Britain"; and "the politically well-connected" public relations firm of Sydney S. Baron and Company. Muldergate projects also provided direct benefits to leading conservative individuals and organizations, such as Christian-right "ministries." In 1986, U.S. evangelical broadcasters "began a pro–South Africa publicity campaign, in collaboration with the South African government." No less a personality of the Far Right than Jerry Falwell spoke publicly on behalf of South African president P. W. Botha and pledged to work to defeat a proposed sanctions bill.

Constructive engagement made for an overall policy context that shaped relations between the United States, apartheid South Africa, Unita, and Renamo. Though the relationship between patron and proxy was always unequal, it was never wholly one-sided. The U.S. endorsement enabled South Africa to act with impunity, but the South African government also used the relationship strategically. It continued to take initiatives that would consolidate relations with the right wing in and out of government. The same was true of Unita in its relations with South Africa and the United States and, to a lesser extent, of Renamo. In effect, constructive engagement recast South African regional policy through a sophisticated blend of covert and overt operations: in Mozambique, for example, South Africa combined an official peace accord—the 1984 Nkomati Agreement—with continued clandestine material support for Renamo terrorism. Less than a year after Nkomati, Mozambican forces captured a set of diaries belonging to a member of the Renamo leadership; the Vaz Diaries detailed continued South African Defense Forces support for Renamo.

Constructive engagement clearly delayed political reform in South Africa by at least a decade. Before the United States encouraged South Africa to intervene in Angola, South Africa's own version of détente with independent Africa had come a long way. Prime Minister John Vorster explained the new strategy to *Le Monde:* "Domestic politics must not obstruct international cooperation." Pretoria's initial response to the approach of independence in Mozambique was not to withdraw into a tight defensive circle, which Boer settlers called the laager, but to open up to the possibility of regional reform. Instead of yet again increasing its support to Ian Smith's Unilateral Declaration of Independence (UDI)—which had hitherto included the presence of "about two thousand" South African policemen in Rhodesia from 1967 to 1975—Pretoria prepared for a transition to majority rule in the former British colony. "South Africa, in search of détente with Black Africa, is prepared to ditch us," the head of Rhodesian intelligence wrote in his diary on December 1, 1974.

The era of constructive engagement coincided in South Africa with a period of rising popular resistance in the decade that followed the 1976 Soweto uprising. Yet the partnership with the United States reinforced those in South African ruling circles who gave priority to fighting the Cold War. As voices calling for internal reform were marginalized domestically and were ignored internationally, the South African military tightened its hold over governmental processes and shifted its regional policy from détente to "total onslaught." The militarization of the apartheid regime and its regional policy is amply detailed in the five-volume report of the postapartheid Truth and Reconciliation Commission. The regional shift from accommodation to aggression echoed a similar global shift in the policy of the Reagan administration, from "containment" to "rollback."

It goes without saying that the Cold War was fought by two superpowers, and both subordinated local interests and consequences to global strategic considerations, but here I am only concerned with the United States. My limited purpose is to illuminate the ways in which the United States embraced terror as it prepared to wage the Cold War to a finish.

The United States and Low-Intensity Conflict

The CIA and the Pentagon called terrorism by another name: "low-intensity conflict" (LIC). The move from counterinsurgency to low-intensity conflict signified a strategic reorientation in U.S. war strategy. It was, first of all, a recognition that the dominant threat to U.S. strategic interests came not directly from Soviet troop concentrations in Europe, but indirectly from Third World insurgencies, which Washington thought were Soviet proxies. "Given the proposition that low-intensity conflict is our most likely form of involvement in the Third World," Colonel John D. Waghelstein, former head of the U.S. military group in El Salvador and a leading proponent of LIC, wrote in *Military Review*, "it appears that the army is still preparing for the wrong war by emphasizing the Soviet threat on the plains of Europe." Second, LIC signaled a determination to move from a defensive posture of "deterrence" to an offensive one. The five years that followed defeat in Vietnam were marked by a string of ideological defeats in at least a dozen other countries, including Angola, Mozambique, Iran, Nicaragua, Ethiopia, and Grenada.

The essence of the Reagan doctrine was "rollback." Instead of coexistence or containment, it advocated a determined, sustained, and aggressive bid to reverse defeats in the Third World. The rallying cry came in 1980 from a Republican group called the Committee of Santa Fe. Observing that "containment of the Soviet Union is not enough," it concluded: "It is time to sound a clarion call for freedom, dignity and national self-interest which will echo the spirit of the people of the United States. Either a Pax Sovietica or a world-wide counter-projection of American power is in the offing. The hour of decision can no longer be postponed."

The intellectual argument for rollback, one that made it respectable in polite circles, came from the neoconservative academic Jeanne Kirkpatrick, first in an article titled "Dictatorships and Double Standards," and then in a book by the same name. Kirkpatrick's argument connected Soviet global expansion with Third World revolutions in a causal relationship. Third World revolutions, she claimed, are illegitimate since they are the products of Soviet expansion rather than of local historical forces fighting repressive dictatorships. Kirkpatrick then drew a distinction between two kinds of dictatorships, left-wing ("totalitarian") and right-wing ("authoritarian"). The difference, she argued, was that totalitarian dictatorships are incapable of reforming from within and so have to be overthrown forcibly from without, whereas authoritarian dictatorships are open to internal reform, which can be tapped through constructive engagement. The intellectual importance of Kirkpatrick's argument cannot be exaggerated. By giving a rationale for why it is fine to make friends with right-wing dictators while doing everything to overthrow left-wing governments, she solved the moral problem associated with rollback.

After Ronald Reagan took office in 1981, the new secretary of state, Alexander Haig, declared, "The escalating setback to our interests abroad, and the so-called wars of national liberation, are putting in jeopardy our ability to influence world events." When reelected in 1984, Reagan confirmed in his speech to the nation: "The tide of Soviet Communism can be reversed. All it takes is the will and the resources to get the job done."

With the shift in military strategy to rollback, a clear distinction was made between counterinsurgency and low-intensity conflict: the ambition of counterinsurgency during the Vietnam era had been to defeat revolutionary insurgents; LIC aimed to undermine revolutionary *governments,* not just movements. In his 1985 State of the Union address, President Reagan boldly pledged to assist anti-Communist forces fighting pro-Soviet governments, "on every continent, from Afghanistan to Nicaragua." Covert LIC operations were to be carried out by specially trained Special Operations Forces. The SOF annual budget had fallen from a peak of more than $1 billion during the heyday of the Vietnam War to a low of less than $100 million in fiscal year 1975. Under Reagan, there was an unprecedented peacetime expansion of the SOF budget, reaching about $1.5 billion in fiscal-year 1986, with even higher projections for the following years. SOF funds had a distinct advantage over those for CIA covert operations: "The Pentagon is not required to report details of the SOF's activities to Congress."

A series of developments in 1985–1986 formalized the shift to LIC as the main military strategy. Beginning with the establishment of a Joint (Army/Air Force) Low-Intensity Conflict Project (JLIC) in 1985, it led to a 1986 publication of a thousand-page report on concepts, strategy, guidelines, and application in the Third World. That same year, 1986, the Pentagon held its first conference on low-intensity warfare and established the Army/Air Force Center for Low-Intensity Conflict, both to "elevate awareness" and to "improve the Army/Air Force posture for engaging in low-intensity conflict." This double reformulation of U.S. policy—defining the

Third World as the core battlefield and moving to the offensive—became widely known as the Reagan Doctrine. With it began an idealization—and *ideologization*—of counterrevolutionary forces and their choice weapon, terror. This was particularly so with regard to the contras in Nicaragua, Unita in Angola, and the mujahideen in Afghanistan. These forces, Secretary of State George Shultz declared in a major address in 1985, are part of a "democratic revolution" that is "sweeping the world today."

Senator Clark's advocacy of a decade earlier, calling for "the ethical element in foreign policy," had tragically been emptied of its ethical and democratic content. Clark's call had capped a dual objective: to end U.S. "political and military interference in the internal affairs of other countries" and to recast U.S. foreign-policy formulation along democratic principles. But the Cold Warriors had learned from the antiwar movement that political advantage came from occupying the moral high ground. The Reaganites incorporated "the ethical element," though rhetorically and demagogically, to promote interference rather than to end it. Previously clandestine forms of interference were now unabashedly proclaimed as the pursuit of freedom: in his 1985 State of the Union address, Reagan described support of the contras as backing "freedom fighters" in their battle to overthrow Third World "communist tyranny." When he signed the International Security and Development Cooperation Act of 1985 (S.960) into law on August 8, 1985, Reagan praised this "assistance for the democratic revolution in Nicaragua." Proxy war, designed by Kissinger as a makeshift and pragmatic way of avoiding congressional oversight, was turned into a full-blown ideological assault under the Reagan administration.

LIC had several attractions: it offered the prospect of waging war without declaring it, without a draft, with few soldiers deployed, and with even fewer returning home in body bags. But, for these very reasons, the domestic political costs of LIC were high and, in time, became higher still: for to wage war without declaring it was also to erode and, ultimately, to undermine the democratic process at home. LIC theorists made no secret of their conviction that an active press and vigilant congressional oversight were significant obstacles to military effectiveness. One is struck by the consistency with which this point of view was articulated, whether in testimony to Congress, in military conferences, or in official reports. Its most dramatic statement came in Colonel Oliver North's July 1987 testimony to the select congressional committee investigating the Iran-contra affair. Repeatedly affirming that U.S. national security justifies the employment of covert paramilitary operations and the calculated dissemination of false and misleading information to conceal such operations from adversaries, North defended the right of some U.S. officials to deceive other U.S. officials. Deadpan and matter of fact, he declared, "There is great deceit [and] deception practiced in the conduct of covert operations. They are at essence a lie." LIC theorist Neil Livingstone summed up that same view to senior officers at the National Defense University at Fort McNair, Washington, D.C.: "The United States will never win a war fought daily in the U.S. media or on the floor of Congress." Some years before, Deputy Assistant Secretary of the Air Force J. Michael Kelly had told a 1983 National Defense University conference attended by Colonel North: "I think the most critical special operations mission we have today is to persuade the American public that the communists are out to get us. If we win the war of ideas, we will win everywhere else." And the JLIC report confirmed, "In order to promote a broad understanding of the issues involved, a carefully created, sophisticated, and ongoing public diplomacy effort is necessary." No matter the language, the message was consistent: first waged in Vietnam, the war for "hearts and minds" was to be brought home, and in this propaganda effort all institutional safeguards that we may think of as key to a functioning democracy—particularly congressional oversight and an independent press—were considered as no more than inconveniences to be set aside in organizing an efficient war effort. When Colonel North declared in his July 10, 1987, testimony that CIA Director William J. Casey had proposed the establishment of an "off-the-shelf, self-sustaining, stand-alone entity" that could perform covert political and military operations without accountability to Congress, Senator Warren B. Rudman observed: "If you carry this to its logical extreme, you don't have a democracy anymore."

Central America: Embracing Terror Openly

With the Sandinista-led Nicaraguan Revolution of 1979, the center of gravity of the Cold War shifted from southern Africa to Central America, although the Reagan administration's foreign policy was very wide ranging. Once Jeanne Kirkpatrick had rationalized the dual strategy of embracing right-wing dictators while targeting left-wing regimes, the Heritage Foundation translated the theoretical maxim into a practical proposal that identified nine countries for rollback: Afghanistan, Angola, Cambodia, Ethiopia, Iran, Laos, Libya, Nicaragua, and Vietnam. In March 1981, CIA Director Casey proposed to Reagan a counterrevolutionary offensive on eight countries—Nicaragua, Afghanistan, Laos, Cambodia, Grenada, Iran, Libya, and Cuba—six of which were taken from the Heritage Foundation's hit list. Whereas the October 25, 1983, invasion of Grenada signaled the ceremonial beginning of rollback, Nicaragua was the real policy test. The CIA was in command from the time agency operatives established contact with anti-Sandinista groups in Florida and Central America and brought them together as a single organization—the FDN (Nicaraguan Democratic Forces)—under the leadership of former dictator Anastasio Somoza's national-guard officials. The FDN became the leading organization in the coalition known as the counter-revolutionaries—or, the contras.

The contras were a CIA progeny from the outset. In November 1981, President Reagan had signed National Security Decision Directive 17, authorizing $19.5 million "for the CIA to create a paramilitary commando squad to conduct attacks inside Nicaragua." In another month, "American agents—some CIA, some U.S. Special Forces—were working through Argentine intermediaries to set up contra safe houses, training centers and base camps along the Nicaraguan-Honduran border." Contras were an exclusive CIA "asset," and the war in Nicaragua was a CIA production, from scripting to editing. Take, for example, the testimony of Arturo Cruz, one of the three leaders of the contras from 1985 until he resigned on March 9, 1987. On his resignation, Cruz condemned the Reagan administration for allowing the contras to be controlled by CIA-appointed military commanders and right-wing politicians. Declaring that contra leaders were really puppets of the United States, he said it would be impossible to turn the contras into a democratic movement. A close parallel can be found in the CIA's relationship to the Royal Lao Army in Vientiane—in Alfred McCoy's words, "the only army in the world, except for the U.S. army, that was entirely financed by the U.S. government"— and to assorted mercenary forces in the Laotian provinces; in southern Africa, the relationship between the apartheid regime in South Africa and Renamo in Mozambique was also similar.

The counterrevolutionary war in Nicaragua was unofficially declared on March 14, 1982, when "CIA-trained and -equipped saboteurs blew up two major bridges in Chinandega and Nueva Segovia provinces." In a matter of months, the contras had established a reputation for brutality and cruelty. By mid-1982, the U.S. Defense Intelligence Agency was reporting contra "assassination of minor government officials." In late 1983, Duane Clarridge, the CIA agent in charge of the covert war, admitted in a closed briefing of the House Intelligence Committee staff that the contras had killed not only "Sandinista officials in the provinces" but also "heads of cooperatives, nurses, doctors and judges." The human-rights monitoring group Americas Watch documented contra forces "systematically engaged in the killing of prisoners and the unarmed" including "indiscriminate attacks, torture and other outrages against personal dignity." By the end of 1985, Nicaragua's Ministry of Health estimated that 3,652 civilians had been killed, 4,039 wounded, and 5,232 kidnapped during contra raids. The point of kidnapping, whether by contras in Nicaragua or Renamo in Mozambique, was to make recruits out of hostages. The *New York Times* reported a mass contra kidnapping of between fifteen and twenty civilians near the town of Sinna on April 27, 1987. The U.S.-based Nicaraguan Association for Human Rights confirmed in July 1987 that, besides executing prisoners and murdering civilians, contras also forcibly kidnapped peasants as recruits.

As run-of-the-mill contra activities—blowing up bridges, torturing and assassinating officials and professionals, kidnapping civilians—became known, the CIA got involved in providing political cover for the contras. Starting in January 1983, the CIA retained a Miami-based public-relations firm for $600,000 per year; the contract said the firm was to "project a positive image" and to "publicize" the FDN "in specific target countries through newspaper/magazine articles." The public-relations effort reached its climax in May when President Reagan christened the contras as "freedom fighters" and soon after upgraded them to "the moral equivalents of our founding fathers," an epithet he was later to bestow on the Afghan mujahideen as well.

While the contras carried out crude acts of face-to-face violence, the CIA organized the kind of large-scale sabotage that was beyond contra operational capability. Even in these instances—such as the "at least twenty-two air, land, and sea raids on vital Nicaraguan installations" carried out between September 1983 and April 1984—the operations were clandestinely conducted by "a specially trained force of 'unilaterally controlled Latino assets' (UCLAs)." "Our mission," explained one Honduran UCLA, was "to sabotage ports, refineries, boats, and bridges and to try to make it appear that the contras had done it." Thus, UCLA-manned speedboats launched from a CIA "mother ship" twelve miles offshore struck the oil facilities at Puerto Sandino on September 8, 1983, and CIA commandos fired mortars and grenades to ignite five storage tanks filled with 3.4 million gallons of fuel on October 10. When President Reagan authorized the mining of Nicaraguan harbors, as part of a National Security Council "harassment" plan, in December 1983, UCLA commando teams, once again operating from a CIA mother ship, deposited the mines in shipping channels. Joint CIA-UCLA teams conducted attacks on oil tanks, port facilities, communications centers, and military positions in the first third of 1984. "Our intention is to severely disrupt the flow of shipping essential to Nicaraguan trade during the peak export period," Oliver North wrote in a "top secret" memorandum, "Special Activities in Nicaragua," dated March 2, 1984. Add to these activities comprehensive economic sabotage, which included halting all bilateral aid, a trade boycott, an economic embargo, and pressure on the World Bank to suspend all lending to the Sandinistas in October 1982, and you have a full understanding of the range of policies the United States mustered to isolate and crush this tiny country, the size of Iowa.

Cocaine, Contras, and the CIA

The mining of Nicaraguan harbors created an uproar in public and in Congress. This was around the same time that other U.S.-supported Third World dictators began losing credibility in the public eye: counterinsurgency in El Salvador began to look like propping up a regime condoning death squads; the public image of the Marcos regime in the Philippines began to resemble that of earlier U.S. protégés like the shah of Iran and Somoza of Nicaragua; and there was growing concern within the Republican Party about the extent of domestic black electoral support being lost on account of constructive engagement with apartheid South Africa. The CIA and the Reagan administration seemed to have overreached themselves. In response, Congress passed the Boland Amendment, attached to the Intelligence Authorization Act for 1984:

> During fiscal year 1984, no more than $24,000,000 of the funds available to the Central Intelligence Agency, the Department of Defense, or any other agency or entity of the United States involved in intelligence activities may be obligated or expended for the purpose or which have the effect of supporting, directly or indirectly, military or paramilitary operations in Nicaragua, by any nation, group, organization, movement, or individual.

With this amendment—admittedly a much milder version of the Clark Amendment—Congress capped contra funding at roughly a quarter of what the Reagan administration considered necessary to establish a proper fighting force. Soon after, Robert McFarlane and Oliver North hunted for additional funding sources: they asked the Saudis for $1 million per month and took a mission to apartheid South Africa with a similar objective. In a concerted effort to circumvent the Boland Amendment, the Reagan administration took two initiatives that were to have lasting impact on U.S. foreign policy. The first was to turn to the drug trade for an illicit source of funds; the second was to turn to the religious right to implement those foreign-policy objectives that Congress had ruled against, thus beginning a trend toward privatizing war.

As in the Golden Triangle of Southeast Asia, so in Central America; the pursuit of war by proxy led to an alliance between the CIA and drug dealers. Even though Nicaragua never produced coca as Laos did opium, CIA assets became key to providing a protective cover for the flow of cocaine from Central America to the United States in return for a reverse flow of materials and armaments from the CIA to the contras. Cocaine production and distribution were controlled by the Medellín cartel in Colombia, whose 1988 annual income was estimated at $8 billion and two of whose leaders, Jorge Ochoa and Pablo Escobar, were placed on the list of the world's richest men by *Forbes* magazine. Alfred McCoy observed in his study on the global drug trade, "The Medellín cartel's rise coincided with the start of the CIA's . . . support and supply of contra guerrillas." Indeed, McCoy noted that "all major U.S. agencies have gone on the record stating, with varying degrees of frankness, that the Medellín cartel used the contra resistance forces to smuggle cocaine into the United States." The minimalist statements came from the State Department, whose view was that "a few people somehow affiliated with the contras may have been involved with cocaine." But "better-informed agencies," such as the CIA and the Drug Enforcement Administration (DEA), were more realistic; they "reported that leading contra commanders were major drug traffickers."

The most detailed account of CIA and contra involvement in the cocaine trade during the two years when the Boland Amendment was in effect (1984–1986) is to be found in the report of Senator John Kerry's Subcommittee on Terrorism, Narcotics, and International Operations, part of a larger 1988 report, *Drugs, Law Enforcement, and Foreign Policy,* by the Senate Committee on Foreign Relations. The report concluded both that "individuals associated with the contra movement" were traffickers and that cocaine smugglers had participated in "contra supply operations." The report cites two particularly important examples of contra- and CIA-linked trafficking of cocaine into the United States. The first is that of Eden Pastora, the ex-Sandinista guerrilla turned commander of the contra southern front when it opened in 1983. Pastora's commanders struck an alliance with George Morales, a leading Colombian smuggler based in Miami. In late 1984, Morales supplied Pastora's front with a C-47 aircraft and money—according to the Senate committee report—"to fly narcotics shipments from South America to sites in Costa Rica and Nicaragua for later transport to the United States." Between October 1984 and February 1986, the C-47 made twenty-four flights from America to southern-front bases along the Nicaragua–Costa Rica border with 156,000 pounds of matériel and returned carrying "unspecified quantities of drugs." The second example of major trafficking is that of a Costa Rica–based American rancher named John Hull. In the words of the committee report, Hull became a "central figure in contra operations when they were managed by Oliver North, from 1984 through late 1986." Scattered across Hull's sprawling ranch were six airstrips from where regular "guns for drugs" flights flew straight across the U.S. border without having to go through any customs checks.

The Senate committee also noted that the CIA had made "payments to drug traffickers . . . for humanitarian assistance to the contras, in some cases after the traffickers had been indicted . . . on drug charges." One such contract pilot for the CIA's "humanitarian aid" flights to the contras was Marcos Aguado, a Nicaraguan who had become a senior officer in the Salvadoran air force. In 1990, after another operative, Norman Menses, was arrested in Nicaragua for trying to transport 750 kilograms of cocaine, Enrique Miranda, a former intelligence officer in Somoza's national guard, testified that "Aguado flew Salvadoran air force planes to Colombia to pick up cocaine shipments and delivered them to US Air Force bases in Texas."

There developed in Nicaragua—as in Laos—a close affinity between covert military operatives and criminal drug syndicates. Both groups specialize in clandestine work and work outside the parameters of the law, far from the glare of publicity and the constraint of public scrutiny. Both shun environments shaped by either a rule of law or a democratic order.

This affinity came to the surface during the Iran-contra affair, most dramatically in the person of Oliver North. In 1989, the National Security Archive (NSA), a Washington-based public-interest group, filed a Freedom of Information Act lawsuit and obtained access to the handwritten notebooks of Oliver North, "the National Security Council aide who helped run the contra war and other Reagan administration covert operations." The NSA released the declassified information on its own Web site. A number of entries from the notebooks show that "North was repeatedly informed of contra ties to drug trafficking," most often by his own liaison with contras, Robert Owen. A memo from Owen dated April 1, 1985, warns North that new southern front units include "people who are questionable because of past indiscretions," citing José Robelo's "potential involvement with drug running" and Sebastian Gonzalez as "now involved in drug running out of Panama." In another entry, dated August 9, 1985, North records a meeting with Owen: "Honduran DC-6, which is being used for runs out of New Orleans, is probably being used for drug runs into U.S." Yet another memo from Owen, dated February 10, 1986, refers to "a plane being used to carry 'humanitarian aid' to the contras that was previously used to transport drugs." The plane belonged "to the Miami-based company Nortex, which is run by Michael Palmer, one of the largest marijuana traffickers in the United States." In an accompanying note, the NSA observes that Oliver North—along with Assistant Secretary of State for Inter-American Affairs Elliott Abrams and CIA officer Alan Fiers—oversaw the Nicaraguan Humanitarian Aid Office (NHAO), which paid Palmer more than $300,000 "to ferry supplies to contras . . . despite Palmer's long history of drug smuggling."

Oliver North was also a key link between the Reagan administration and the Panamanian dictator Manuel Noriega, whose collaboration with Colombian drug traffickers had been the subject of a series of *New York Times* articles in June 1986. Soon after, Noriega approached North, suggesting a deal for help in cleaning up his official record. In an e-mail to Reagan's national security adviser, John Poindexter, dated August 23, 1986, North laid out Noriega's proposal: if U.S. officials can "help clean up his image" and lift the ban on arms sales to the Panamanian Defense Forces, Noriega will "take care of the Sandinista leadership for us." North then suggested "paying Noriega a million dollars—from 'Project Democracy' funds raised from the sale of U.S. arms to Iran—for the Panamanian leader's help in destroying Nicaraguan economic installations." North's notebook contains details of his September 22 meeting with Noriega in a London hotel. The two "discussed a commando training program in Panama, with Israeli support, for the contras and Afghani rebels" and "spoke of sabotaging major economic targets in the Managua area." The NSA commentary adds: "These plans were apparently aborted when the Iran-Contra scandal broke in November 1986."

The Iran-Contra Scandal

Faced with congressional limitations on support to contras, the Reagan administration took a second initiative. This, too, turned out to be of lasting significance. The initiative involved expanding the search for proxies, from overseas groups to domestic ones. The religious right was no longer dominated by a few centralized organizations, such as the Moral Majority and Christian Voice, as had been the case in the 1970s; the 1980s saw the formation of numerous grassroots organizations, each with a specific purpose. Christian-right activism in foreign policy focused on Central America and began with Guatemala, where General Efrain Ríos Montt had been converted to Pentacostalism by a group of young Californians who had brought their Gospel Outreach church to Guatemala after a devastating earthquake. Following the 1982 coup that installed Montt as dictator of Guatemala, Pat Robertson and other Christian-right leaders lobbied successfully for the resumption of U.S. military aid to the country. When Montt's army annihilated entire Indian villages, Gospel Outreach members defended the "scorched earth" campaign in religious terms. One enthusiastic pastor put it: "The Army doesn't massacre the Indians. It massacres demons, and the Indians are demon possessed; they are communists. We hold Brother Efrain Ríos Montt like King David of the Old Testament. He is the king of the New Testament."

The contra war "became a laboratory for the administration's use of private organizations," both religious and secular. Here, too, Oliver North turned out to be a key link between the administration and organizations on the religious right. By 1984, leading contra fund-raisers in the United States fell into three categories: paramilitary mercenary outfits, Christian-right "ministries," and the secular political network of conservative lobbies. Key among the Christian-right supporters were Pat Robertson—who had already used his tax-exempt television broadcast to raise $3 million for the FDN—and the founder of the Unification Church, Reverend Sun Myung Moon, whose *Washington Times* had established the Nicaraguan Freedom Fund. Another important Christian-right organization in the contra-support network was Concerned Women for America (CWA), which was otherwise active in providing legal counsel for parents who sought to remove "secular humanist" books from public schools. Appearing at its 1987 convention, President Reagan thanked the CWA for its grassroots support of the contras. Sara Diamond concludes her study of right-wing movements in the United States with the observation that the congressional investigation of the Iran-contra scandal "neglected Oliver North's role in recruiting Christian right activists for the multi-tentacled contra aid network."

It is now widely known that North had formed a private network to fund the contras after official aid was sharply reduced. At the heart of this network was the Israeli connection, and its most ambitious initiative involved the sale of arms to Iran, with the proceeds used to purchase war supplies for the contras. Israel emerged as a significant military supplier to El Salvador, Guatemala, and

Nicaragua in the late seventies and early eighties after those countries were found guilty of human rights violations and the Carter administration terminated military aid to all three. As "a quid pro quo for El Salvador's decision to move its embassy from Tel Aviv to Jerusalem," Israel supplied the military regime "with over 80% of its weaponry for the next several years, including napalm for use against the Salvadoran civilian population." In Guatemala in 1983, as the government carried out massacres of Indian villagers, a *Time* magazine correspondent reported the "the Israelis have sold the government everything from anti-terrorism equipment to transport planes" and that "army outposts in the jungle have become near replicas of Israeli army field camps." Finally, Israel moved into Nicaragua as soon as the Carter administration cut off aid: "Israel sold Somoza 98% of the weapons he used against the Nicaraguan population" between September 1978 and his ouster the following July.

The first major Israeli arms deliveries to the contras began shortly after the pullout of Argentine trainers and suppliers from Central America in the aftermath of the Falklands War. *Time* magazine reported that Argentine advisers were replaced by "retired or reserve Israeli army commanders . . . hired by shadowy private firms." Haifa University professor Benjamin Beit-Hallahmi confirmed that "when the CIA was setting up the contra organization in 1981, the Mossad was also there, carrying out the training and the support for the first units."

Israel's military links with Iran began with the Iraq-Iran War. As Israeli defense minister Ariel Sharon told the *Washington Post* in May 1982, justifying Israeli arms sales to Tehran, "Iraq is Israel's enemy and we hope that diplomatic relations between us and Iran will be renewed as in the past." Four months later, he told a Paris press conference, "Israel has a vital interest in the continuing of the war in the Persian Gulf, and in Iran's victory." Retired General Aharon Yariv, formerly Israel's head of military intelligence, was even more candid when he told a conference at Tel Aviv University in late 1986 that "it would be a good idea if the Iran-Iraq wars ended in a tie, but it would be even better if it continued." Israel and the United States shared the same strategic objective: to prolong the Iraq-Iran War as long as possible. To realize that objective, each armed a different side.

Most observers agreed that, in the face of chilled relations with both the United States and the Soviet Union, Israel had emerged as an important supplier of parts and arms for the Islamic government of Iran. In March 1982, the *New York Times* cited documents indicating that Israel had supplied half or more of all arms reaching Tehran in the previous eighteen months, amounting to at least $100 million in sales. Foreign intelligence sources told *Aerospace Daily* in August 1982 that Israel's support was "crucial" to keeping Iran's air force flying against Iraq. Israeli sources told *Newsweek* that "they sold the Iranians much of the light weaponry and ammunition that the Israeli army had captured during its invasion of Lebanon; subsequently, they sold overhauled jet engines, spare-parts for American-made M-48 tanks, ammunition and other hardware—$100 million worth in 1983 alone."

The Israelis both openly defied the official American ban on the supply of U.S. arms to Iran and tried to get the Reagan administration to deal with the Iranians. In return, they agreed to take on at least a part of the burden of supplying the contras as Congress began to put restrictions on the supply of U.S. military aid. The heart of the deal that came to be known as Iran-contra was that the United States agreed to sell arms to Iran, either directly or through Israel, at prices sufficiently inflated to use the difference to purchase arms for the contras. After a White House briefing, Representative Jim Wright (D-TX) was able to provide a breakdown of one such transaction: Iran had paid the Israelis $19 million: $3 million of that had gone back to the Pentagon, $4 million went to arms brokers, and $12 million went to the Swiss account for the contras. Some of the money went to the Israeli government, which, according to North, established the prices that Iran would have to pay. Most observers agreed that the idea for the deal came from the Israelis. The normally cautious *Times* of London said that "the Senate Intelligence Committee had been given secret evidence strongly suggesting that the plan to divert money from the Iran arms operation to the Nicaraguan Contras was first put forward by Mr. Shimon Peres, then the Israeli Prime Minister." Yo'el Marcus wrote in the Israeli daily *Ha'aretz*: "There is even room to fear that Israel is the moving force behind the whole idea of assistance to Iran. Evidence of this lies in the fact that as early as July 1980 the Jewish lobby was actively trying to convince the administration that the shipment of military spare parts and equipment to Iran would help in getting the hostages [members of the U.S. Embassy in Tehran] released! . . . It is exactly the same thesis, only now with different hostages." The reference was to the kidnapping, among others, of the CIA's Beirut station chief William Buckley in March 1984. Buckley was a prize catch: according to Jonathan Marshall, Peter Dale Scott, and Jane Hunter, "Buckley's encyclopedic knowledge of terrorism, and familiarity with every CIA agent in Lebanon, made him a priceless catch, particularly since the destruction of the CIA station in the Beirut embassy bombing had left the United States with very few eyes and ears in the region." This crisis influenced the Reagan administration to deal with the Islamic regime of Iran. North's memo to the president, delivered in summary form by National Security Advisor John Poindexter on January 16, 1986, ended: "They [Israel] also point out . . . [that] this approach through the government of Iran may well be our only way to achieve the release of the American hostages held in Beirut."

The Iran-contra scandal broke on November 25, 1986, when Reagan appeared at a nationally televised press conference to confess that he "was not fully informed on the nature of the activities undertaken in connection with this [Iran] initiative" and to announce the dismissal of Poindexter and North. Then Attorney General Edwin Meese followed with the real bombshell: funds from the Iran arms sales had been diverted, possibly illegally, to the contras in Nicaragua. The attorney general had revealed nothing less than a conspiracy at the highest levels of government to break the law and contravene public policy on Iran, terrorism, and military aid to the contras. No longer a question of faulty judgment, this was about breaking the law.

The Sunday Telegraph of London cited one former official in early 1989 as saying that the White House "suppressed" hundreds of documents on "Israeli mercenaries who, with the knowledge of the Israeli and the U.S. governments, flew weapons and ammunition to Tegucigalpa [Honduras] . . . at a time when Congress had banned military aid. The arms were then distributed to contra bases on the Nicaraguan border." Claiming that these documents were "crucial to understanding the whole scandal," a congressional source concluded: "The American public never knew. It is a cover-up."

The resulting Iran-contra scandal could have taken on the proportions of Watergate, which ended Nixon's presidency, but it did not. Part of the reason must lie in the alliances built by the pro-Israel lobby in Congress, which had over the years turned into an antidétente lobby. Fearful that American détente with Russia was weakening American backing of Israel, supporters of the Jewish state were willing to ally with one and all, liberals or conservatives, to weaken the rapprochement with the Soviet Union. On the one hand, they joined hands with conservatives who considered the Kissinger line soft on the Soviet Union; on the other, they lined up with liberals who regarded his silence on human-rights violations within the Soviet Union as amoral and inconsistent with American values. Faced with Israel's involvement in the Iran-contra scandal, could it be that congressional liberals hesitated to press matters further precisely because Israel was involved?

Even before the Boland Amendment expired in October 1986, President Reagan was calling for a renewed contra offensive against the Sandinistas. Few outside of official Washington would have thought of Nicaragua—this small, impoverished nation just emerged from under the boot of an American-blessed dictatorship in 1979—in the terms that Reagan used in his February 4, 1986, State of the Union address: "This is a great moral challenge for the entire free world. Surely no issue is more important for peace in our own hemisphere, for the security of our frontiers, for the protection of our vital interests than . . . Nicaragua." The point of the escalating rhetoric was to convince the American public that this bloody war of attrition against this tiny country was, somehow, in the national interest. The scandal was that as soon as the Boland Amendment expired on October 17, 1986, the portion of the CIA budget allocated for the contras rose to $100 million.

The contra war combined elements of the old and the new. As in Laos, the covert war was financed through illicit trade. The proxy war came to include a range of domestic constituencies, most significantly the religious right. Finally, it was in Nicaragua that the Reagan administration learned how to combine covert and overt methods of work into a single coherent strategy, thereby joining terrorism to electoral politics, so as to translate the pursuit of terror into a political victory.

The CIA's embrace of terror tightened during the two years the Boland Amendment was in effect. How far CIA thinking had come from the days of Vietnam and counterinsurgency is clear from the training manual it published in 1985 for the contras, titled *Psychological Operations in Guerrilla Warfare.* The manual called for combining a range of tactics, from the "neutralization" of civilian officials to "armed propaganda." It advised "the selective use of violence," including involving the population in acts of violence: "It is possible to neutralize carefully selected and planned targets, such as court judges, magistrates, police and state security officials, etc. For psychological purposes, it is necessary to gather together the population affected, so that they will be present, take part in the act, and formulate accusations against the oppressor." While calling for selective terror as a way of eroding popular confidence in government, the manual advised against "explicit terror," lest the population be alienated: "If the government police cannot put an end to the guerrilla activities, the population will lose confidence in the government which has the inherent mission of guaranteeing the safety of citizens. However, the guerrillas should be careful not to become an explicit terror, because this would result in a loss of popular support." When it came to the practice of terror, governments and private groups shared the same minimal objective: to put into question the ability of a government in power to ensure security of person and property for the population it claimed to represent.

The parallel between Renamo in Mozambique—particularly after South Africa became Renamo's principal patron in 1980—and the contras in Nicaragua is indeed striking. Both began as counterrevolutionary movements created by a foreign power looking for proxies in a war in which it could not intervene directly. Both embraced terror as a strategy. Their practice made little sense from the point of view of winning or taking power. No one—including the CIA—really expected the contras to win the war against the Sandinistas. The point of this war, this terror, was not to win but to bleed the government, to show it as incapable of protecting the population from terror and simultaneously to invite its repression—two different but effective ways of discrediting the government. Testifying before the World Court on September 8, 1985, David MacMichael, a CIA national intelligence analyst on Central America from 1981 to 1983 who later became critical of the contra War, explained that the CIA expected that contra raids would provoke the Sandinistas into three kinds of aggressions: (1) "clamp down on civil liberties within Nicaragua itself, arresting its opposition, demonstrating its allegedly inherent totalitarian nature and thus increase domestic dissent within the country"; (2) provoke "cross border attacks by Nicaraguan forces and thus serve to demonstrate Nicaragua's aggressive nature and possibly call into play the Organization of American States"; and (3) provoke "reaction against United States citizens, particularly against United States personnel within Nicaragua and thus serve to demonstrate the hostility of Nicaragua towards the United States."

The point of harnessing terror as part of an electoral campaign was to turn it into a form of blackmail that could be switched off and on at will. This is how the Nicaraguan election was turned into a referendum on terror. The idea was that if the right dose of terror could be delivered with effectiveness and combined with impunity, it would be only a matter of time before the population was convinced that the only way to end terror was to grant terrorists their political objective: power. Meanwhile, so long as the terror continued, those responsible for giving it a political cover continued to disclaim political responsibility. Just as the South African and American press routinely described mounting deaths in southern Africa as evidence of "black-on-black violence"—consistently downplaying its overall context—so the United States, too, looked for "deniability" by describing terror as a matter of "Nicaraguans fighting against Nicaraguans," an internal Nicaraguan affair for which Washington had no responsibility.

The United States' embrace of terror can be plotted as a learning curve that went through three successive phases of the late Cold War, from southern Africa to Central America and central Asia. Each phase can be identified with a distinct lesson. If the patronage of terror in the opening phase was shy, more like the benign and permissive tolerance of the practices of an aggressive regional ally—apartheid South Africa—the United States moved to a bold and brazen embrace of terror when it came to the counterrevolutionaries in Central America, combining it with patronage of an illicit trade in cocaine as the preferred way of financing its covert operations. It was, however, in the closing phase of the Cold War that the United States came to see the embrace of terror as the means to an international public good. It did this in two ways: by privatizing and by internationalizing the main operations in the war. Whereas both tendencies were already present in U.S. support of the contras, each truly blossomed only with the anti-Soviet war in Afghanistan, which was so ideologized that it was seen less and less as a national-liberation struggle and more and more as an international religious crusade: a jihad.

Chapter Three

AFGHANISTAN: THE HIGH POINT IN THE COLD WAR

In an article he wrote in *Dawn,* the Pakistani political thinker and activist Eqbal Ahmad draws our attention to an American television image from 1985. On the White House lawn, President Ronald Reagan is introducing, with great fanfare, a group of Afghan men, all leaders of the mujahideen, to the media: "These gentlemen are the moral equivalents of America's founding fathers." This was the moment when America tried to harness extreme versions of political Islam in the struggle against the Soviet Union.

The half decade that followed defeat in Vietnam witnessed other setbacks in U.S. foreign policy. This trend was illustrated dramatically in 1979 when popular revolutions swept away two U.S.-backed dictatorships, one in Nicaragua, the other in Iran. At the end of the same year, the Soviet Union invaded Afghanistan. Who would have guessed that the Soviet Union would collapse only a decade later, leaving the United States as the sole, triumphant superpower? If 9/11 cut short the celebration of that victory, it also posed the question: At what price was the Cold War won? To answer this question requires focusing on the Reagan presidency, for it was Ronald Reagan who claimed that the defeat of U.S.-backed dictatorships in the Third World was evidence that the Soviet Union was "on a roll," and it was Reagan who demanded that all possible resources be marshaled to "roll back" the Soviet Union, "by all means necessary." Afghanistan, more than any other location, was the high point of the Cold War.

The Afghan War made the counterrevolutionary operation in Nicaragua pale by comparison, both in the extent of resources mustered and in the gravity of its aftereffects. There were 100,000 Soviet ground troops in Afghanistan at the height of the war. Afghanistan presented the United States with an opportunity to hand the Soviet Union its own Vietnam. Reagan formulated this into a strategic objective, thereby approaching the Afghan War from a perspective more global than regional. As it stretched through the near decade of the Reagan presidency, the Afghan War turned into the bloodiest regional conflict in the world. This largest CIA paramilitary operation since Vietnam also turned out to be the longest war in Soviet history.

The revolutions of 1979 had a profound influence on the conduct of the Afghan War. The Iranian Revolution led to a restructuring of relations between the United States and political Islam. Prior to it, America saw the world in rather simple terms: on one side was the Soviet Union and militant Third World nationalism, which America regarded as a Soviet tool; on the other side was political Islam, which America considered an unqualified ally in the struggle against the Soviet Union. Thus, the United States supported the Sarekat-i-Islam against Sukarno in Indonesia, the Jamaat-i-Islami against Zulfiqar Ali Bhutto in Pakistan, and the Society of Muslim Brothers against Nasser in Egypt. The expectation that political Islam would provide a local buffer against secular nationalism was also broadly shared by U.S. allies within the region, from Israel to conservative Arab regimes. Until events proved the foolhardiness of the project, Israel hoped to encourage an Islamist political movement in the Occupied Territories and play it off against the secular nationalism of the Palestine Liberation Organization (PLO). Israeli intelligence allowed Hamas to operate unhindered during the first intifada—letting it open a university and bank accounts and even possibly helping it with funding—only to confront a stronger Hamas as the organizer of the second intifada. In Egypt, Anwar Sadat appeared as a liberator of political Islam after the death of Nasser. Between 1971 and 1975, Sadat released Islamists who had been languishing in jail and gave them, first, the freedom to publicize their views and, later, the freedom to organize. I cite these instances not to tarnish and discredit the movements concerned because they were supported by American or Israeli intelligence, but to show how the unintended consequences of misinformed, cynical, and opportunistic actions can boomerang on their perpetrators.

The impact of the Iranian Revolution was dramatized by the humiliating saga of the American embassy hostages. The first student occupation of the embassy occurred shortly after Khomeini's return to Iran on February 14, 1979, but Khomeini and Prime Minister Mehdi Bazargan moved quickly to expel the occupiers. Eight months later, circumstances changed radically: when the U.S. government welcomed the deposed shah to New York for medical treatment, Khomeini responded with criticism of the United States as "the Great Satan." Within a month, some three thousand Iranian students stormed the U.S. embassy in Tehran and took ninety hostages. This time, Khomeini and the government responded differently. After the release of women and black Marine guards, the remaining fifty-two American diplomats were held for 444 days.

The Iranian Revolution introduced a new political development on the world scene: here was an Islamist regime that was not only Islamist and anti-Communist but at the same time fervently nationalist, determined to act independently of all foreign influences, particularly the United States. The more this became clear, the more official America expanded its search for friends in the neighborhood. Soon, secular but brutal regimes like that of Saddam Hussein in Iraq were recruited as American allies. While the second embassy occupation was in progress, the forces of Saddam Hussein invaded southwest Iran on September 20, 1980—with open encouragement from the United States. The Iraqi war against Iran saw the first post-Vietnam use of chemical weapons in war, and America was the source of both the weapons and the training needed to use them.

The revolution in Iran taught the United States to distinguish between two faces of political Islam: the revolutionary and the elitist. The revolutionary side saw the organization of Islamic social movements and mass participation as crucial to ushering in an independent Islamist state. In contrast, the elitist side distrusted popular participation; its notion of an Islamist state was one that would *contain* popular participation, not encourage it. Before the Iranian Revolution complicated the picture by sharpening the difference between these sides in Iran, the United States had operated with a simple formula, one that identified the revolutionary face of political Islam with Iran and the Shi'a sect in Islam, and the elitist face with majority-Sunni pro-American regimes such as those in Saudi Arabia and Pakistan.

Afghanistan: The High Point in the Cold War

The Nicaraguan Revolution was the source of a different kind of lesson: how to organize and pursue a counterrevolutionary war by means both overt and covert. This first significant attempt to roll back a nationalist pro-Soviet Third World government taught the Reagan administration how to harness support from diverse quarters toward a single objective. Two lessons from the contra experience were particularly useful: the first was a benign attitude toward the drug trade as a source of cash to carry out a clandestine war; and the second was the need to involve the entire neighborhood—Christian-right ministries, the network of secular conservative political lobbies, and paramilitary mercenary outfits—in the war effort.

Secret American aid to opponents of the pro-Soviet regime in Kabul had begun before the Soviet army invaded Afghanistan. CIA and State Department documents seized during the embassy takeover in Tehran reveal that the United States had begun quietly meeting Afghan-rebel representatives in Pakistan in April 1979, eight months before Soviet military intervention. This much was confirmed by Zbigniew Brzezinski, President Carter's national security advisor, in a later interview with the Paris-based *Le Nouvel Observateur* (January 15–21, 1998):

Q: The former director of the CIA, Robert Gates, stated in his memoirs [*From the Shadows*] that American intelligence services began to aid the Mujahidin in Afghanistan 6 months before the Soviet intervention. In this period, you were the national security advisor to President Carter. You therefore played a role in this affair. Is that correct?

Brzezinski: Yes. According to the official version of history, CIA aid to the Mujahidin began during 1980, that is to say, after the Soviet army invaded Afghanistan, 24 Dec. 1979. But the reality, secretly guarded until now, is completely otherwise: Indeed, it was 3 July 1979 that President Carter signed the first directive for secret aid to the opponents of the pro-Soviet regime in Kabul. And that very day, I wrote a note to the president in which I explained to him that in my opinion this aid was going to induce a Soviet military intervention.

The passage from the Carter to the Reagan presidency also exacerbated the shift in U.S. foreign policy from containment to rollback. In Afghanistan, as in Nicaragua, the Carter administration had preferred a two-track approach, combining the carrot and the stick, approving moderate levels of covert support for anti-Communist allies, whether governments or groups, alongside a search for a negotiated settlement. Containment, in this sense, was guided by the search for coexistence. In contrast, the Reagan administration had absolutely no interest in arriving at negotiated settlements. Rather than coexistence, the point of the Reagan policy was payback: everything must be done to turn the Afghan War into the Soviet Union's Vietnam. The single objective was to bleed the Soviet Union white. The CIA was determined that nothing come in the way of the "real task" in Afghanistan: "killing Russians." Among the more influential "bleeders" in Washington was Reagan's assistant secretary of defense, Richard Perle. He would later have a second coming as a prominent hawk on the George W. Bush team after 9/11.

If the Reagan administration was predisposed to groups with hard-line ideological opposition to the Soviet Union and no interest in a compromise settlement, successive Pakistani governments had a pathological distrust of Afghan nationalism. This became clear when the Afghan king, Zahir Shah, was deposed in a bloodless coup by his cousin and former prime minister, Mohammad Daud, in July 1973. Daud put together a republican alliance of sections of the military and a wing of the Communist Party named after its newspaper, *Percham* (banner). The new nationalist government took up the popular cause of Pashtunistan, which demanded a homeland for the Pashtun people. Not only were roughly half of Afghanistan's population ethnic Pashtuns, millions of Pashtuns also lived in Pakistan's North-West Frontier Province (NWFP), on the other side of an artificial border drawn by the British at the height of their colonial empire in India. Fearful of Afghan nationalism, Pakistani governments were open to supporting antinationalist forces in Afghanistan, and Zia ul-Haq's was no exception. The ideological opposition to nationalism, including to Daud's authoritarian version, came mainly from Communists and Islamists, mostly university students and professors who were strongly international in their outlook. Increasing popular opposition to Daud's rule led to a second military coup known as the Saur Revolution that brought both factions of the Communist Party, Percham and Khalq (also named after its newspaper), into government. With this revolution of April 17, 1978, Communist "internationalism" became officially respectable, and Islamist "internationalism" was labeled subversive. Moderate and extremist Islamist radicals fled Kabul University for refuge in Pakistan, where they were welcomed.

The 1978 Communist coup also created a decisive shift in U.S. relations with Pakistan. The Carter administration had cut aid to Pakistan in 1977, a response to both its dismal human-rights record at home—dramatized by the army's judicial murder of an elected prime minister, Zulfiqar Ali Bhutto—and the global implications of its accelerated nuclear program. The coup and the Soviet invasion of Afghanistan changed all this: "literally days after the Soviet invasion, Carter was on the telephone with Zia offering him hundreds of millions of dollars in economic and military aid in exchange for cooperation in helping rebels." Zia held out for more, and the Carter-Zia partnership remained lukewarm. The real warming came with the Reagan administration, which offered Pakistan "a huge, six-year economic and military aid package which elevated Pakistan to the third largest recipient of U.S. foreign aid"—after Israel and Egypt.

During the Reagan presidency, there was sustained cooperation between the CIA and Pakistan's Inter Services Intelligence (ISI), and neither party had much interest in a negotiated settlement. Both intelligence agencies came to share a dual objective: militarily, to provide maximum firepower to the mujahideen and, politically, to recruit the most radically anti-Communist Islamists to counter Soviet forces. The combined result was to flood the region not only with all kinds of weapons but also with the most radical Islamist recruits. They flocked to ISI-run training camps in Pakistan, where they were "ideologically charged with the spark of holy war and trained in guerrilla tactics, sabotage and bombings." The Islamist recruits came from all over the world, not only Muslim-majority countries such as Algeria, Saudi Arabia, Egypt, and Indonesia, but also such Muslim-minority countries as the United States and Britain. There is the well-known example of Sheikh Abdullah Azzam, dubbed by Lawrence Wright, writing in *The New Yorker,* the "gatekeeper of the Jihad" in the mid-eighties. "A Palestinian theologian who had a doctorate in Islamic law from Al-Azhar University," Sheikh Azzam "went on to teach at King Abdul Aziz University, in Jidda, where one of his students was

Osama bin Laden." Azzam traveled the globe under CIA patronage. He appeared on Saudi television and at rallies in the United States. A CIA asset who appeared as the embodiment of the holy warrior and "toured the length and breadth of the United States in the early and mid-1980s recruiting for holy war, ostensibly only in Afghanistan," Azzam was also one of the founders of Hamas. Azzam's message was clear: participation in the jihad is not just a political obligation but a religious duty. The point of the jihad is not only to kill the enemy, the Russian, but also to invite "martyrdom." In a 1988 recruitment video examined by Wright, Azzam says: "I reached Afghanistan and could not believe my eyes. I traveled to acquaint people with jihad for years. . . . We were trying to satisfy the thirst for martyrdom. We are still in love with this." Azzam's formula for the holy war was simple: "Jihad and the rifle alone: no negotiations, no conferences, and no dialogues." It neatly echoed the combined CIA-ISI objective.

The Islamic world had not seen an armed jihad for nearly a century. But now the CIA was determined to create one in service of a contemporary political objective. Of course, the tradition of jihad is contentious. Doctrinally, the tradition of jihad as "just war" can be located in the "lesser jihad," not in the "greater jihad." Historically, the tradition of "lesser jihad" itself comprises two different—and conflicting—notions. The first is that of a just war against occupiers, whether nonbelievers or believers. There were four such just wars: Saladin's jihad against the Crusaders in the twelfth century, the Sufi jihad against enslaving aristocracies in West Africa in the seventeenth century, the Wahhabi jihad against Ottoman colonizers in the Arabian peninsula in the eighteenth century, and the Mahdi's anticolonial struggle against the combination of Turko-Egyptian and British power in late nineteenth-century Sudan. The first was against occupying nonbelievers, the second against oppressive believers, the third against occupying believers, and the fourth, against a combination of occupiers, believers and nonbelievers. The second, conflicting, tradition is that of a permanent jihad against doctrinal tendencies in Islam officially considered "heretic." This is a tradition with little historical depth in Islam. Associated with the slaughter of Shi'a civilian populations in Iran and Iraq carried out by the Ikhwan faction of the Wahhabi movement in the eighteenth century—not to be confused with the later Egyptian Ikhwan (Society of Muslim Brothers)—this tradition is more akin to the Inquisition in Christianity than to any historical practice of jihad in Islam. The notion of a standing jihad—a state institution in defense of state interests—is identified less with historical Islam than with the later history of the House of Saud and the state of Saudi Arabia. Precisely because of its association with sectarian practices enshrined in the history of a state with such close ties to official America, an armed standing jihad was particularly appealing to CIA planners.

This is the setting in which the United States organized the Afghan jihad and that informed its central objective: to unite a billion Muslims worldwide in a holy war, a crusade, against the Soviet Union, on the soil of Afghanistan. The notion of a crusade, rather than jihad, conveys better the frame of mind in which this initiative was taken. A secondary objective was to turn a doctrinal difference between two Islamic sects—the minority Shi'a and the majority Sunni—into a political divide and thereby to contain the influence of the Iranian Revolution as a Shi'a affair. The Afghan jihad was in reality an American jihad, but it became that fully only with Reagan's second term in office. In March 1985, Reagan signed National Security Decision Directive 166, authorizing "stepped-up covert military aid to the mujahideen, and it made clear that the secret Afghan war had a new goal: to defeat Soviet troops in Afghanistan through covert action and encourage a Soviet withdrawal."

The redefined war was taken over by CIA chief William Casey, who undertook three significant measures in 1986. The first was to convince Congress to step up American involvement by providing the mujahideen with American advisers and American-made Stinger antiaircraft missiles. The second was to expand the Islamic guerrilla war from Afghanistan into the Soviet republics of Tajikistan and Uzbekistan, a decision reversed when the Soviet Union threatened to attack Pakistan in retaliation. The third was to step up the recruitment of radical Islamists from around the world to come train in Pakistan and fight alongside the mujahideen.

The second and third decisions intensified the ideological character of the war as a religious war against infidels everywhere. Even more than Nicaragua, Afghanistan was to be an ideological battlefield. It was Islamic in a triple sense. First, the mobilization of the war targeted a worldwide Islamic public, in all aspects: financial, material, and human. Second, the mobilization was carried out, as far as possible, through Islamic institutions, ranging from banks and charities to mosques and evangelical organizations. Third, the war was (at least in theory) to be expanded to Soviet Asia, the part of the Soviet Union with historically Muslim populations.

How did right-wing Islamism, an ideological tendency with small and scattered numbers before the Afghan War, come to occupy the global center stage after 9/11? The answer lies in the Afghan jihad, which gave it not only the organization, the numbers, the skills, the reach, and the confidence but also a coherent objective. Before the Afghan jihad, the right wing of political Islam was divided into two camps: those identified with pro-American regimes, as in Saudi Arabia and Pakistan, and those opposed to these same regimes, seeing them as American stooges that had betrayed the Palestinian cause. Unlike Islamists who organized political parties and sought to galvanize ordinary people into political activity, however, the right-wingers had no program outside of isolated acts of urban terror. Until the Afghan jihad, right-wing Islamists out of power had neither the aspiration of drawing strength from popular organization nor the possibility of marshaling strength from any alternative source. The Reagan administration rescued right-wing Islamism from this historical cul-de-sac. The American jihad claimed to create an Islamic infrastructure of liberation but in reality forged an "infrastructure of terror" that used Islamic symbols to tap into Islamic networks and communities. To understand the deep-seated effects of the decision to ideologize the war as Islamic, it is necessary to look at different aspects of the mobilization that was the American jihad.

The blueprint for the Afghan jihad was worked out by the CIA, in collaboration with the ISI of Pakistan. For the actual conduct of the war, the CIA acquired weapons and specialists in guerrilla warfare from different countries and delivered them, along with intelligence and surveillance information on Afghanistan, to the ISI. The ISI was responsible for transport of weapons to the border, supervised the training of Afghan fighters inside Pakistan, and coordinated their operations inside Afghanistan. While ISI was the main regional proxy in the operation, the second line included the intelligence services of Saudi Arabia and Egypt, with the intelligence services of Britain, China, the Philippines, and even Israel also involved. The basic lesson of Indochina, southern Africa, and Central America was applied with great care: this was to be an operation in which the CIA would be at more than arm's length. It would be a proxy war run through third and fourth parties.

As different tasks were subcontracted to different agencies, the blueprint of the war unfolded in a compartmentalized fashion. The point was to ensure the direct involvement of as few Americans as possible; fewer still were in direct contact with the mujahideen or their field commanders. While subcontracting removed American presence from the ground, and thus the possibility of any direct damage to American personnel, its unintended consequence was to give substantial freedom to the subcontractors to bypass central command and deal directly with agencies such as the CIA or DEA. The result was a lack of coherence in overall American policy.

Beyond the front-line proxy states and their intelligence agencies, increasingly the intermediaries were private institutions, both religious and secular. The overall effect was progressively to privatize the war on an international basis. From this dynamic emerged the forces that carried out the operation we know as 9/11.

Had the anti-Soviet crusade been organized in a national framework, the CIA would have looked for mainly Afghani recruits to wage it. But with the war recast as an international jihad, the CIA looked for volunteers from Muslim populations all over the globe.

Outside of Pakistan, the Arab countries were the main source of volunteers, who became known as Afghan-Arabs. The non-Afghani recruits were known by hyphenated identities, as Afghan-Algerians, Afghan-Indonesians, and so on. A network of recruitment centers was set up, linking key points in the Arab world—Egypt and Saudi Arabia—with Pakistan. Eventually, they spread as far as Sudan to the south, Indonesia to the east, Chechnya to the north, and

Kosovo to the west. Sensitive to the critique from within the religious right that they had failed to support the Palestinian struggle meaningfully, members of the Saudi establishment encouraged local dissidents to join the Afghan jihad, and the Egyptian government looked the other way as local Islamists made their way to Afghanistan. A third major Arab source of recruitment was Algeria. Martin Stone writes that "the Pakistani embassy in Algeria alone issued 2,800 visas to Algerian volunteers during the 1980s." The numbers recruited and trained were impressive by any reckoning: the estimate of foreign radicals "directly influenced by the Afghan jihad" is upwards of one hundred thousand. The Afghan-Arabs constituted an elite force and received the most sophisticated training. Fighters in the Peshawar-based Muslim "international brigade" received the relatively high salary of around $1,500 per month.

The CIA looked for a Saudi prince to lead this crusade but was unable to find one. It settled for the next best, the son of an illustrious family closely connected to the Saudi royal house. We need to remember that Osama bin Laden did not come from a backwater family steeped in premodernity but from a cosmopolitan family. The bin Laden family endows programs at universities such as Harvard and Yale. Bin Laden was recruited, with U.S. approval at the highest level, by Prince Turki al-Faisal, then head of Saudi intelligence. According to Pakistani journalist Ahmed Rashid, Osama bin Laden first traveled to Peshawar in 1980 and met mujahideen leaders there, and for the next two years he returned frequently with Saudi donations for the cause. In 1982, he decided to settle in Peshawar. In 1986, bin Laden worked as the major contractor to build a large CIA-funded project: the Khost tunnel complex deep under the mountains close to the Pakistani border. The Khost complex housed a major arms depot, a training facility, and a medical center for the mujahideen. It is the Khost complex that President Clinton decided in 1998 to bomb with Tomahawk cruise missiles. It is also in the Khost complex—the famed mountain caves—that the United States later fought al-Qaeda remnants in its own Afghan War.

Though Osama bin Laden had been a student of Sheikh Abdullah Azzam, the first Afghan-Arab gatekeeper of the jihad in the mid-eighties, a break between Azzam and bin Laden came toward the end of the Afghan jihad. The parting of the ways was the result of a disagreement in 1989 over the future of the jihad: bin Laden "envisioned an all-Arab legion, which eventually could be used to wage jihad in Saudi Arabia and Egypt," whereas Azzam "strongly opposed making war against fellow-Muslims." Soon after, Azzam and two of his sons were blown up by a car bomb as they were driving to a mosque in Peshawar. A meeting was held toward the end of 1989 in the town of Khost to decide on the future of the jihad. One of the ten at the meeting was a Sudanese fighter named Jamal al-Fadl. He testified in a New York courtroom in one of the trials connected with the 1998 bombings of the American embassies in East Africa that a new organization was created in that meeting to wage jihad beyond the borders of Afghanistan. That organization was al-Qaeda, "the Base." Bin Laden thus emerged as the organizer and patron of the most prominent privatized arm of the American jihad.

There is little published information on the pattern, scope, and method of the CIA's international recruitment to its jihad. If the volunteers were recruited by "CIA agents," these agents were more often than not neither directly employed nor directly paid by the CIA, nor even always acting in the knowledge that they were CIA proxies. The little available information suggests that the recruitment of foreign volunteers—perhaps not on the level of Osama bin Laden but certainly many others—was privatized through Islamic religious and charitable bodies. Would it be surprising if recruiters received no special payment, and commitment turned out to be the chief mode of harnessing volunteer energies?

To get an idea of the type of Islamic religious and charitable bodies that were knowingly or unknowingly turned into recruiting agencies for the Afghan jihad, we can turn to John Cooley's study of one international Islamic missionary organization, the Tablighi Jamaat, with headquarters in Pakistan and branches all over the world, including in North America. Founded in 1926 by a Muslim scholar, Maulana Mohammad Ilyas, to "purify" borderline Muslims "who had retained many of the customs and religious practices from their Hindu past," the Tablighi Jamaat had grown large enough to attract more than a million Muslims from ninety countries to their annual conference near Lahore, Pakistan, in 1988, the last year of the Afghan War. That same year, their convention in Chicago attracted more than six thousand Muslims from around the world.

The Tablighi Jamaat was neither set up nor functioned as a terrorist organization. This mainstream religious group was, however, among those used by the CIA as a conduit in its recruitment. It is difficult to tell how many of these recruits were mercenaries looking for advantage, how many were adventurers looking for a thrill, and how many enlisted out of conviction, in response to a call to fight for the independence of an Islamic people from a "godless evil empire" determined to impose a secular code of conduct on them. Of those recruited by the Tablighi Jamaat from Tunisia, "a few more than 160" were recruited for religious courses in Lahore; of these, "about 70" completed military training, "some

15 to 20" actually fought in the jihad, and "a handful of these died fighting," according to Cooley. Only when Sheikh Muhammed al-Hamidi, a religious teacher who had immigrated to France, "was charged with trying to recruit mercenaries for the Afghan Mujahidin and was later imprisoned for three years," did it become clear that "the Tablighi recruiting network was spreading from North Africa to France."

In the United States, too, the CIA took cover behind legitimate charitable and religious Muslim organizations. To what extent these were subverted in the process, we shall probably never know. One instance will suffice to highlight this development. According to Cooley, the al-Kifah Afghan Refugee Center on Atlantic Avenue in Brooklyn, New York, was turned into a key center for "recruiting and fund raising for the Afghanistan jihad" and came to be called the "Al-Jihad" center by those who worked there. Among the leading recruiters at the center were Sheikh Abdullah Azzam and Sheikh Omar Abdel Rahman. Both were prominent Islamists, and both had sustained records of collaboration with the CIA. Sheikh Azzam, as we have seen, was a founder of Hamas and the leading recruiter of Afghan-Arabs for the CIA. Sheikh Rahman, a blind Egyptian prayer leader, was a founder of the Egyptian Islamic Group. He had "sent his sons to fight in Afghanistan" and was at the same time known to have "recruited for the CIA." Sheikh Rahman, who had relocated to the United States in the eighties, was "convicted in the successful World Trade Center bombing of February 1993 and the subsequent aborted conspiracy in June 1993 to bomb UN headquarters, traffic tunnels, bridges, FBI headquarters and government offices, as well as to assassinate pro-Israel officers and legislators."

Training for the Afghan jihad was divided into the training of trainers and the training of fighters. Whereas the main training for the Afghan jihad took place in the string of traditional Koranic schools or madrassahs opened up under General Zia in Pakistan, the training of trainers—and of some high-level mujahideen recruits—also took place at a number of camps in the United States. Cooley's list includes the High Rock Gun Club in Naugatuck, Connecticut; Fort Bragg, North Carolina; CIA's Camp Perry in Williamsburg, Virginia; a CIA-used Army Special Forces site, Harvey Point, North Carolina; Fort A. P. Hill, Virginia; and Camp Pickett, Virginia.

Probably the most subversive effect of the privatized jihad was on the madrassahs, many of which were turned into politico-military training schools. The point was to integrate guerrilla training with the teachings of Islam and thus create "Islamic guerrillas." The London-based Indian journalist Dilip Hiro commented on the curriculum of the madrassahs: "Predominant themes were that Islam was a complete sociopolitical ideology, that holy Islam was being violated by atheistic Soviet troops, and that the Islamic people of Afghanistan should reassert their independence by overthrowing the leftist Afghan regime propped up by Moscow." The madrassahs not only opened their doors to Islamic radicals from around the world but also taught that the Islamic revolution in Afghanistan would be but a precursor to revolution in other Muslim-majority countries, particularly those in Soviet Central Asia. By the late 1980s, leading Deobandi madrassahs in Pakistan "began to reserve places specifically for Central Asian radicals, who received a free education and a living allowance." These were among the first of the students to be prepared for a wider war, and from them would come the Taliban.

The mujahideen operated an Educational Center for Afghanistan during the 1980s. Pervez Hoodbhoy gives the following examples from children's textbooks designed for it by the University of Nebraska under a $50 million USAID grant that ran from September 1986 through June 1994. A third-grade mathematics textbook asks: "One group of maujahidin attack 50 Russian soldiers. In that attack 20 Russians are killed. How many Russians fled?" A fourth-grade textbook ups the ante: "The speed of a Kalashnikov [the ubiquitous Soviet-made semiautomatic machine gun] bullet is 800 meters per second. If a Russian is at a distance of 3200 meters from a mujahid, and that mujahid aims at the Russian's head, calculate how many seconds it will take for the bullet to strike the Russian in the forehead." The program ended in 1994, but the books continued to circulate: "US-sponsored textbooks, which exhort Afghan children to pluck out the eyes of their enemies and cut off their legs, are still widely available in Afghanistan and Pakistan, some in their original form."

The madrassahs were both private and government-funded, and ranged from those who thought of Islamic piety in religious terms to those for whom Islam was also a political calling. In spite of their proliferation, military training was mainly carried out in army camps. The trainees were divided into two groups: Afghan mujahideen and non-Afghan jihadi volunteers. Brigadier Muhammad Yusuf, a chief of the Afghan cell of ISI for four years, confirmed: "During my four years, some 80,000 mujahiddin were trained." Ahmed Rashid estimates that thirty-five thousand Muslim radicals from forty-three Islamic countries fought for the mujahideen between 1982 and 1992. United States authorities estimated that "at least 10,000" received "some degree of military training." A *Los Angeles Times* team of reporters that did a four-continent survey of the fallout of the Afghan jihad estimated that "no more than 5,000 had actually fought." Between the withdrawal of Soviet troops in February 1989 and the collapse of Kabul's Communist government in April 1992, another round of "at least 2,500 foreigners" received "military instruction of some sort." That made for a total of 7,500, no mean figure: "Largely out of sight of the world, in training camps in Afghanistan and Pakistan, something akin to a radical Islamic foreign legion was taking shape." Around this core was a larger group: tens of thousands more studied in the thousands of new madrassahs in Pakistan. Eventually, Rashid concludes, "more than a hundred thousand Muslim radicals around the world had direct contact with Pakistan and Afghanistan." However most madrassah graduates were not destined for Afghanistan but for the internal political contest in Pakistan. Tariq Ali gives an estimate of 2,500 madrassahs with an annual crop of 225,000 students, many of whom had been taught literacy in primers that stated that the Urdu letter *tay* stood for *tope* (cannon), *kaaf* for *Kalashnikov, khay* for *khoon* (blood), and *jeem* for *jihad*.

The real damage the CIA did was not the providing of arms and money but the *privatization* of information about how to produce and spread violence—the formation of private militias—capable of creating terror. Cooley notes that CIA training in its U.S. camps ranged from infiltration techniques to ways of extracting prisoners or weapons from behind enemy lines to more than sixty assorted "deadly skills." The skills passed on by trainers to fighters included "the use of sophisticated fuses, timers and explosives; automatic weapons with armor-piercing ammunition, remote-control devices for triggering mines and bombs (used later in the volunteers' home countries, and against the Israelis in occupied Arab territory such as southern Lebanon)." There were also local Afghan skills—such as throat cutting and disemboweling—that the CIA incorporated in its training.

Afghanistan: The High Point in the Cold War

The team of *Los Angeles Times* reporters who carried out an investigation into the aftermath of the Afghan War "over four continents" found that the key leaders of every major terrorist attack, from New York to France to Saudi Arabia, inevitably turned out to have been veterans of the Afghan War.

One of those charged in 1995 for the conspiracy to bomb the UN building, FBI headquarters in lower Manhattan, and the Lincoln and Holland tunnels linking Manhattan with New Jersey was Claments Rodney Hampton-el, a hospital technician from Brooklyn, New York, who had come home after being wounded in the arm and leg in Afghanistan. Both the "hands-on ringleader" of the 1993 World Trade Center bombing, a Brooklyn taxi driver named Mahmud Abouhalima, and the alleged mastermind of the bombing, Kuwaiti-born Ramzi Ahmed Yousef, had fought in the Afghan War against the Soviets. In 1995, Pakistani authorities arrested and extradited to the United States the twenty-eight-year-old youth named Yousef, according to the *Los Angeles Times,* "the most notorious example yet of this lethal, unanticipated by-product of the Afghan War." Charges leveled against him include FBI charges of "an alleged plot to simultaneously bomb about a dozen Delta, Northwest and United Airlines jumbo jets over the Pacific," Philippine government accusations of "plotting to assassinate Pope John Paul II during a January 1995 visit," and Pakistani charges of an aborted plan in 1993 to kill the prime minister, Benazir Bhutto.

When France, with a population of three million Muslims, endured a series of eight bomb attacks in the summer of 1995, a law enforcement officer in Paris commented, "Almost all of the leaders of the people we have arrested for terrorism have passed by Afghanistan or Pakistan. The know-how was learned there. How to operate clandestinely as well." When a pickup truck stuffed with explosives was detonated outside a three-story building in the Saudi capital, Riyadh, on November 13, 1996, killing five Americans, "three of the four Saudi militants arrested for that attack admitted to having received firearms and explosives training in Afghanistan and to having participated in combat" there. When a mammoth truck bomb demolished an eight-story barracks at the King Abdulaziz Air Base in Dhahran, Saudi Arabia, on June 25, 1996, killing nineteen U.S. airmen and wounding 250 others, General J. H. Binford Peay, head of the U.S. Central Command, told hearings of the Senate Armed Services Committee looking into the Dhahran bombing, "Recently we have seen growth in 'transnational' groups, comprised of fanatical Islamic extremists, many of whom fought in Afghanistan and now drift to other countries with the aim of establishing anti-Western fundamentalist regimes by destabilizing traditional governments and attacking U.S. and Western targets."

Others were more candid. "Your government participated in creating a monster," Mahfoud Bennoune, an Algerian sociologist, told a *Los Angeles Times* correspondent in Algiers, "Now it has turned against you and the world: 16,000 Arabs were trained in Afghanistan, made into a veritable killing machine."

Financing the Jihad Through the Drug Trade

When the Carter administration began to ferry arms to the mujahideen in Afghanistan, there was immediate opposition from Dr. David Musto, a Yale University psychiatrist who was also a White House adviser on drug policy. Musto and another medical member of the White House Drug Council asked in a the *New York Times* op-ed piece, "Are we erring in befriending these tribes as we did in Laos when Air America (chartered by the Central Intelligence Agency) helped transport crude opium from certain tribal areas?" Years later, Musto recalled in an interview with Alfred McCoy, "I told the [White House Drug] Council that we were going into Afghanistan to support the opium growers in their rebellion against the Soviets. Shouldn't we try to avoid what we had done in Laos?"

There were two reasons why Musto's concerns went unheeded. First, precisely because Afghanistan's drug lords were in open rebellion against the new Soviet-supported regime, the CIA counted on them as readily available and dependable allies. Second, as the CIA knew too well from experience, nothing could rival the drug trade as a reliable source of big money for covert warfare. The Afghan War was funded from multiple sources, external and internal, state and private. When it began, it was fueled by state contributions. As early as February 1980, Zbigniew Brzezinski secured pledges of financial support from Saudi Arabia, "which eventually would match the US government financial input 'dollar for dollar.' " After President Reagan issued National Security Directive 166 in March 1985, the Afghan jihad turned into the largest covert operation in the history of the CIA. In the fiscal year 1987 alone, according to one estimate, clandestine American military aid to the mujahideen amounted to $660 million—"more than the total of American aid to the contras in Nicaragua." Noting that this sum was "more than what Pakistan itself was receiving from Washington," Steve Galster at the National Security Archive calculated that Congress ultimately provided "nearly 3 billion dollars in covert aid for the mujahideen, more than all other CIA covert operations in the 1980s combined."

Besides these external funds, there were funds generated by the mujahideen through the drug trade. Organized and centralized under CIA control, the drug trade combined the peasant's market wisdom with the mujahideens' capacities for extortion and entrepreneurship. Alfred McCoy traced the different steps in the drug economy, beginning with peasant production: "As the Mujahideen guerrillas seized territory inside Afghanistan, they ordered peasants to plant opium as a revolutionary tax." It no doubt helped that for the grower the price of opium was five times that for wheat. Also, there was no dearth of processing facilities: "Across the border in Pakistan, Afghan leaders and local syndicates under the protection of Pakistan intelligence operated hundreds of heroin laboratories." Writing in *The Nation* in 1988, Lawrence Lifschultz pointed out that the heroin laboratories, located in North-West Frontier Province, were operated under the protection of General Fazle Haq, an intimate of General Zia. The next link in the chain was transport, which was provided by trucks from the Pakistani army's National Logistics Cell (NLC), which "arrived with CIA arms from Karachi" and "often returned loaded with heroin—protected by ISI papers from police search." *The Herald* of Pakistan had reported as early as September 1985 that "the drug is carried in NLC trucks which come sealed" and "are never checked by the police" and that "this has been going on now for about three and a half years." Finally, the CIA provided the legal cover without which this illicit trade could not have grown to monumental proportions:

> During this decade of wide-open drug-dealing, the U.S. Drug Enforcement Administration in Islamabad failed to instigate major seizures or arrests. . . . U.S. officials had refused to investigate charges of heroin dealing by its Afghan allies "because U.S. narcotics policy in Afghanistan has been subordinated to the war against Soviet influence there."

Afghanistan: The High Point in the Cold War

Prior to the Afghan jihad, there was no local production of heroin in either Afghanistan or Pakistan. The production there was of opium, a very different drug, which was directed to small, rural, regional markets. By the end of the Afghan jihad, the picture had changed drastically: the Pakistan-Afghanistan borderlands became the world's leading producers of both opium and processed heroin, the source of "75 percent of the world's opium, worth multi-billion dollars in revenue." In a report released in early 2001, the United Nations International Drug Control Program traced the rapid expansion of Afghan opium production to exactly 1979, the year the U.S.-sponsored jihad began: "It is no coincidence that Afghanistan began to emerge as a significant producer of illicit opium in precisely the period of protracted war that began in 1979, and still persists." The big push came after 1985. Accounting for less than 5 percent of global opium production in 1980, the region accounted for 71 percent of it by 1990, according to this same report. The fate of Afghanistan resembled that of Burma, another Asian mountainous region that had been the site of CIA intervention at the beginning of the Cold War. "Just as CIA support for Nationalist Chinese (KMT) troops in the Shan states had increased Burma's opium crop in the 1950s," concluded Alfred McCoy, "so the agency's aid to the mujahideen guerrillas in the 1980s expanded opium production in Afghanistan and linked Pakistan's nearby heroin laboratories to the world market."

The heroin economy literally poisoned Afghani and Pakistani life. The figures who thrived in this cesspool had been hailed by Ronald Reagan as "moral equivalents of America's founding fathers." The worst example was Gulbuddin Hikmatyar, who received more than half of CIA covert resources, estimated to be worth $2 billion over the ten-year war, and quickly came to dominate the Afghan mujahideen. Long known as a militant "fundamentalist," Hikmatyar was not a clergyman but a student in the highly competitive American-sponsored Faculty of Engineering at Kabul University, "who had led student demonstrations in Kabul during the late 1960s to oppose the king's secular reforms." The *New York Times* reported—though only after the Afghan jihad had ended—an incident in the early 1970s when "he had dispatched followers to throw vials of acid into the faces of women students who refused to wear veils." Accused of murdering a leftist student, Hikmatyar served a prison sentence and fled to Pakistan. His opportunity came with the republican coup of 1973 in Afghanistan. Fearing that the new government might encourage Pashtun separatism in Pakistan's North-West Frontier Province, the Pakistani government ordered the army to train a clandestine Afghan rebel group. From then on, Hikmatyar became the Pakistani army's favorite "contract revolutionary." When introduced to the CIA by the ISI, Hikmatyar was leading an armed guerrilla force called Hizb-i-Islami, a creation of the ISI that had little support inside Afghanistan. Over the next decade, his group received "more than half of all arms" supplied by the CIA. With a guaranteed long-term subsidy, the Hizb-i-Islami grew into the mujahideen's "largest guerrilla army," one that Hikmatyar used "to become Afghanistan's leading drug lord."

Hikmatyar's chief rival was Mullah Nasim Akhundzada, known as the "King of Heroin." Mullah Nasim controlled "the best-irrigated lands in the Northern Helmand valley," once Afghanistan's breadbasket, "and decreed that half of all peasant holdings . . . be planted to opium." He "issued opium quotas to every landowner" and responded "by killing or castrating those who defied his directives." When the *New York Times* correspondent Arthur Bonner spent a month in early 1986 traveling in Helmand, he found extensive poppy fields in every village and town.

Mullah Nasim's elder brother, Mohammed Rasul, explained, "We must grow and sell opium to fight our holy war against the Russian nonbelievers." While Mullah Nasim had the opium-poppy fields of Helmand, Hikmatyar had six heroin refineries. Situated at Koh-i-Sultan at the southern end of Helmand, just inside Pakistan, these refineries processed the opium into heroin. At the height of the Afghan jihad, in 1988–1989, Hikmatyar's forces "challenged Mulla Nasim's rule over the Helmand opium harvest." The savage turf war lasted into the spring of 1989, after the snows melted. Both sides absorbed huge casualties. This, and not any encounter with Soviet or Afghan government forces, turned out to be the largest single battle in the Afghan jihad. In the end, Mullah Nasim won and kept control of the valley.

The ISI gave Hikmatyar "a free hand to rule the Afghan refugee camps that sprawled around Peshawar." Speaking before a congressional committee, Barnett Rubin, a highly respected specialist on Afghan affairs at the Center for International Cooperation at New York University, cited a UN refugee worker who had described Hikmatyar's rule as "a reign of terror." Hikmatyar ran the camps like a drug lord. He used violence as the measure of all relationships. Stating that this was a jihad, he took no prisoners: instead of welcoming defectors from the government side as would a guerrilla army interested in winning support, his forces simply killed them. From the start of the covert war in 1979, "other mujaheddin leaders charged that Hekmatyar's followers were using violence to take control of rival resistance groups."

It is true that Hikmatyar was not an original CIA product, but he was introduced to the CIA's Islamabad station chief, John Joseph Reagan, by the ISI at the very start of the covert war in May 1979, before Soviet troops had entered Afghanistan. Most writers on Afghanistan have concluded that the CIA's margin of maneuver was limited by the ISI. Yet we must take into account that Hikmatyar remained the primary recipient of CIA arms largesse for a decade, from 1979 through 1981, when the supply increased under the first Reagan administration, to 1985, when it ballooned massively under the second Reagan administration, and until the war ended. Islamabad, the nerve center of the Afghan jihad, grew into one of the largest CIA stations. Why did the CIA's affair with Hikmatyar flourish for a decade? I have suggested that the sustained preference that both the CIA and the ISI exhibited for Hikmatyar was a result of a shared objective: neither agency was interested in a compromise settlement; both preferred anti-Communist radical Islamists who shared their desire for "killing Russians" and bleeding the Soviet Union white.

The Bankers of the Jihad

The privatization of the jihad covered all key operations, from recruitment to funding. One of the paymasters of the jihad was the enormously successful Pakistani bank, Bank of Credit and Commerce International (BCCI), set up by the Pakistani tycoon Agha Hassan Abedi. Established in 1972, BCCI collapsed in 1991, soon after the end of the Afghan War, precipitated by charges of fraud, bribery, and conspiracy in American courts. With fourteen thousand employees and offices in seventy countries, BCCI was incorporated in two tax havens and used two sets of auditors, allowing it to avoid publishing meaningful consolidated accounts. As international regulators proceeded to close many BCCI branches, some $9.5 billion of depositors' money was found to be missing. The New York prosecutor called it "the largest bank fraud in New York financial history."

This opinion was not shared by all, who felt the BCCI was

framed, having served a purpose throughout the Afghan War, including a large number of depositors among whom both Agha Hassan Abedi and BCCI continued to retain loyal support. Was the BCCI one in a line of such crooked banks as the Castle Bank, through which the CIA had funneled cash for anti-Castro operations in Cuba and that it used whenever it needed the services of corrupt or criminal banks for overseas operations? Or was it one among Agha Hassan Abedi's several initiatives, undertaken during a brilliant career dedicated to breaking the colonial monopoly of western institutions but corrupted by the CIA-brokered alliance? Or was it, most likely, both? It was possible BCCI's crime had been that it had worked both sides of the fence, being available for covert operations by all those in need: from the Palestinian Abu Nidal group, to Pakistani, Argentinean, and Libyan initiatives to acquire nuclear weapons (as *Time* magazine charged), to CIA and DIA covert operations. Most certainly, though, the CIA's decision to privatize the Afghan jihad led to the emergence of several rogue private actors, among which al-Qaeda was one and BCCI another.

Given the privatized nature of the Afghan jihad, it should come as no surprise that the congressional subcommittee charged with investigation into "the BCCI Affair" found it extremely difficult to elicit information from both the CIA and the Bank of England. The subcommittee complained that whereas "initial information" supplied by the CIA was "untrue," information supplied later was "incomplete." The subcommittee concluded that "the CIA knew more about BCCI's goals and intentions concerning the U.S. banking system than anyone else in government," and yet "it failed to provide the critical information it had gathered to the correct users of the information—the Federal Reserve and the Justice Department." Worse still, the CIA continued to use both

BCCI and First American, BCCI's secretly held U.S. subsidiary, even "after the CIA knew that BCCI as an institution was a fundamentally corrupt criminal enterprise."

The subcommittee faced a similar stone wall with the Bank of England. Even after it "learned of BCCI's involvement in the financing of terrorism and in drug money laundering" in 1988 and 1989 and was advised of "evidence of fraud" by its auditors, Price Waterhouse, the bank tentatively agreed "to permit BCCI to restructure as three 'separate' institutions" in London, Abu Dhabi, and Hong Kong. Despite a 1989 investigation by District Attorney Robert Morgenthau, in April 1990 the Bank of England permitted BCCI "to move its headquarters, officers and records out of British jurisdiction to Abu Dhabi," with "profound negative consequences for investigations of BCCI around the world." When the U.S. Federal Reserve attempted to investigate BCCI, it, too, faced "lack of cooperation" from the Serious Fraud Office of the British government.

CIA denials about links with BCCI could not stand in the face of British and American investigative reports. The media—particularly such networks as ABC—reported that CIA accounts in BCCI London branches were used to pay "scores of British subjects and residents who had worked as informants for the CIA." Soon after, *The Financial Times* cited the Pakistani finance minister's confirmation that "the CIA used BCCI branches in Pakistan to channel money, presumably through the ISI, to the Afghan jihad." The trickle of information on CIA-BCCI links turned into a flood as Senator John Kerry's investigating committee reported "that a Senate aide who worked to supply the Moujahideen with Stinger missiles and other weapons, Michael Pillsbury, kept a close relationship with BCCI front-man Muhammad Hammoud." Finally, on February 23, 1992, NBC reported that Agha Hassan Abedi had been meeting CIA director William Casey "secretly for three years in Washington's Madison Hotel." Soon after, the CIA's acting director admitted to collusion between the agency and BCCI.

The more the larger picture became known, the more it became clear that BCCI's connection with the CIA predated the Afghan jihad. BCCI was a regular conduit used by Saudi intelligence to channel funds for covert CIA operations: Saudi funds were known to have been regularly deposited in secret BCCI accounts in Switzerland, London, and Miami, for use by CIA's proxies in southern Africa and Central America. The congressional investigation listed a whole host of U.S. and foreign officials who "float in and out of BCCI at critical times in its history." The names included former CIA directors Richard Helms and William Casey, principal U.S. foreign agents such as Adnan Khashoggi and Manucher Ghorbanifar, and Saudi intelligence officials such as Kamal Adham and Abdul Raouf Khalil. The Saudi-BCCI link was exposed in the plea bargain reached in the 1992 federal trial in New York. When Kamal Adham, the Saudi chief of intelligence, pleaded guilty to charges of conspiracy and agreed both to pay a fine of $105 million and to disclose some of BCCI's labyrinthine global operations—but not before his lawyers and associates had hinted that further "disclosures about Afghanistan" might have come in the absence of a plea bargain.

Cost to Pakistan

The Afghan jihad had a deeper effect on the Pakistani state and society than it did on any other country outside of Afghanistan. The military claimed that the creation of a national security state would in reality be the building of an Islamic state. Zia ul-Haq was convinced that Pakistan would not survive unless it was as regimented as Israel: "Pakistan is like Israel, an ideological state. Take out Judaism from Israel and it will collapse like a house of cards. Take Islam out of Pakistan and make [it] a secular state; it would collapse. For the past four years we have been trying to bring Islamic values to this country." The imperative was clear: Pakistan could be held together only by an ideological project.

The heart of the national security state was the ISI, also the executive agency for the Afghan jihad. Given the proxy nature of its jihad, the CIA was aware that it needed the full cooperation of the ISI to be effective in Afghanistan and, more generally, in Soviet central Asia. The more the anti-Soviet jihad grew, the more the ISI moved to the center of governmental power in Pakistan. The Islamization of the anti-Soviet struggle drew inspiration from the Islamization of the Pakistani state under Zia and in turn reinforced it. The ISI came to see itself as the defender and the custodian of Islam. The Islamization of state agencies continued after Zia's death. Blasphemy laws, as well as the 1979 Hudud Ordinance, which put extraordinary emphasis on corporal punishment and tended to subordinate the judiciary to executive control, remained in place. The Jamaat-e-Ulema-Islam (JUI), a key party in the alliance behind the Afghan jihad, became a part of Prime Minister Benazir Bhutto's governing coalition in 1993. The JUI was the party of Pakistani Deobandis and was the sponsor of the Taliban, the ideological product of Deobandi madrassahs. Entry into government gave the JUI its first opportunity to build close relations with both the ISI and the army. The harvest came soon after: when the Taliban took power in Kabul in 1995, they handed over the training camps to the JUI.

Two related processes intensified the negative impact of the Pakistani state on its society. Intimate links with the CIA gave the ISI access to state-of-the-art surveillance, allowing it to closely monitor the Pakistani people; also, the easy availability of arms led to the proliferation of armed factions and an associated "Kalashnikov culture." Central to the ISI's impact on Pakistani society was its patronage of a number of jihadi organizations, which in reality were paramilitary forces that claimed the mantle of Islam. The two most important such groups were Lashkar-i-Tayyaba (Soldiers of Medina) and Harkat ul-Ansar (Volunteers Movement). Lashkar-i-Tayyaba was estimated to have fifty thousand militants and was "the leading group in the 'jihad' to 'liberate' Indian Kashmir." Harkatul Ansar was formed to support the Afghan jihad, and its members were the most dedicated of the Taliban. Its leader was Osama bin Laden, and it was once funded by the United States. When declared a "terrorist" organization by the United States in 2001, it promptly changed its name to Harkatul Mujahideen and continued to function without missing a step. Thus, the Afghan jihad came to be joined to the Kashmiri jihad.

The madrassahs did not close after the Soviet withdrawal from Afghanistan in February 1989. The post-Soviet graduates of these madrassahs were known as the "second wave" of militants. The *Los Angeles Times* interviewed one of them, twenty-two-year-old Iftikar Haider. His life story gives us a glimpse into the kind of impulse that could lead a young man into the ranks of the jihad. "The sole child of a poor family that fled to Gujranwala in Pakistan from India after losing its farm and most of its members in the blood bath of the Indian partition," Haider "grew up hearing gruesome tails of Hindu and Sikh cruelty toward Muslims from his father, a low-level worker in the government Agricultural Department." Haider underwent his first military training in 1990. His life took a fateful turn on December 6, 1992, the day a "mob of Hindu zealots in the northern Indian town of Ayodhya tore down an unused mosque built on the site where, the Hindu god-king Ram was born." It was estimated that twelve hundred people, mostly Muslims, died in the month of communal rioting that followed. The following February, Haider enlisted with Markaz-ud-Daawa-Wal-Irshad, one of the jihadi groups, and infiltrated Indian-administered Kashmir. Two of his comrades-in-arms were killed, but Haider was captured and confined in the high-walled prison in Kot Bhalwal outside Jammu in southern Kashmir, where he was interviewed by the *Los Angeles Times* reporter. Even in captivity he was "alert, clear-eyed and unremorseful." He told the reporter, "My religion says that whosoever is an oppressor must be combated. Even if he is a Muslim, like Hosni Mubarak [the Egyptian President] or Moammar Kadafi [the Libyan leader], we should fight them. Wherever there is oppression, Markaz-ud-Daawa-Wal-Irshad will be fighting for the oppressed." To the reporter who interviewed him, Haider "sounded like an Islamist version of righteous Tom Joad, protagonist of John Steinbeck's *The Grapes of Wrath.*"

The more the jihadi culture grew, the more it inflamed doctrinal differences inside Pakistan, turning them into political differences to be settled through armed confrontation. Both major religious sects—Sunni and Shi'a—developed their own paramilitary groups during the 1980s: the Sunni organized the Sipah-e-Sahaba (Soldiers of the First Four Caliphs) and the Shi'a responded in kind, with Sipah-e-Muhammad (Soldiers of Muhammad). As the sectarian conflict raged, it turned Pakistani society into a microcosm of Afghanistan. As in Afghanistan, the Pakistani jihadi culture tended to go hand in hand with the drug culture, and the effect of the heroin and opium trade was devastating. The increase in local heroin processing led directly to an increase in its local consumption. The number of officially registered heroin addicts in Pakistan rose from 130 in 1977 to 30,000 in 1988, but the UN

Drug Control Program estimated that the actual heroin-addicted population had gone from negligible in 1979 to 1.3 million by 1985, "a much steeper rise than in any [other] nation." By 1997, the UNIDCP estimate had risen to 1.7 million heroin addicts. As Pakistani society reeled from a combination of militarization and a rapidly spreading drug culture, it became clear that even if the Afghan jihad was over, its effects on Pakistan society were not.

The Outcome: Taliban

The CIA jihad made no effort to create a single organization out of the myriad of Afghan mujahideen groups. This was a consequence of, on the one hand, the extremely sectarian character of Islamist ideology that came to dominate the Afghan jihad and, on the other, the political objectives that guided the Americans.

There were seven mujahideen groups in all. They reflected every kind of fissure, internal and external, to which the Afghan resistance was subject. The internal differences in the Afghan jihad were of two different kinds. The first involved regional (north vs. south), linguistic (Farsi vs. Pashtun), and ethnic (Pashtun vs. non-Pashtun) differences. Historically, Afghan society managed its cultural diversity through a highly decentralized polity and society. A centralizing state project was likely to exacerbate rather than contain these differences. The lesson of history is clear: cultural differences need not translate into political differences.

A different kind of internal division arose from doctrinal differences, as between Shi'a and Sunni. Doctrinal distinctions, too, did not have to translate into ideological and political differences. That this happened was a direct consequence of the nature of the political ideology that came to dominate Afghan politics and the state. The overriding ideological difference among the seven mujahideen groups was between two political points of view: traditionalist nationalists and Islamist ideologues. The traditionalists generally came from the religious leadership, whereas the ideologues came mainly from the ranks of political intellectuals. Traditionalists tended to treat doctrinal distinctions—as those between Shi'a and Sunni—as nonpolitical; in contrast, the tendency of ideologues was to turn doctrinal and cultural differences into political divisions. To understand why Islamist ideologues—and not Muslim traditionalists—emerged in charge of Afghanistan through the civil war, we need to understand not just the internal composite that was Afghan society but also how external forces played upon internal differences.

Two political objectives, one regional, the other global, shaped U.S. policy in Afghanistan. The regional objective was to contain the influence of the Iranian Revolution. This was accomplished with two regional alliances against Iran, one with Pakistan and Saudi Arabia, the other with Iraq. Whereas the United States saw Islamist social movements as a threat, it was eager to reinforce Islamist—Sunni, not Shi'a—state projects. This American strategy provided a political opening for the intelligence agencies of Pakistan and Saudi Arabia to promote exaggeratedly anti-Shi'a Sunni doctrines, chief among them the Wahhabi doctrine from Saudi Arabia and the Deobandi doctrine from Pakistan.

The strategic shift in the U.S. perspective as the Cold War progressed from "containment" to "rollback" coincided with the transition from the Carter to the Reagan presidency. Determined to increase the tally of dead Russians in Afghanistan, the Reagan administration showed no interest in a negotiated or compromise settlement. It wanted to ally itself with internationalist, militantly anti-Communist Islamist ideologues rather than moderately pragmatic Muslims, a view shared by the ISI. Both were uninterested in

Afghan nationalism, the United States because it feared nationalists might compromise the anti-Soviet war and Pakistan because it feared that Pashtun nationalism would erode its territorial integrity. This shared view of the patron and the proxy, CIA and ISI, effectively marginalized mainstream traditionalist/nationalist Muslim organizations and elevated highly ideological but exiled Islamist factions, even if they were on the fringes of Afghan society. The simple fact was that whereas traditionalists understood their struggle in a national frame of reference, ideologues found meaning in the struggle as the beginning of an international jihad.

Close observers of the Afghan jihad have tended to conclude that the ISI was able to take advantage of its position as sole agent to translate its own preference for state-centered political Islam into policy, while the American course of action was one of benign neglect. Thus, Ahmed Rashid wrote:

> When the CIA funneled arms to the Afghan Mujahideen via Pakistan's Inter-Services Intelligence (ISI), the ISI gave preference to the radical Afghan Islamic parties—which could more easily be turned into an engine of anti-Soviet jihad—and pushed aside moderate Afghan nationalist and Islamic parties. At that time the CIA made no objections to this policy.

But the absence of a stated CIA objective did not mean a lack of a clear CIA preference. Ironically, this objective was so central to U.S. policy that it led to a high level of tolerance for groups not particularly well disposed to the United States. As early as 1985, during a visit to address the UN, Gulbuddin Hikmatyar refused to meet President Reagan, arguing that "to be seen meeting Reagan would serve the KGB and Soviet propaganda," which "insisted that the war was not a jihad, but a mere extension of US Cold War strategy."

The seven resistance groups that made up the Afghan jihad were divided into two opposing political constellations, one traditional-nationalist, the other Islamist. Barnett Rubin has sketched their historical formation and political perspective in some detail. The leadership of the traditionalist bloc came from the historic elite of Afghanistan, who were either heads of the Sufi orders (the Qadariyya or the Naqshbandi tariqa) or traditional *alims* (legal scholars) versed in Islamic jurisprudence. None of these three mainstream groups received external assistance of any significance. The National Islamic Front of Afghanistan, led by the head of the Qadariyya Sufi order, was considered too "nationalist" and "insufficiently Islamic" to receive funds. The Afghan National Liberation Front was led by the family that headed the Naqshbandi tariqa. It was more of a centrist group that pledged both to defend "national traditions" and to establish "an Islamic society"; it, too, "hardly existed as a military force." The only traditional-nationalist group with a military presence on the ground was called the Movement of the Islamic Revolution. Led by a respected alim who both ran a large traditional madrassah and controlled huge landholdings, its commanders (in particular, Mullah Nasim Akhundzada of the Helmand Valley) were also among the largest drug lords inside Afghanistan.

In contrast to these three traditional-nationalist groups whose leadership came from the historical tribal and religious elite of Afghanistan, leaders of the four Islamist groups came from students and faculty active in the Jamiat-i-Islami, the parent Islamist organization at Kabul University in the 1970s. The first split from the Jamiat came in 1975 and led to the formation of Hikmatyar's Hizb-i-Islami (Hizb). A later split from the Hizb led to the creation of the Khalis faction. The fourth Islamist organization was led by Abd al-Rabb al-Rasul Sayyaf, who had studied at Al-Azhar University in Cairo and then joined the sharia (law) faculty at Kabul University. He had been Burhaneddin Rabbani's deputy in the Jamiat in the 1970s.

The key parties in the Islamist constellation were the Jamiat and the Hizb. After the split with Hizb, Jamiat had turned into the "main voice for non-Pashtuns, especially Persian speakers." Jamiat field commanders were autonomous and retained control over their men's weapons. Led by the most successful of the commanders, Ahmed Shah Massoud, Jamiat developed into "the most powerful party of the resistance" over the course of the war. In spite of that, the Jamiat was not the preferred recipient for CIA support. There was one important reason for this: Jamiat represented the moderate center in Islamist politics, and the CIA backed not just Islamist ideologues but extremists over moderates.

The key extremist party was the Hizb, which "represented the most radical part of the student movement" and was "the most revolutionary and the most disciplined of the Islamic parties." Unlike other leaders in the Jamiat, Gulbuddin Hikmatyar had a political background that included participation in both the Communist and the Islamist movements: he had begun political life in high school as a member of the Percham faction of the Communist party and then gone on to the Muslim Youth Movement. One wonders whether Hikmatyar brought the discipline of Communist youth organizations to Hizb, for Hizb was distinguished from other Islamist parties by its modern organization. It stressed party supremacy over loyalty to individual commanders, so that weapons were the property of the party and not of individual commanders, as in other organizations. Recruitment and promotion were based more on individual ideology and skills than on social background. Hizb was also the only party to have internal election of leaders, although the right to vote was restricted to members who had joined before the 1978 Communist coup. In Rubin's judgment: "Hikmatyar's radical Islamism (and hence anticommunism) and the superior organization of his party made the Hizb the favorite of not only the Pakistani and the Arab Islamists—including the ISI officers—but also moderate Pakistani generals and the operations wing of the CIA." This preference gave the Hizb privileged access to Afghan refugee camps in Pakistan, to American refugee aid, and to refugee schools. We have also seen that Hikmatyar was the drug lord who owned seven heroin-processing plants on the Pakistani side of the border. Yet even though it was the recipient of more than half of CIA funds, estimated at $2 billion over the ten-year war, the Hizb was not the most active in the guerrilla war, a fact that led to the formation of a splinter group, the Khalis faction, calling for greater involvement in guerrilla action.

As to unity, most initiatives came from individuals outside the CIA/ISI and the radical Islamists they patronized. Serious overtures usually came from moderates within and from Saudi Arabia, except that Saudi interest was limited to an alliance behind their favored leader, Sayyaf. The first Saudi effort at unity was in 1981. It led to a brief alliance, which ended when the three traditionalist-nationalist parties left, "complaining of rampant corruption and discrimination by Sayyaf." Only remnants of these parties, lured by the scent of Saudi money, stayed behind. This is why, in spite of the fact that only four organizations stayed in the alliance, the record speaks of the ISI-favored alliance as the Peshawar Seven. Later, when traditionalist-nationalist leaders proposed coming together under a unifying leader such as King Zahir, Pakistan, reluctant to flirt with Afghan nationalism and determined to put an

Islamist in power in Kabul, refused him a visa. Unity among the Islamists continued to be elusive. Rebel leaders had admitted to U.S. officials as early as 1979 that trying to create a unified Afghan resistance was like "putting five different animals in the same cage."

In this setting, in which America was backing groups with no internal support or the possibility of organizing it, the United States and its allies had to support a myriad of groups if only to ensure that the jihad continued to have an even chance. The support of different groups turned out to be support for several wars fought by rival groups. This is why as soon as the Soviet army withdrew from Afghanistan and victory seemed at hand, the CIA-supported jihad mutated into a civil war. With the traditionalist-nationalists marginalized, the Soviet withdrawal of 1989 led to a turf battle between different Islamist groups, pitting the extremists led by Gulbuddin Hikmatyar and the Hizb against the moderates in the Jamiat led by Burhaneddin Rabbani and his spectacularly successful field commander, Ahmed Shah Massoud. When the international press reported that Hikmatyar had slaughtered thirty members of a rival mujahideen group, the president of the interim government was so outraged that he denounced Hikmatyar, by then his own foreign minister, as a "criminal" and a "terrorist."

As the turf war culminated in a seesaw battle for Kabul, the civil war turned vicious. When it became obvious that Hikmatyar's forces were losing ground, the Pakistani army shifted its backing to the Taliban, a group mainly comprising students it had trained since 1980 in madrassahs in the North-West Frontier Province. The ISI saw the Taliban as amenable to tight control and thus a preferable substitute for the now discredited Islamist coalition led by Hikmatyar. With the Cold War over, the focus of official America also narrowed to a pecuniary dimension: oil. And for

American oil interests—particularly Unocal, the giant oil company that hoped to build a trans-Afghan pipeline from Central Asia to the Indian Ocean as an alternative to going through Iran—any group that could offer security in Afghanistan would do. On October 4, 1996, the *Los Angeles Times* reported that a new rumor was making rounds of Kabul—"many are sure that the Clinton administration is supporting the Taliban, the victorious Islamic militia"—and added that the conspiracy theory was "plausible, given the great mystery that shrouds the Taliban's rise and rapid advance: How did a ragtag force that emerged in late 1994 among Muslim religious students in the southern region of Kandahar and adjacent areas of Pakistan grow so quickly that, two years later, it has become master of three-quarters of Afghanistan? Who paid for its weaponry, ammunition and vehicles? Who organized its training and logistics? Is intelligence or military assistance received from outside one of the reasons the Taliban has enjoyed astonishing, and relatively bloodless, successes over experienced moujahedeen who, for nearly a decade, fought occupying Soviet troops?" It cited "generous support" from Pakistan but still wondered whether the United States was involved. A ranking UN official said: "The U.S. wants law and order in Afghanistan, and the Taliban now seem like the best bet." A local director of a foreign charity was equally cynical: "There are two different things—American state interests and human rights. For the politicians running America, human rights take second place." And a Kabul university graduate who worked as a translator asked the reporter, "How can your country want to deal with people who whip women for not conforming to their dress code?" After a State Department meeting with a visiting Taliban delegation on February 3, 1997, a senior U.S. diplomat explained his government's point of view: "The Taliban will probably develop like

Saudi Arabia. There will be Aramco, pipelines, an emir, no parliament and lots of Sharia law. We can live with that."

If the assortment of mujahideen groups were the ideological products of the Cold War—trained, equipped, and financed by the CIA and its regional allies—the Taliban arose from the agony and the ashes of the war against the Soviet Union. The Taliban was a movement born across the border in Pakistan at a time when the entire population of Afghanistan had been displaced, not once but many times over, and when no educated class to speak of was left in the country. A *talib* was a student in a religious school, and the movement of students, Taliban, was born of warfare stretching across decades, of children born in cross-border refugee camps, of male orphans with no camaraderie but those of other boys in madrassahs, which initially provided student recruits to defend the population at large—ironically, women and young boys in particular—from the lust and the looting of mujahideen guerrillas. Without understanding that the Taliban provided the population effective protection against the likes of Gulbuddin Hikmatyar, warlords turned drug lords, it is difficult to understand why the population turned to the Taliban. The promise that made the Taliban popular and brought it to power was that it would establish law and order. Tragically, though, the Taliban, born of a brutalized society, was to brutalize it further. An old man in a mosque in Kandahar, an architectural ruin of an ancient city of gardens and fountains and palaces, confided about the Taliban to Eqbal Ahmad, "They have grown in darkness amidst death. They are angry and ignorant, and hate all things that bring joy to life."

Ahmed Rashid noted that "the Taliban reflect none of the major Islamicist trends that were earlier prevalent in Afghanistan or that emerged during the jihad of the 1980s." Not one of the three major impulses that define Islam in central Asia and its environs could be found in the Taliban. They did not follow either of the traditional Central Asian paths—the mystical Islam of the Sufis or the scholarly Islam of the ulama. And they were not inspired by the social and political radicalism of the political Islamist group born at the start of the twentieth century, the Society of Muslim Brothers, the one that was closest to the moderate Islamists led by the Jamiat. Their ideology of Deobandi Islam was a Pakistani import. The Taliban's international agenda was an adoption as well as an adaptation, a hand-me-down from the alliance with Osama bin Laden and al-Qaeda. In Ahmed Rashid's words, "the tens of thousands of Pakistani militants, and the thousands of Central Asians, Arabs, Africans, and East Asians who have fought for the Taliban since that time, have brought with them a global perspective of Islamic radicalism that the Taliban have adopted as their own."

Both those who see the Taliban as an Islamic movement and those who see it as a tribal (Pashtun) movement view it as a premodern residual in a modern world. But they miss the crucial point about the Taliban: even if it evokes premodernity in its particular language and specific practices, the Taliban is the result of an encounter of a premodern people with modern imperial power. When I asked two colleagues, one an Afghani and the other an American student of Afghanistan, how a movement that began in defense of women and youth could turn against both, they suggested I put this outcome in a triple context. First, the experience of the enforced gender equity of the Communists; second, the combination of traditional male seclusion of the madrassahs with the militarism of the jihadi training; and finally, the fear of Taliban leaders that their members would turn into rapists, following the notorious example of the mujahideen. Eqbal Ahmad recognized the tragedy of the Afghani people, historically adapted to a highly decentralized and localized mode of life but subjugated to two highly centralized state projects during the Cold War: first, Soviet-supported Marxism; then, CIA-supported Islamization. "The Ideologies of war—marxism and fundamentalism—are alien to Afghan culture," he wrote in 1991. "Afghanistan is a diverse and pluralistic society; centralizing, unitary agendas cannot appeal to it."

Cost to the Muslim World

The CIA was key to the forging of the link between Islam and terror in central Asia and to giving radical Islamists international reach and ambition. The groups it trained and sponsored shared a triple embrace: of terror tactics, of holy war as a political ideology, and of a transnational recruitment of fighters, who acquired hyphenated identities.

Tens of thousands of jihadi fighters, trained in the Afghan War, scattered with the end of the war. Subsequent developments in disparate locations testify to the overall impact of the Afghan jihad as well as to the importance of local histories and local grievances. The Afghan War realized the dream of Abdul A'la Mawdudi and Sayyid Qutb: it trained and linked together an international jihadi vanguard of Algerian-Afghans, Egyptian-Afghans, Indonesian-Afghans, Filipino-Afghans, British-Afghans, and so on. The importance of the vanguard was that its members shared an experience that shaped their ideological and political perspective. But the shared perspective could not ensure a local following. To cultivate that required the vanguard to address local issues. This single fact explains the difference between crime and political terrorism: unlike crime, political terror must bid for popular support. To deny that support for terrorist groups requires addressing grievances—and thus issues—that give terrorists so many opportunities to recruit followers. Terror, unlike crime, has to be fought politically, not just militarily. The political dimension of terror, and the fight against it, is best highlighted by recent events in Algeria and Egypt.

Algeria

When Algeria held its first national ballot after independence in 1991, the Islamic Salvation Front (FIS) won 180 out of 231 seats in the first round. A second round to decide more than two hundred other seats was to be held on January 16, 1992. The secular establishment, including the ruling National Liberation Front (FLN) and the army, was alarmed: not only were the Islamists only twenty-eight seats short of a majority already, there was a real possibility they would win the two-thirds majority that would have allowed them to rewrite Algeria's constitution. The army stepped in, nullified the electoral process, and took power. Algeria's ruling party and army were not the only ones to be alarmed; their anxiety was shared by Algeria's former colonial power, France. Significant sectors of political society in France, including many on the left, supported the demand that the electoral process in Algeria be nullified to prevent the FIS—which they described as "Islamofascist"—from coming to power.

The FIS were not democrats, but neither were the FLN and the military. The FIS, however, had the demonstrated support of the majority of Algerian people. The rise of FIS signaled the entry of an Islamist element into politics, but that element could not be equated with political terrorism. The difference between political Islam and political terrorism became clear as the nullification of the electoral process set the stage for the onset of a vicious civil war between Islamists and secularists and, in that context, a contest between different Islamist political tendencies. Once the parliamentary road was blocked, a debate and a struggle for power ensued between those in the FIS leadership who had pioneered that road and those in the Armed Islamic Group (GIA) and other organizations calling for an armed jihad as the only way to establish an Islamic state in Algeria.

Chadli Bendjedid, a prominent figure in the Algerian independence movement, served three terms as president, from 1979 until his resignation in January 1992. Two different generations, each the product of an armed struggle, proved key to the formation of extremist Islamist groups in the post-Chadli crisis. The older generation tended to be shaped by Algeria's particularly brutal armed struggle for national independence against French colonialism after the Second World War. Reports from Algeria confirm not only the totally ruthless attempt by the government to repress the Islamist insurgency but also raise questions about how many of the massacres attributed to Islamists are actually the work of *agent provocateurs*. As always, we cannot ignore the link between state terror and societal terror. When it comes to the proliferation of terror in society, the influence of the Afghan-Algerian veterans seems to be more important. The Algerian sociologist Mahfoud Bennoune insists that "the nucleus of the terrorist movement in Algeria had combat experience in Afghanistan." Cooley estimates that "between 600 and 1000 Algerians with combat experience returned home." In the 1990s, John-Thor Dahlburg, who reported for the *Los Angeles Times* from Algeria, put together biographies of some of the more important ones, of which here are three.

Probably the most important leader to come out of the

Afghan-Algerian ranks was Kamerredin Kherbane. Kherbane left the Algerian military in 1983 to join the Afghan jihad. There, he met Osama bin Laden and representatives of Islamic Rescue Organization, a support group, and discussed with them the possibility of raising an "Afghan Legion" to lead the struggle for an Islamic state in Algeria. Kherbane went on to serve on the FIS's executive council in exile. Another is the notorious Aisa Messaoudi, known as "Tayeb al-Afghani" (Tayeb the Afghan). Messaoudi returned from Afghanistan after 1989 and became an active member of FIS. After the 1991 election was nullified, he organized the armed slaughter of border guards in a barrack in Guemar, a palm-bordered oasis on the Tunisian border. This gruesome event has come to mark the start of the armed uprising and the civil war in Algeria, as well as the birth of the notorious GIA. Dahlburg reported that the group used "the same tactics employed against Russians in Afghanistan": they hacked their victims to death with knives and swords and burned others with blowtorches.

Another GIA leader key to defining the use of terror in the civil war was Si Ahmad Mourad, also called Jaffer al-Afghani. Mourad became known for expanding the ranks of those targeted from government agents to civilians—foreigners, intellectuals, journalists, women, even children—and for the savagery of those attacks. The justification was simple: violence must be used to intimidate indifferent rural masses. The emphasis on the use of terror reportedly caused one of the first serious splits in the GIA, one between national and international fragments. As the nationalists pursued the gruesome civil war at home, the internationalists, wary of slaughter and bloodshed in their own country, turned to terrorism abroad.

Egypt

Islamist politics in Egypt was defined by the historical legacy of the Society of Muslim Brothers and the ideological legacy of Sayyid Qutb. We have seen that the society was historically more of a reformist than an extremist organization. Their ideological shift came with the radicalization of Sayyid Qutb in prison. Qutb's prison writings constituted a break with the reformist thought of Hassan al-Banna and a link with the Indian Islamist Abdul A'la Mawdudi. To understand the growth of a terrorist group in practice, we need to trace the links between radical Islamism in Egypt and the American jihad of the 1980s. Egyptian involvement in the American jihad flowed from Anwar al-Sadat's determination to move Egypt from being pro-Soviet to being pro-American. He became an enthusiastic supporter of the American jihad, second only to Pakistan and Saudi Arabia. But for the Islamist recruits that his intelligence services sent to join the American jihad, Sadat's commitment was belied by his willingness to sign a peace treaty with Israel, thus betraying the Palestinian cause by contributing to its isolation. Ironically, Sadat was killed by jihadists in October 1981, at a time when Egyptian state support for the Afghan jihad was reaching its high point.

One of the leaders of the jihadist group was Ayman al-Zawahri, a surgeon trained at one of the country's leading universities. Soon after Sadat's assassination, al-Zawahri escaped Egypt and arrived in Peshawar to join Osama bin Laden. With the Gulf War and the entry of American troops into Saudi Arabia, al-Zawahri's view that Sadat had betrayed the Islamist cause came to be shared by bin Laden, who now thought similarly of the House of Saud. The unipolar world that emerged from the fall of the Soviet Union no doubt influenced the radical shift in how the al-Qaeda leadership came to see its erstwhile benefector, America. Al-Zawahri wrote in his memoir that he considered the Afghan jihad as "a training course of the utmost importance to prepare the Muslim mujahideen to wage their awaited battle against the superpower that now has sole dominance over the globe, namely, the United States."

Afghan-Egyptians came to public attention on November 17, 1997, when an Egyptian gunman—who security officials said was trained in the Afghan guerrilla camps—led five others in the mass murder of fifty-eight foreign tourists and at least four Egyptians on the banks of the Nile at Luxor in Upper Egypt. As in Algeria, the methods used by terrorists were gruesome—such as throat cutting and disemboweling—and suggested training in the Afghan jihad. The Luxor attack was not an isolated incident; it came on the heels of at least 150 murders of unarmed civilians in 1996 and 1997—killings that in several cases were led, according to Egyptian police, by "Afghan war veterans."

Perhaps more important than the skills the jihad fighters were taught was the training that obliterated the distinction between soldier and civilian and justified any target so long as attacking it increased chances of victory. Foreigner or local, intellectual or soldier, judge or police officer, woman or man, child or adult, all were considered fair game. Those recruited as volunteers for the American jihad included all types of characters: from honest believers acting out of commitment to unemployed youths looking for adventure to hardened criminals in search of victims. Not all were enthusiastic converts to the tactics of terror taught by their new mentors. Depending on past experience, some—such as criminals and outcasts—were likely to embrace these skills more readily than others. This may also explain why the fallout of the American jihad tended to lead to greater brutality than had been characteristic of the original Afghan edition.

The legitimization of violence against civilians was a direct consequence of something the CIA manual called training in "strategic sabotage," which was categorized as either simple or indirect. The manual explained simple sabotage as "personalized, surreptitious interdiction by individuals and small groups to damage or destroy installations, products or supplies" and indirect sabotage as different ways of reducing production in enemy territory. Part of simple sabotage was training in "demolition and arson." More important, simple and indirect forms of strategic sabotage really distinguished between two different ways of undermining civilian support for the enemy. The time-honored forms of terror against women—kidnap and rape—were formalized and thus normalized in the annals of the Afghan jihad as "marriages of convenience." "Time and again," writes Cooley, "these same techniques appear among the Islamist insurgents in Upper Egypt and Algeria, since the 'Afghani' Arab veterans began returning there in the late 1980s and early 1990s."

The Islamist terror that we are witnessing today is more a mutation than an outgrowth of Islamic history, the result of a triple confluence: ideological, organizational, and political. The ideological element was the product of an encounter between Islamist intellectuals (Mawdudi, Qutb) and different Marxist-Leninist ideals that embraced armed struggle in the postwar period. The organizational element was a direct consequence of the American decision to organize the Afghan jihad as a quasi-private international crusade. The political element is a consequence of the demonization of Islam and its equation with terrorism, a tendency that emerged after the Cold War and gathered steam after 9/11. This demonizing point of view questions whether a historically grounded modernity is even possible in the postcolonial Islamic world. Best identified with Bernard Lewis, it equates modernity with secularism, secularism with Westernization, and Westernization with subjugation. Because it sees a necessary contradiction between Islam and modernity, this point of view also sees a necessary contradiction between modernity and democracy wherever Muslim populations reside.

The Cold War and Radical Islam

The twentieth century saw three nuanced differences within political Islam. The first is a schism between reformists and radicals. Radicals are convinced that no meaningful social reform will be possible without the conquest of state power: thus the centrality of jihad in radical Islamist discourse. The second is a deepening wedge between two strands of radicalism, one society-centered, the other state-centered. Whereas society-centered Islamists claim to balance the struggle for justice (jihad) with that for democracy in the state (ijtihad), state-centered Islamists have little confidence in popular organization and action and consider the gates of ijtihad forever closed. Their perspective is defined by a single-minded dedication to the pursuit of justice. Finally, the Cold War bred, hothouse fashion, terrorist elements from within state-centered political Islam. Islamist terror combined two hitherto hostile points of view: a deep hostility to contemporary Islamic states from those like Qutb who had been savagely repressed in jails, and a deep distrust of popular organization and action shared by terrorist groups.

This is why it is necessary to distinguish Islamist terror from radical Islamism. Radical Islamist social movements of the twentieth century were part of an ongoing search for an effective response to a twin dilemma: imperial occupation and social reform. Like the Society of Muslim Brothers in Egypt, their starting point was reform. They were not looking for a doctrinal response in spiritual matters but a political and social response to a this-worldly dilemma. Driven more by intellectuals than by clergy, these movements argued that Islam is not "a mere religion" but is more like a political ideology that addresses all aspects of our social existence. The concern of Islam is not only theology and ethics but also politics and law, economy and social justice, even foreign policy. Though it began by calling for the building of a supranational Muslim community (umma), as had the poet and philosopher Muhammed Iqbal in early-twentieth-century India, radical Islamism sprouted different national versions as it adapted to different nation-states. Like Hizbullah and Hamas, it occasionally resorted to terror—violence against civilians—without embracing it as a consistent policy. The shift from a supranational commitment to an orientation defined by the political community within state boundaries has been the most dramatic in movements such as Hizbullah, which has entered the electoral process and given up the idea of establishing an Islamic state, and Hamas, whose critique of the PLO is less and less that it betrayed Islam and more and more that it betrayed the Palestinian people.

Hizbullah

The founding of Hizbullah was a direct reaction to the Israeli invasion of Lebanon in June 1982 and the subsequent introduction of western troops under the banner of the Multi-National Forces (MNF). Iran responded to this by dispatching fifteen hundred Revolutionary Guards to the Syrian-controlled Bekaa valley. Soon after, Hizbullah was secretly organized under Iranian sponsorship. Hizbullah's short history can be divided into two phases. The first, the military resistance against Israeli occupation, lasted from 1982 to 1985, the year of Israel's withdrawal from southern Lebanon. During this time, Hizbullah created two organizations: Islamic

Resistance, said to be responsible for "suicide attacks against Western and Israeli targets," and Islamic Jihad, "which led more conventional attacks against Israeli troops in the south." In this first phase, Hizbullah aimed to establish an Islamic republic in Lebanon, ruled by Islamic law as part of an Islamic state larger than Lebanon.

The shift in Hizbullah's ideological and political orientation toward a secular notion of the state was the result of a leadership struggle that followed two major changes in the region. The first was the end of Israeli occupation in Lebanon and, following it, the end of the civil war (1985–1989) between Hizbullah and Amal, two organizations vying for political leadership of the Shi'a community in Lebanon. The second was the leadership change in Iran after the death of Ayatollah Khomeini, which led to a less-ideological political orientation. The new party leadership in Lebanon under Sheikh Fadlallah "called constantly for a dialogue with Christians . . . on the values shared between Muslims and Christians, and Hizbullah officials called for establishing a non-confessional system without defining it in explicit terms, thus leaving the characteristics of the system open to debate." This was tantamount to a call for the secularization of politics in Lebanon. In Lebanon's parliamentary elections of 1992, "the first open elections in more than two decades," Hizbullah backed non-Shi'a candidates, both Sunni and Christian, in an attempt to broaden its appeal. Hizbullah won eight seats, including those won by two Sunni and two Christian candidates.

The Hizbullah case reinforces the lesson of the contemporary civil war in Algeria: that reform is better engineered from within than imposed from without. The revocation of a democratic process in Algeria, triggered by the refusal to honor the results of the 1991 election, had been motivated by a secular fear that its outcome would hand over power to religious extremists, eventually endangering both secularism and democracy. It recalls a similar sidestepping of the democratic process in Vietnam out of fear that it would deliver power to Communists who would deny the same rights to their opponents. This kind of reasoning ignores the fact that the tension between democratic processes and undemocratic outcomes is one that is integral to every democracy, most recently evident in the American election of 2000. It cannot be an argument for abrogating democracy, only for devising effective safeguards to entrench the process in the face of outcomes that may undermine it. Second, it masks a dogma that equates secularism with an already existing institutional arrangement, particularly the kind of arrangement that came to define European political life beginning in the seventeenth century. Predicated on a notion that the only mode of global coexistence for different cultures (now civilizations) is parallel existence—tolerance—this dogma is certainly premature and does not exhaust other historical possibilities that also lay emphasis on engagement and critique.

Iran

Algeria and Iran reveal contrasting examples of radical political Islam in contemporary history. Both underscore the importance of letting social movements—whether religious or secular—work through internal ideological and political struggles in an autonomous fashion. When they have been allowed to operate within legal frameworks, social and political movements, though not necessarily democratic, have strengthened the conditions for democracy by expanding participation in the political process. The possibilities of this are best glimpsed in Iran, where the broad Islamist movement has given rise both to democratic demands and to a growing feminist movement.

The point is made by Richard Bulliet, a social historian of

medieval Islam at Columbia University. "The revolutionary regime," he points out, "came to power intent on reversing the Shah's liberal legislation concerning women" and "quickly accomplished this goal and mandated severe restrictions on women's dress, employment, and behavior." Yet only "two decades later, an active Islamic feminist movement in Iran has seen a woman take her place at the cabinet table as director of women's affairs and another attain the rank of vice president." In addition, "the parliament has put in place a body of legislation that makes the Iranian laws of marriage and divorce among the most liberal in the Islamic world." Bulliet writes with an understanding that Algeria and Iran provide official America with two contrasting options. He is also quite clear as to which option to take: "The Algerian must not become a regional norm supported actively or tacitly by the United States." At the same time, Iran is less a model than a lesson. The lesson is that of democracy: instead of thinking of modernity as an import into Islam, one needs to be sensitive to the emergence of an Islamic modernity, arising from processes within Islamic societies.

Islamist politics are driven by two very different movements. Radical Islamists see the reorganization of society as the only way to change the state, while conservative Islamists see the seizing of power as the sole way to change either state or society. Not always democratic, radical Islamists like Hizbullah or the FIS in Algeria demand that everyone—including women—participate in public life. In contrast, conservative movements not only oppose female presence in public life but also tend to be violently sectarian. Both radical and conservative Islamists claim to adhere to sharia (a rule of law), but the conservative notion of sharia excludes any meaningful space for democracy. The difference lies in their respective attitude to ijtihad, an institution that allows for legal principles to be interpreted in light of changing historical contexts. Conservative, state-centered Islamists are vigorous defenders of a rule of law, but they understand law as divine law and see any form of democracy as corruptive of it. This is why the true dividing line between society- and state-centered Islamists is not the commitment to a rule of law but to popular participation in state affairs.

Islamist statism has arisen from different routes. One is the endeavor of unpopular regimes—such as the Zia dictatorship in Pakistan—to legitimize power. The other route—the main one in these times—is exemplified by the late Cold War project in central Asia, the American jihad. Whereas the imperative to seek popular support in a democratic contest has forced radical Islamist movements like Hizbullah to develop national roots, the absence of that possibility—and, in some instances, the fear of that same contest—has led statist movements to turn supranational. Not only did this kind of imperative tie Zia's state to the American jihad, it also led to the formation of an international cadre of uprooted individuals who broke ties with family and country of origin to join clandestine networks with a clearly defined enemy.

One can conclude, therefore, that political Islam is a modern political phenomenon, not a leftover of traditional culture. To be sure, one can trace several practices in political Islam—opium production, madrassah education, and the very notion of jihad—to the era before modern colonization. In fact, opium, madrassah education, and al-jihad al-akbar were all reshaped and remade within modern institutions as they were put in the service of a global American campaign against the "evil empire."

Political Islam is a diverse movement with multiple and even contradictory elements. I have argued that it is useful to distinguish between society-centered and state-centered movements, with moderates and radicals on each side. Inasmuch as they are committed to a strategy of change that calls for increased popular participation in politics, society-centered movements resemble Latin American social movements inspired by Christian liberation theology. In contrast, state-centered movements try to contain popular political participation and see the state—rather than society or any sector of it—as the true subject of historical change. Rather than being vehicles for popular pressures from below, they reflect elite-driven attempts to dam the flow of popular participation.

State-centered Islamist political movements should not be equated with terrorism. As long as authoritarian movements remain confined within national borders and adhere to even a semblance of a rule of law—as with the Zia dictatorship in Pakistan, the House of Saud in Saudi Arabia, and the Taliban in Afghanistan—the potential for terror remains sheathed. The emergence of terror goes along with the erosion of a rule of law. The distinction between a lawful dictatorship and terror outside the law will help us distinguish between the Taliban, on the one hand, and the mujahideen, on the other. In Afghanistan, after the Soviet Union was defeated, terror was unleashed on the Afghani people in the name of liberation. Eqbal Ahmad observed that the Soviet withdrawal turned out to be a moment of truth, rather than of victory, for the mujahideen. As mujahideen factions coalesced into two rival forces, one more extreme and ideological than the other, and fought for power, they shelled and destroyed their own cities. Precisely when they were ready to seize power, the mujahideen lost the struggle for the hearts and minds of their own people. That was the explanation of how a "liberation" force could lose power literally at the moment of having taken it, to a student force that had not participated in the war of "liberation." Once the Taliban began to run the state, its brutality took the form of a harshly patriarchal rule, the main targets of which were young people and women.

In contrast, al-Qaeda was a transnational movement whose violence was unrestrained by any form of law. Al-Qaeda members, originally recruited from dozens of countries around the world, found they had no home to return to when the jihad ended. John Cooley gives the example of North African recruits, many of whom "feared to return" and "stayed in the postwar training program for future terrorists, financed mostly by private Saudi and other Arab funds." Rootless, bewildered, and embittered hostages to a social condition that made them more or less prone to political nihilism, they were the strike force against the empire they had come to understand, in language they shared with Reagan, as "evil." The source of privatized and globalized terrorism in today's world, the international jihadis are the true ideological children of Reagan's crusade against the "evil empire."

Chapter Four

FROM PROXY WAR TO
OPEN AGGRESSION

E ven after the Soviet Union collapsed and the Cold War ended, America's low-intensity conflict against militant nationalist regimes continued well into the next decade, right up to 9/11. From a Reaganite point of view, this made perfect sense. Was it not the Reagan administration that had concluded that the real threat of war did not lie on the plains of Europe but in the Third World, where successful insurgencies were leading to militant nationalist regimes, which (it claimed) were nothing but Soviet proxies? The Reagan response was proxy war. Built on the Nixon Doctrine—"Asian boys must fight Asian wars"—as applied by Henry Kissinger, its effect was to redesign American war strategy. Instead of a possible confrontation with Soviet ground troops in Europe, it prepared to wage low-intensity conflict against militant nationalist regimes in the Third World.

By 9/11 the methods changed drastically, from low-intensity

proxy war to high-intensity direct warfare. That shift was made possible by a changed political climate in post–9/11 America: not only had security become a concern, but this concern was received initially with empathy from most of the world. For the Bush administration, this was a golden opportunity to shed the inhibitions of the Cold War and declare open season on militant nationalism. From this point of view, a war against militant nationalism would conclude the unfinished business of the Cold War. The ambition to smash militant nationalism was summed up as a call for "regime change" and—in true Reaganite fashion—"democratization." In a flash of less than two years, the United States moved from the invasion of Taliban-ruled Afghanistan to that of Saddam Hussein–ruled Iraq. Whereas the Taliban had been pinpointed as hosts of al-Qaeda, there was little legitimate effort to connect the invasion of Iraq to the terror that was 9/11. This is because the "war on terror" had moved on, from addressing broadly shared security concerns to targeting militant nationalism.

The trajectory of proxy war in the rough decade from the end of the Cold War to 9/11 is best illuminated on the common ground of Iraq. America's post-Vietnam preoccupation with low-intensity proxy war reached its high point in Iraq, where it was waged in the entirely novel form of a multilateral proxy, taking the form of UN sanctions, mitigated by an "oil-for-food" program, justified in the language of humanitarian intervention but at a cost of hundreds of thousands of innocent children's lives. After 9/11, Iraq, more than Afghanistan, became the real launching pad for a brazen U.S. intervention undertaken in the midst of international opposition, including in the halls of the UN.

Iraq: Collective Punishment in War and Peace

The two decades of proxy war, from the Iraq-Iran War of the 1980s to the regime of UN sanctions, provide a background to the invasion of Iraq and highlight a novel development in U.S. strategy in the region. If U.S. attitude to the Iraq-Iran War recalls a time-tested strategy of big powers fueling and sustaining a local conflict in order to weaken both sides, the regime of sanctions that followed the Gulf War was a remarkable development in the history of low-intensity conflict: for the first time, the proxy was not bilateral but multilateral. Whereas the sanctions regime demonstrated the success with which the United States turned the UN into a multilateral proxy, the invasion of Iraq demonstrated that approach's limits and, ultimately, failure.

To understand how Iraq became central to U.S. strategy in the Middle East, we need to return to Iran in 1979. We have seen that postwar U.S. foreign policy operated on the simple assumption that Islam was an anti-Communist and antinationalist force; the Iranian Revolution changed this by giving the United States the taste of a nationalist Islamist regime. To contain Iranian nationalism and the force of its example, the United States turned to Iraq. Neither the brutal dictatorship that Saddam Hussein ran at home nor his determination to create a modern and independent state made much difference at the time. The relationship between the United States and Iraq was marked by three phases in the two decades that followed. The first phase was an alliance in which the United States supported Iraq in the war against Iran, but it was also a setup, designed to keep the war going rather than to bring it to a swift conclusion. The second phase, the Gulf War that followed Saddam's occupation of Kuwait, was a war of vengeance. The third phase was a vicious low-intensity, high-casualty campaign conducted through the offices of the UN; in reality, this was nothing short of an officially conducted and officially sanctioned genocide, primarily of children, most under five.

On September 22, 1980, when Saddam Hussein invaded Iran with enthusiastic U.S. support, he initiated a war that saw the first use of chemical weapons since the U.S. invasion of Vietnam. Nicholas D. Kristof of the *New York Times* reported that "the United States shipped seven strains of anthrax to Iraq from 1978 to 1988." Training in the use of chemical and biological agents had been provided to Iraqi military officers as early as the 1960s. An official army letter published in the late 1960s noted that "the U.S. army trained 19 Iraqi military officers in the United States in offensive and defensive chemical, biological and radiological warfare from 1957 to 1967." At the time Iraq got access to U.S. chemical and biological weaponry, the U.S. military was advertising these weapons not only as less expensive but also as more humane. Harvard professor Matthew Meselson, codirector of the Harvard-Sussex Program on Chemical-Biological Warfare Armament and Arms Limitation, explained: "The argument was you would lose fewer American lives if you fought a war because you would knock the enemy out right away."

Further, a report in the February 2003 issue of *Foreign Policy* says the United States provided Iraq satellite imagery of Kurdish militias and Iranian troops so the Iraqis could target both more effectively. A central figure in Reagan's effort to court Saddam was the person who was one of the most hawkish on Iraq after 9/11: Defense Secretary Donald Rumsfeld, who, as Reagan's envoy, met Saddam Hussein in December 1983 and Tariq Aziz, then the foreign minister, on March 24, 1984, the very day the UN released its report on Iraq's use of poison gases against Iranian troops.

American assistance to Saddam Hussein ranged from commercial credits to political protection. When Saddam began gassing the Kurdish minority in Iraq in May 1987, the United States was already providing Iraq with aid worth $500 million per year. In spite of public revelations about the use of chemical weapons, the United States doubled aid to the regime. Additionally, the United States blocked attempts to raise the topic in the UN Security Council. But when Saddam Hussein's forces gassed Iraqi Kurds for a second time, after the September 1988 cease-fire with Iran, the brutality received wide publicity, including in the American press. Compelled to acknowledge the crime, the United States asked that the UN response be limited to appointing a fact-finding team to confirm the event.

Chemical weapons from the United States were not just unleashed on those for whom they were meant. In at least one disasterous instance during the 1991 Gulf War, over 100,00 American soldiers were exposed to Sarin nerve gas when the U.S. military improperly blew up chemical weapon sites in Khamasiyah. Today, hundreds of thousands of Gulf War veterans are sick—estimates range "up to half"—many suffering from a variety of symptoms collectively known as Gulf War Syndrome. Matters came to public attention after the current invasion of Iraq when a class-action suit, introduced on behalf of over 100,000 Gulf War veterans in August 2003, named "11 companies and 33 banks alleged to have helped Iraq with its chemical weapons program in the 1980s, despite knowledge Saddam Hussein was actively using WMD against both Iranians and his own people."

This alliance between the United States and Saddam Hussein is better understood by looking at the Ba'athist and the Islamist regimes in Baghdad and Tehran. Two forms of nationalism, one secular and the other religious, they represented the more successful attempts at state building in the region. Washington's support of Baghdad in the war was an indication of which it thought was the greater danger. But Washington's real strategic objective was to bleed *both* to death. The sentiment behind it was brazenly articulated by Kissinger in the middle of the Iraq-Iran War, perhaps because he was already out of office: "We hope they kill one another."

Saddam Hussein's invasion of Kuwait ended the alliance. Hussein became an example of the price that must be paid by any regime that violates the terms of its alliance with the United States. The 1991 Gulf War was literally a punishment. It was the first time the United States applied the military doctrine it had forged in Laos during the long war from 1964 to 1974: "to compensate for the absence of ground forces by an aerial bombardment of unprecedented intensity, without regard to the 'collateral damage.'" The political prerequisite was that collateral damage must not become public, as it had in Laos. Then as it "panned the Ho Chi Minh trail in the jungles of the south" and "the heavily populated areas of the Plain of Jars in the north," the bombing aroused great concern in antiwar circles in the United States. A group of Cornell University scientists pointed out that the bombing violated the principle of proportionality—"that a reasonable proportionality exist between the damage caused and the military gain sought"—under international law. In his introduction to the scientists' report, the Pulitzer Prize–winning *New York Times* journalist Neil Sheehan concluded: "The air war may constitute a massive war crime by the American government and its leaders." It is this doctrine of aerial bombing, without regard to the principle of proportionality or to consequences for the civilian population, that the United States applied during the Gulf War in Iraq, after it, in Kosovo, and then in Afghanistan.

The Gulf War was waged with little restraint, and in the

process the United States committed many war crimes. Former attorney general Ramsey Clark charged that the administration used "all kinds of weapons in violation of international law," from explosives to depleted uranium to cluster bombs. As Iraq's infrastructure was comprehensively targeted, little thought was given to civilian casualties, which were explained away as "collateral damage." Eric Hoskins, a Canadian doctor who was also coordinator of a Harvard team on Iraq, reported that the bombardment of 1991 had "effectively terminated everything vital to human survival in Iraq—electricity, water, sewage systems, agriculture, industry and health care." Thomas Friedman, the chief diplomatic correspondent of the *New York Times,* openly claimed that "the best of all worlds" for the United States would be another Saddam-like dictator, "an iron-fisted Iraqi junta without Saddam Hussein." But George H. W. Bush hesitated to replace Saddam Hussein, uncertain of what consequences regime change would have had for the region. Bush faced a double dilemma. On the one hand, the Kurdish minority was the group best organized among the Iraqis to take advantage of Saddam's overthrow, but its objective was a Kurdish state that would also include parts of Turkey, a close U.S. ally in the region. On the other hand, there was also the possibility that Iraq's majority Shi'a population, which had religious and cultural ties to Iran, would assert itself, surely dimming America's hopes of isolating Iran. So Bush feared bringing even a semblance of democracy to Iraq. The alternative was to continue punishing Iraq in peacetime, so as to keep the regime from arming effectively against anyone but its own population.

Even after this punishing war, the idea persisted that Iraq was a danger to the region, capable of mounting an invasion, as with Kuwait, and a danger to the world, capable of unleashing weapons of mass destruction. In the worst-case scenario, Iraq was said to be close to possessing a nuclear device. The editor of the *Bulletin of Atomic Scientists* commented after the 2003 Iraq War that "many of the charges that had been dangled in front of [the media] failed the laugh test, but the more ridiculous, the more the media strove to make the whole-hearted swallowing of them a test of patriotism." These fictions supported the argument that Iraq must be policed and punished simultaneously. That combination was carried out by the United States and Britain through the intermittent aerial bombardment that continued even after the Gulf War ended. By the time the second war against Iraq started in 2003, the peacetime bombing of Iraq had lasted longer (since 1990) than had the U.S. invasion of Vietnam or the war in Laos. In October 1998, U.S. officials told the *Wall Street Journal* they would soon run out of targets: "We're down to the last outhouse." That was two months before President Clinton, bedeviled by the Monica Lewinsky scandal and faced with a vote in the House of Representatives indicting him for perjury and obstruction of justice, decided to unleash a round-the-clock bombing of Iraq. Round-the-clock bombing began on December 16, 1998, and ended on December 19. The mission was called Operation Desert Fox, also the nickname of German Field Marshal Erwin Rommel. The U.S. government reported that American and British forces flew more than 650 strike and strike-support sorties, that navy ships and submarines fired 325 cruise missiles, and that an additional 90 cruise missiles were fired by U.S. Air Force B-52s.

The intermittent bombing of Iraq ran parallel with an indefinite regime of economic sanctions. The UN adopted economic sanctions as part of its 1945 charter, as a way of maintaining global order. Since then, sanctions have been used fourteen times, twelve of those since the collapse of the Soviet Union. But Iraq represents the first time a country has been comprehensively sanctioned since the Second World War, meaning that virtually every aspect of its exports and imports was controlled by the UN and subject to a U.S. veto.

The UN Security Council imposed comprehensive multilateral economic sanctions in resolution 661 on August 6, 1990. All exports from and imports to Iraq were banned, with exemptions for medical supplies and, in some instances, foodstuffs. Resolutions 665 and 670 that same year imposed a marine and air blockade to enforce the sanctions. The sanctions regime was renewed, with the same humanitarian caveats, in resolution 687 (1991). A further set of resolutions in 1991 permitted the sale of petroleum and petroleum products, up to $1.6 billion every six months, but it was not implemented until resolution 986 (1995) set up the oil-for-food program.

The rationale for the sanctions regime kept on shifting. First, it was meant as a lever to get Iraq to withdraw from Kuwait. When Iraq withdrew, the rationale shifted to the need to disarm it, particularly of chemical and biological weapons of mass destruction. The real objective was to compromise its sovereignty. When a proposal was floated as early as 1991 that UN-controlled Iraqi oil sales be used to purchase humanitarian goods, Iraq objected on the grounds that the proposal would undercut its sovereignty and reduce the government to an internal civil administration. The sanctions regime continued even longer than the Iraqis had expected. As the concomitant humanitarian crisis deepened, Iraq and the UN finally came to agreement on the oil-for-food program.

This regime signified a truly novel and sinister development in the history of low-intensity conflict. Waged as a human-rights campaign, it claimed to soften a punishment meted out according to a rule of law with provisions for "humanitarian goods" supervised by on-the-ground "UN Humanitarian Aid Coordinators."

In reality, it unleashed the mass murder of hundreds of thousands, mainly children, in the full and callous knowledge that the victims were not the target and a cynical acceptance that sanctions so effectively centralized the official export-import trade that it put the surviving population at the mercy of the very regime it claimed to target. Done in the name of the UN, it turned the UN into an American proxy for low-intensity conflict.

Since no foreign loans or foreign investment—and no access to foreign exchange—were permitted, this is how the program worked: Iraq was allowed to sell a set amount of oil over six months (initially $1.2 billion net, later $3 billion net). The revenues went directly into a UN account. The United States and Britain required that nearly one third of this (30 percent from 1996 to 2000, 25 percent thereafter) be diverted into a compensation fund to pay outsiders for losses allegedly incurred because of Iraq's invasion of Kuwait. Another 10 percent went to pay for UN operating expenses in Iraq. The remainder was controlled solely by the UN controller who disbursed funds to contractors and suppliers of foodstuffs and basic medicines approved by the sanctions committee. But as a working paper prepared for the UN Sub-Commission on the Promotion and Protection of Human Rights noted, "Of the revenue from sale, only about half ended up going towards the purchase of humanitarian goods, the majority of the rest going towards reparations and administrative costs." Finally, the sanctions regime treated the northern Kurdish part of Iraq preferentially—both in the funds provided and the degree of autonomy allowed its local administrators—to the central and southern parts. Whereas child mortality decreased in the three northern governorates during the period of the sanctions regime, it increased in the fifteen governorates of central and southern Iraq.

The effect of comprehensive sanctions was deadly. Because

they followed on the heels of a war that had targeted and destroyed Iraq's physical infrastructure, there was a veritable social and demographic disaster. Yet public knowledge of the humanitarian crisis was slow in coming. Part of the reason lay in the fact that the UN human-rights rapporteur on Iraq was limited to identifying human-rights violations by the government of Iraq; the rapporteur was prohibited by mandate from looking at human-rights violations as a result of the sanctions. At the same time, the oil-for-food program lacked an evaluation component and therefore also lacked a trigger mechanism that would force a response if conditions deteriorated. As the dimensions of the humanitarian crisis became known, two nonpermanent members of the Security Council, Canada and Brazil, pushed through a resolution in 1998 mandating the UN to assess humanitarian conditions in Iraq. The result was the 1999 UNICEF demographic survey, which for the first time brought to light comprehensive and credible evidence of the human tragedy wrought by the sanctions regime.

Before 1999, there had been two kinds of studies: forty-three independent studies on the nutritional status of Iraqi children carried out over fifteen years, and data on the number of deaths in hospitals, compiled by the Iraqi Ministry of Health from 1993. These studies and claims were evaluated by Richard Garfield, professor of clinical international nursing at Columbia University and chair of the human-rights committee of the American Public Health Association. Garfield considered the Iraqi ministry's statistics highly unreliable both because most deaths are not reported to hospitals and because not all deaths in hospitals can be attributed to the sanctions. When it came to independent studies, he found that, though reliable, they were too local in focus. But Garfield acknowledged that the 1999 UNICEF survey "provides the first reliable mortality estimates for Iraq since 1991."

UNICEF data showed "that the rate of mortality more than doubled" among children under five years in the fifteen governorates of central and southern Iraq, "from 56 per 1000 births in 1984–89 to 131 per 1000 during 1995–99." The result was an estimated five thousand "excess child deaths" every month above the 1989 presanctions rate. Writing in the summer of 2000, Garfield gave 300,000 as "a conservative estimate of 'excess deaths' among children under five." Even worse, of those alive, more than 22 percent of young children were chronically malnourished.

Even in this age of mass murder, the gravity of these figures should not escape our attention. Noting that "even in cases of extreme economic decline like the Great Depression in the United States, there was no increase in the rate of mortality," Garfield underlined the gravity of the Iraqi disaster as "the only instance of a sustained, large increase in mortality in a stable population of more than 2 million in the last two hundred years." Where death stalked, life was miserable: Iraq's ranking in the UN Development Program (UNDP) Human Development Index fell from 55 out of 130 in 1990 to 126 out of 150 in 2000.* By 2000, there was a consensus in both the UN and the human-rights community about the excess child deaths directly linked to sanctions: the June 2000 report to the UN Sub-Commission on the Promotion and Protection of Human Rights acknowledged that the total deaths "directly attributable to the sanctions" ranged "from half a million to a million and a half, with the majority of the dead being children." Even the minimum estimate was three times the number of Japanese killed during the U.S. atomic-bomb attacks.

---

*The 1990 Index was compiled from low to high, and the 2000 Index from high to low. Thus, Iraq, ranked 76th in 1990 out of 130, would be 55th if the Index had been compiled from high to low, as in 2000.

The moral indefensibility of the sanctions regime was clear as early as 1996, when Madeleine Albright, U.S. ambassador to the UN, was asked by Lesley Stahl on the TV program *60 Minutes* about the price of "containing" Saddam: "We have heard that a half million children have died. I mean, that's more than died in Hiroshima. And, and you know, is the price worth it?"

Madeleine Albright responded: "I think this is a very hard choice, but the price, we think the price is worth it."

How and by whom was such a death toll justified for so long? This question was the subject of research by Joy Gordon, professor of philosophy at Fairfield University, who studies the ethics of international relations. She described both her research experience and its findings in a cover story in *Harper's Magazine* that explored "economic sanctions as a weapon of mass destruction."

The simple fact is that the United States consistently used its veto on the Security Council's 661 Committee, the body "generally responsible for both enforcing the sanctions and granting humanitarian exemptions," to minimize the humanitarian goods entering the country. It was not required to give a reason for the veto, but the reason it gave most often was concern over dual use, civilian and military, claiming that the goods in question—those necessary to provide electricity, telephone service, transportation, even clean water—could also be used to enhance Iraq's military capabilities.

Gordon found that as of September 2001 the United States had blocked "nearly 200 humanitarian contracts," including "contracts that the U.N.'s own agency charged with weapons inspections did not object to." The most notorious were those needed to repair the damaged water and sanitation systems, given that most excess child deaths were "a direct or indirect result of contaminated water." Yet U.S. officials blocked contracts for water tankers, "on the grounds that they might be used to haul chemical weapons instead." As of September 2001, "nearly a billion dollars' worth of medical-equipment contracts—for which all the information sought had been provided—was still on hold."

The United States was able to block even contracts approved by UN monitors on the ground because UN procedure allowed it. The only time the United States felt compelled to justify its veto was when it was forced to do so by publicity in the American press, as indeed happened in March 2001, when the *Washington Post* and Reuters reported that the United States had placed a hold on $280 million of "medical supplies, including vaccines to treat infant hepatitis, tetanus, and diphtheria, as well as incubators and cardiac equipment." Washington's rationale was "that the vaccines contained live cultures, albeit highly weakened ones," and that the Iraqi government "could conceivably extract these, and eventually grow a virulent fatal strain." The veto persisted in spite of testimony from European biological-warfare experts "that such a feat was in fact flatly impossible," and in spite of "pressure behind the scenes from the U.N. and from members of the Security Council." Only when confronted with adverse publicity did the United States abruptly announce it was lifting the veto in this specific instance.

UN administrators on the ground argued that they had developed an aggressive monitoring system to guard against dual use of imports. In a 1999 interview, the UN humanitarian-aid coordinator in Baghdad, Hans Von Sponeck, pointed out: "We have to control every gas cylinder that comes into this country. We have a number and we must make sure that 'gas cylinder 765' is there and the other one is over there. If you can do it with that detail, surely you can also do it with computers that are necessary for high school or university students that need to learn how to interact with modern technology."

Forced to take responsibility for a policy they could neither defend nor influence, many of those in charge of implementing Iraq policy at the UN opted to resign, one after another. The first to resign was Denis Halliday, an Irishman who was the assistant secretary general and humanitarian coordinator in Iraq for thirteen months. He resigned in September 1998, declaring: "We are in the process of destroying an entire society. It is as simple and terrifying as that. It is illegal and immoral." His successor, Hans Von Sponeck, who served as humanitarian coordinator until March 2000, was "driven out by U.S. charges of turning soft on sanctions-hit Iraq," a UN official told Agence France-Presse. The resignation followed Von Sponeck's warning in a CNN interview that the UN program was failing to meet even the "minimum requirements" for Iraq's 22 million people: "How long should the civilian population, which is totally innocent on all this, be exposed to such punishment for something they have never done? As a UN official, I should not be expected to be silent to that which I recognize as a true human tragedy that needs to be ended." Two days later, Jutta Burghardt, head of the World Food Program in Iraq, also resigned, stating: "I fully support what Mr. Von Sponeck is saying."

The more the UN's refusal to modify the sanctions regime in spite of the scale of human carnage in Iraq became public knowledge, the greater the outrage in the human-rights community. Human Rights Watch wrote of the sanctions, "The continued imposition of comprehensive economic sanctions (against Iraq) is undermining the basic rights of children and the civilian population generally," and called on the UN Security Council to "recognize that the sanctions have contributed in a major way to persistent life threatening conditions in the country." Save the Children (UK) described the economic sanctions as "a silent war against Iraq's children."

We have seen that the rationale for sanctions shifted over the years: they were later said to be necessary to force Iraq to disarm, particularly because of chemical and biological weapons. Iraq had been armed with weapons of mass destruction during the period of its military collaboration with the United States, which had ended with the Gulf War. There followed a period of disarmament and a debate over how effective the disarmament had been. Among those with hard facts that could help answer this question were the weapons inspectors. Scott Ritter, a marine intelligence officer who was the chief weapons inspector from 1991 to 1998, was the most doubtful that Saddam Hussein's regime any longer represented a significant, let alone an imminent, threat. Ritter resigned in protest that the U.S. government had sabotaged his mission, placing nine American intelligence officers on the inspection team as far back as 1992. Ritter told CNN on July 17, 2002:

> As of December 1998 we had accounted for 90 to 95 percent of Iraq's weapons of mass destruction capability. We destroyed all the factories, all the means of production and we could not account for some of the weaponry, but chemical weapons have a shelf-life of five years. Biological weapons have a shelf-life of three years. To have weapons today, they would have had to rebuild the factories and start the process of producing these weapons since December 1998.

In his view, this was a remote possibility, since "no one has substantiated the allegations that Iraq possesses weapons of mass destruction or is attempting to acquire weapons of mass destruction." Hans Blix, the last of the chief weapons inspectors, also confirmed that there was no evidence that Iraq possessed weapons of mass destruction.

Iraq claimed it had destroyed all its prohibited weapons between 1991 and 1994, either unilaterally or in cooperation with the inspectors. The inspectors were able to verify that unilateral destruction had taken place on a large scale but could not quantify the amounts destroyed. So they recorded the material as "neither verified destroyed nor believed to still exist," an ambiguity that the United States and Britain seized on to claim the existence of hidden "stockpiles."

If truth be told, it was not the Saddam Hussein regime but successive U.S. administrations that freely resorted to using weapons of mass destruction beginning with the 1991 Gulf War. We have seen that Professor Joy Gordon described economic sanctions after the Gulf War "as a weapon of mass destruction." During the invasion of Iraq, the United States used at least two others: an updated version of incendiary bombs brand-named napalm during the Vietnam war, now called Mark-77 firebombs, and depleted uranium. Mark-77 firebombs were dropped on Iraqi troops near the Iraq-Kuwait border at the start of the war. Although the use of napalm was banned by the United Nations in 1980, the United States never signed the agreement. The United States considers the use of Mark-77 firebombs legal for a variety of reasons. To begin with, they are no longer identified by the brand name napalm. Yet this latest generation of incendiary bombs, first developed during the Second World War and used on Japanese cities, is acknowledged to be far more destructive of human life than napalm. Mark-77 firebombs explode into massive fireballs. "Incendiaries create burns that are difficult to treat," explained Robert Musil, the director of Physicians for Social Responsibility, a Washington-based group that opposes the use of weapons of mass destruction. He described the Pentagon's distinction between napalm and Mark-77 firebombs as "pretty outrageous" and "clearly Orwellian." The Pentagon's response came from Colonel Mike Daily of the Marine Corps: even though he acknowledged that the Mark-77 has "similarly destructive" effects on humans, he emphasized that it has "significantly less of an impact on the environment."

Depleted uranium (DU) is the radioactive and highly toxic waste product that remains after natural uranium has been "enriched." Like incendiary firebombs, the first use of uranium in munitions occurred in the Second World War: it was pioneered by the Nazis. During the two Gulf Wars, the U.S. used DU in ammunitions as varied as armor plate, anti-tank penetrators, and cruise missiles. Economic considerations alone are unlikely to be an obstacle to the use of DU. According to Damacio Lopez of the International Depleted Uranium Study Team, testifying to the European Parliament for an immediate ban on the military use of DU: "In Iraq over 1.5 million soldiers and civilians have died of natural causes since the 1991 Gulf War, one third of them children under the age of five. Leukemia, cancer, birth defects and rare diseases have increased at an alarming rate in this country. Studies conducted by Iraqi scientists have found higher levels than that permitted by international standards for U-238 and its products in drinking water of various city supplies and in the Tigris River. Vegetables, fish and meat in southern Iraq are showing levels of radiation contamination as well." Since DU enters the food chain and contaminates water, and is said to have a "half-life of four and a half billion years," it will "continue to harm all forms of life in contaminated areas till the end of time" if not cleaned up. Since uranium is known to increase the incidence of lung cancer when inhaled, and bone cancer, leukemia, and genetic defects when ingested, the consequences will be nothing less than drastic—not only for Iraqis, Kuwaitis, and Afghanis promised "democracy" through American power, but also for America's sons and daughters, urged to don uniforms in the pursuit of humanitarian missions in distant battlefields. Just as with incendiary firebombs, the use of weapons containing DU violates humanitarian law. In a 1996 advisory opinion, the International Court of Justice affirmed that "states must never use weapons that are incapable of distinguishing between civil and military targets." Willful killing is a grave breach—a war crime—under Articles 51, 52, and 85 of Protocol Additional 1 of the four Geneva Conventions.

Propaganda has been an integral part of war in modern times. The history of America's war with Iraq, from the Gulf War to the 2003 invasion of Iraq, has seen the upgrading of propaganda from distortion and exaggeration of known facts to the deliberate invention of lies. Decisive in persuading members of Congress to vote for the Gulf War was a statement by a Kuwaiti "nurse" who claimed to have seen Iraqi soldiers looting the maternity department of a Kuwaiti hospital and killing babies. Later, it came to light that the "nurse" was actually the daughter of the Kuwaiti ambassador in Washington, and her account was fabricated for the Rendon Group, a media consultancy firm employed for the war, by Michael K. Deaver, a former media adviser to Ronald Reagan. During the Gulf War, it was often claimed that the Iraqi army was the fourth most powerful in the world and therefore truly a threat to peace—in and beyond the region. On February 20, 2002, the *New York Times* revealed that the Pentagon had, on orders from Donald Rumsfeld and Undersecretary for Defense Douglas Feith, created the Office of Strategic Influence (OSI) with a mandate to generate false news to serve U.S. interests. Coordinated by an air force general, Simon Worden, the OSI was authorized to engage in disinformation, particularly to foreign media. Its activities included a contract worth $100,000 a month with the Rendon Group. The OSI was officially dissolved after these revelations but subsequent developments—particularly the "rescue" of Private Jessica Lynch—raised questions about whether this was indeed the case, or whether its mandate had been taken up by another agency.

The by now well-known story of Jessica Lynch's "rescue" was splashed across the U.S. media in April 2003. According to the official account, she was ambushed on March 23, fired at the Iraqis until her ammunition ran out, then was hit by a bullet, stabbed, tied up, and taken to a hospital in Nasariyah where she was supposedly beaten by an Iraqi officer. A week later, she was freed by U.S. Special Forces who broke into the hospital, overcame resistance from her guards, rescued her, and flew her by helicopter to Kuwait. That same evening, President Bush announced her rescue to the nation in an address from the White House. Eight days later, the Pentagon supplied the media with a video of the rescue, one that easily matched the standard of the best of Hollywood action movies.

When the war ended, journalists—including those from the *New York Times,* the *Toronto Star, El Pais,* and the BBC—went to Nasariyah to find out the truth. The Iraqi doctors they interviewed told them that Lynch's wounds, a fractured arm and leg and a dislocated ankle, were not caused by bullets but by an accident in the truck in which she had traveled. American doctors who later examined her also confirmed this fact. Rather than being mistreated, the Iraqi doctors had shown her the utmost consideration. "She had lost a lot of blood," explained Dr. Saad Abdul Razak, "and we had to give her a transfusion. Fortunately, members of my family have the same blood group: O positive. We were able to obtain sufficient blood. She had a pulse rate of 140 when she arrived here. I think that we saved her life." At considerable risk, the doctors contacted the U.S. Army to inform them that the Iraqi army had retreated and that Lynch was waiting to be claimed. Two days before the Special Forces arrived, the doctors had even taken her in an ambulance to a location close to U.S. lines. But U.S. soldiers opened fire and almost killed her. When Special Forces arrived, equipped with special equipment for a pre-dawn raid, members of the hospital staff were surprised. Dr. Amnar Uday told the BBC's John Kampfner: "It was like in a Hollywood film. There were no Iraqi soldiers, but the American Special Forces were using their weapons. They fired at random and we heard explosions. They were shouting 'Go! Go! Go!' The attack on the hospital was a kind of show, or an action film with Sylvester Stallone." A former assistant of director Ridley Scott, who had worked on the film *Black Hawk Down*, filmed the "rescue" with a night-vision camera. Robert Scheer of the *Los Angeles Times* reported that the images were then sent for editing to U.S. Central Command in Qatar, then for checking by the Pentagon, and then distributed worldwide.

In the United States, the saving of Jessica Lynch has come to represent the most heroic moment of the 2003 conflict in Iraq. And yet the story of her rescue is as much a lie as the two major reasons given for launching the war on Iraq: Saddam Hussein's weapons of mass destruction (WMD) or the links between the Iraqi regime and al-Qaeda. The very notion of "weapons of mass destruction" was invented as a scare to go alongside the notion of an "evil" regime whose arsenal must evoke deep fear. At the heart of the debate on the quality of intelligence that justified the invasion of Iraq is an ad hoc and secret agency created by the Bush administration: the Office of Special Plans (OSP) based in the Pentagon. The OSP was the subject of an extended piece by Seymour M. Hersh, a veteran investigative journalist at *The New Yorker*.

According to Hersh, OSP was conceived by Paul Wolfowitz, the deputy secretary of defense, overseen by Undersecretary of Defense William Luti, and directed by Adam Shulsky. Set up in the days after 9/11, OSP's job was to analyze data received from security services—including the CIA and the Pentagon's DIA—and to produce summaries to be passed on to the White House. But a Pentagon adviser told Hersh that OSP "was created in order to find evidence of what Wolfowitz and his boss, Defense Secretary Donald Rumsfeld, believed to be true—that Saddam Hussein had close ties to al-Qaeda, and that Iraq had an enormous arsenal of chemical, biological, and possibly nuclear weapons that threatened the region and, potentially, the United States." To make this case, OSP turned to defectors sought out by an umbrella Iraqi exile group, the Iraqi National Congress, led by Ahmad Chalabi, with whom Wolfowitz and Perle had "a personal bond . . . dating back many years." As the small group of analysts at OSP went beyond coordinating existing information to generating new information, they eclipsed existing intelligence-gathering agencies. The former chief of Middle East intelligence at the DIA, W. Patrick Lang, told Hersh: "The D.I.A. has been intimidated and beaten to a pulp. And there is no guts at all in the C.I.A." In one year, Hersh concluded, OSP had "brought about a crucial change of direction in the American intelligence community" and "helped to shape public opinion and American policy toward Iraq"—Hersh noted a February 2003 poll showing that 72 percent of Americans believed it was likely that Saddam Hussein was personally involved in the 9/11 attacks.

OSP's main contentions were directly disputed by the joint congressional inquiry into the suicide hijackings of 9/11, that concluded that "U.S. intelligence had no evidence that the Iraqi regime of Saddam Hussein was involved in the attacks, or that it had supported al-Qaeda." Georgia senator Max Cleland, a member of the congressional committee that produced the report, got to the point: "The administration sold the connection to scare the pants off the American people and justify the war. What you have seen here is the manipulation of intelligence for political ends." Representative Jane Herman, ranking Democrat on the House Intelligence Committee and a California moderate who had voted for the Iraq war, said Bush had no right to declare, as he did on March 17, that "intelligence gathered by this and other governments leaves no doubt that the Iraq regime continues to possess and conceal some of the most lethal weapons ever devised." Representative Herman drew conclusions for the future: "It is clear that there were flaws in U.S. intelligence. WMD [were] not located where the intelligence community thought [they] might be. Chemical weapons were not used in the war despite the intelligence community's judgment that their use was likely. I urge this administration not to contemplate military action, especially preemptive action, in Iran, North Korea or Syria until these issues are cleared up." Senator Cleland accused the administration of deliberately delaying the report's release to keep up the momentum for the war: "The reason this report was delayed for so long—deliberately opposed at first, then slow-walked after it was created—is that the administration wanted to get the war in Iraq in and over. Had this report come out in January like it should have done, we would have known these things before the war in Iraq, which would not have suited the administration."

During the war, no evidence of a stockpile or the use of weapons of mass destruction came forth. This meant either that the regime had no such weapons or that, if it did, it was responsible enough not to use them, even in the face of certain defeat. One wondered which fact would be more damning for the invaders. After the war, the administration deployed a fourteen-hundred-member inspection team, the Iraq Survey Group under General Dayton, but it too failed to come up with any evidence of WMD stockpiles. Perhaps anticipating this possibility, soon after the war, Wolfowitz, in an interview in *Vanity Fair* magazine, said that the United States had focused on alleged weapons of mass destruction as the primary justification for invading Iraq because it was politically the most convenient: "For bureaucratic reasons we settled on one issue, weapons of mass destruction, because it was the one reason everybody could agree on."

One might ask why the United States targeted the Hussein regime if it was not an imminent threat in military terms. Iraq has the world's second-largest proven stocks of oil, after Saudi Arabia. But oil cannot provide the full explanation, or even the bulk of it. Iraq's real significance is political. Just as after 1991 Iraq was turned into an example of the punishment that can be meted to a regime that dares go outside the framework of a U.S.-defined alliance, so the significance of Iraq after 9/11 again extends beyond the country itself. In attacking Iraq, the Bush administration hoped to achieve more than just a regime change: Iraq presented another chance to redraw the political map of the entire region, something the United States has tried several times before—the highlights being the Israeli invasion of Lebanon, which failed to create a buffer Christian state; the alliance with Iraq against Iran in the 1980s; and the war in Afghanistan. The overthrow of the Saddam Hussein regime is meant to change the balance of forces in the Middle East. Writing in April 2003 under the auspices of the Jerusalem Center for Public Affairs, Israeli major-general Ya'akov Amidror put it bluntly: "Iraq is not the ultimate goal. The ultimate goal is the Middle East, the Arab world and the Muslim world. Iraq will be the first step in this direction; winning the war against terrorism means structurally changing the entire area."

The United States seeks to replace defiant regimes and intimidate others, imposing a new regional order by creating pro-American regimes, first in Iraq, and then in an apartheid-style Bantustan-like state of Palestine, presenting regime change as a strategy for "democratization." And yet the thrust of this administration's policy shift is global, not just regional, in spite of the sometimes shrill rhetoric that equates terrorism with Islam. The policy shift is driven by Protestant "fundamentalism," which has a parochial orientation but global consequences, and neoconservatism, which is marked by global ambitions. Its target is militant nationalism, in the Middle East and beyond. Though the methods have changed after 9/11, with proxy war giving way to outright invasion, the objective remains the same as under the Reagan administration: to target and liquidate militant nationalism through regime change.

Dispensing with the Rule of Law Internationally

The defining feature of modern Western imperialism—particularly British and French—was the claim that expanding domains were key to spreading the rule of law internationally. Even the most brutal of dictatorships that were self-consciously western, such as Nazi Germany and apartheid South Africa, insisted that they were upholders of the rule of law.

From this perspective, the George W. Bush administration's open disdain for the rule of law is unmatched in the history of Western imperialism. At the same time, the contemptuous dismissal of rules, agreements, treaties, even institutional arrangements goes along with a self-proclaimed mission to spread "democracy" globally. Unlike those who rationalized global Western domination earlier, but very much like the Reagan administration, the Bush administration claims that there is sharp opposition between rule of law and democracy, two values that have hitherto been seen as cornerstones of Western civilization. So post-9/11 America has scuttled any possibility of an international rule of law and has claimed impunity for American power in the name of spreading democracy internationally. Will this growing contempt for international law be a defining feature of this administration, the stamp of a coalition of secular neoconservatives and Protestant fundamentalists, or are these forces expressing a growing Jacksonian consensus in post–9/11 America? Is this an anomaly or a turning point?

During the Cold War, the United States dealt with the UN at arm's length, limiting participation and cooperation to issues, agencies, and periods that suited American interests. It paid dues if and when it considered necessary and in the amount it chose to pay. It left UN agencies whose purposes it opposed, such as UNESCO, and rejoined them to gain temporary favor, as it did with UNESCO after eighteen years absence. Once the Cold War was over and the United States stood as the world's sole superpower, it felt free to renounce treaties it considered no longer in accord with its interests, at the same time openly coercing the assignment of leading personnel in UN agencies.

Top-level international civil servants who have insisted that America abide by a rule of law have been targeted and left with one choice: resign or be sacked. The most prominent of these was, of course, the former secretary-general of the UN, Boutros Boutros-Ghali, whose passionately naïve conviction that the end of the Cold War would clear the way for an international rule of law led to frequent disagreements with Madeleine Albright and ultimately a clear message from the Clinton administration that his candidacy would be vetoed should he seek a second term.

Other high-level post–9/11 victims of U.S. power include Mary Robinson, the former Irish president, who retired after only a one-year renewal of her contract as the UN high commissioner for human rights; Robert Watson, the much-respected chair of the Intergovernmental Panel on Climate Change; and Jose Mauricio Bustani, the head of the Organization for the Prohibition of Chemical Weapons (OPCW), only a year after he had been unanimously elected to a second five-year term.

Boutros Boutros-Ghali came to the UN with impeccable establishment credentials: he had accompanied Sadat to Jerusalem and was one of the architects of the Camp David Accords. His differences with the United States emerged soon after the Gulf War, which the United States saw as a model for future UN operations: "the UN proposes, on Washington's initiative, and the US disposes." Boutros-Ghali was of the view that the end of the Cold War would free the UN from the constraint of East-West rivalries. In a number of documents, he presented proposals for "preventive diplomacy," including setting up "rapid deployment units which would allow the UN to nip potential conflicts in the bud, and even levy taxes to finance its operations." As the cost of UN peacekeeping operations increased fourfold from 1992 to 1996 (from $600 million to $2.6 billion), and Washington withheld its dues (amounting to $2.9 billion), Boutros-Ghali denounced the "dishonesty" of those "who made the UN ineffective by depriving it of essential funds while refusing to pay the funds due to it on the pretext that it was ineffective." It was when Boutros-Ghali began to assert his independence in practice that Washington's patience ran out. He criticized Washington's preoccupation with Bosnia—"a war of the rich"—and its neglect of Somalia, where "one third of the population was likely to die of hunger," and Rwanda, where he accused the United States of "standing idly by" and "only getting involved when the massacres had already decimated the population." Many believe Washington's anger peaked in April 1996 when Boutros-Ghali "insisted on publishing the findings of the UN inquiry implicating Israel in the killing of some hundred civilians who had taken refuge in a United Nations camp in Kanaa in south Lebanon." In the end, Washington successfully replaced Boutros-Ghali with another African, Kofi Annan, the UN's undersecretary-general for peacekeeping during the Rwanda genocide, who, not surprisingly, turned out to be much more attuned to Washington's bidding. Kofi Annan's rise came in the wake of two major crisis faced by the UN, the first in the former Yugoslavia, the second in Rwanda. Whereas Boutros-Ghali had been unwilling to follow the NATO command and approve American demands for aerial bombing of the Serbs on a scale more than symbolic, Kofi Annan readily obliged when he stood in for Boutros-Ghali. In Richard Holbrooke's words, he then "became Secretary General in waiting." But it was Rwanda that demonstrated that Annan's willingness to serve the United States apparently knew no bounds: as Alexander Cockburn noted, "in deference to the American desire to keep Sarajevo in the limelight, he suppressed the warning of the Canadian General Romeo Dallaire that appalling massacres were about to start in Rwanda."

Mary Robinson also incurred the wrath of the United States for her endorsement of the results of the 2001 UN World Conference Against Racism—which debated Israel's racist treatment of Palestinians and slavery as a "crime against humanity"—leading both the United States and Israel to walk out. Robert Watson infuriated the oil lobby when an independent scientific panel he chaired reached a consensus stating that human activity is a factor in climate change; he also led efforts to establish international norms on fossil fuel usage. The significance of oil interests in shaping U.S. policy was exposed in a leaked memo from Exxon-Mobil that asked the White House: "Can Watson be replaced now at the request of the U.S.?" As director-general of the OPCW, Jose Mauricio Bustani increased the number of signatories to the international convention banning chemical weapons from 87 to 145 in his first five years in office. *The Guardian* credited Bustani with achieving "the fastest growth rate of any multilateral body in recent times" and lauded him for having "done more in the past five years to promote world peace than anyone else on earth." Bustani even received a congratulatory note from U.S. Secretary of State Colin Powell but soon ran into problems with the U.S. government. The reason was that he insisted on the independence of his office, resisting American demands that they decide the nationality of OPCW inspectors assigned to American facilities and opposing U.S. legislation that gave the president powers to block unannounced inspection of American facilities and banned OPCW inspectors from removing chemical samples from inspection sites. His biggest crime, though, was to try to persuade Iraq to sign on to the chemical-weapons convention, with the consequence that if OPCW inspectors were let into Iraqi facilities, Washington would be deprived of a quasi-legal justification for military action against Iraq. The United States first asked the Brazilian government to recall Bustani, but it refused on the grounds that he had been elected and not appointed; it then asked Bustani to resign, which he refused to do; it finally pressured the executive council of the OPCW to sack him, which it did. Bustani told the kangaroo court set up for the purpose:

> By dismissing me, an international precedent will have been established whereby any duly elected head of any international organization would at any point during his

or her tenure remain vulnerable to the whims of one or a few major contributors. They would be in a position to remove any Director-General, or Secretary-General, from office at any point in time.

More than the Cold War, it is the period after it that has led to a breakdown in international rules governing the use of force. Recall that the Security Council never authorized the use of force against Yugoslavia in the case of Kosovo. The UN Charter prohibits the use of force except for self-defense, unless approved by the Security Council. The Kosovo War was led by NATO, which never really claimed defense as its rationale. When Robin Cook, the British foreign secretary, told Madeleine Albright that he had "problems with our lawyers" over using force against Yugoslavia without Security Council approval, Albright responded, "Get new lawyers!"

Asked whether the United States was explicitly seeking Security Council approval to attack Iraq in 2003, Secretary Powell cited Kosovo as precedent for acting without such authority. But when discussing the consequences for Iraq of a possible breach of resolution 1441, Powell had no hesitation in claiming that the Security Council "can decide whether or not action is required," but the United States will "reserve our option of acting" and will "not necessarily be bound by what the Council might decide at that point." In other words, Powell was arguing that the council's decisions are binding on Iraq but not on the United States.

Its cavalier attitude to a rule of law in the international arena is evident in the ease with which the United States has felt free to withdraw from treaties, considered far more binding than resolutions. Ramsey Clark is perhaps the harshest critic of American resistance to an international rule of law. In a letter he sent to all members of the UN Security Council on September 20, 2002, Clark listed the treaties renounced by American administrations since the end of the Cold War:

> The U.S. has renounced treaties controlling nuclear weapons and their proliferation, voted against the protocol enabling enforcement of the Biological Weapons Convention, rejected the treaty banning land mines, endeavored to prevent its creation and since to cripple the International Criminal Court, and frustrated the Convention on the Child and the prohibition against using children in war. The U.S. has opposed virtually every other international effort to control and limit war, protect the environment, reduce poverty and protect health.

The sad fact is that the emergence of the United States as the world's only superpower has gone hand in hand with its demand to be exempt from any international rule of law. At the same time, the United States has not hesitated to call for a selective application of the rule of law, seeking to use the law as an instrument to hold *others* accountable. This much is clear if we contrast the U.S. opposition to the International Criminal Court to its attitude toward the establishment of international tribunals in select cases.

The International Criminal Court was set up to try individuals for the world's most heinous atrocities: genocide, war crimes, and systematic human-rights abuses. American concerns that those with vindictive intentions might turn this into an opportunity to take American soldiers or civilians to court were registered and incorporated into the treaty when it was written. The ICC is thus to be a court of the last instance. It can step in only when countries are "unable or unwilling" to prosecute mass murderers or perpetrators of other systematic abuses. Nonetheless, Washington asked the Security Council to approve a complete and indefinite exemption for U.S. nationals from the court's jurisdiction and even threatened to veto the renewal of UN peacekeeping operations in Bosnia and elsewhere if it did not get its way. After two weeks of bitter negotiations and opposition by the European Union and others, a compromise was reached: the council agreed to grant an exemption to all individuals from countries that had not ratified the treaty—but for one year only.

Outraged by the move, Canada, one of the prime movers behind the court, denounced this arm-twisting as itself illegal. Unable to keep the ICC from becoming reality, the Bush administration devised a new strategy: to sign bilateral agreements whereby both signatories pledge not to hand over to the ICC nationals accused of crimes against humanity. On May 6, 2003, the Sierra Leone parliament became the first to ratify such an agreement. An Amnesty International statement condemning this "impunity deal" stated: "This is a completely unacceptable decision especially at a time when [Sierra Leone] is starting the process of dealing with mass human rights abuses that have taken place in the recent past." But by mid-June 2003, thirty-seven countries had signed such agreements. Except for India, Israel, Egypt, and the Philippines, the rest are small, poor countries, most heavily dependent on U.S. aid.

Its dogged opposition to the ICC not withstanding, the United States has been eager to establish international tribunals in limited contexts, such as Rwanda, Bosnia, and Cambodia. The Cambodian case illuminates particularly well the United States' self-interested policy. When the war in Indochina ended, America did not have a single and consistent approach to dealing with war crimes in the region. Whereas no international tribunal was mandated to try U.S. war crimes in Vietnam or Laos, the United States supported the call for an international tribunal to try Khmer Rouge leaders for war crimes. When it came to drafting the terms of the tribunal, Washington demanded that the mandate of the court be restricted to the period from 1975 to 1979. Had the years before or after been included, the United States would have run the risk of itself being charged with war crimes. Any scrutiny of the pre-1975 period would have directed the court's attention to the years of U.S. carpet bombing in Indochina, just as an investigation of the post-1979 period would have brought to light the political cover the United States provided the Khmer Rouge, both at the UN and internationally, against the Vietnamese, who invaded Cambodia in 1978.

Its reluctance to be held accountable internationally does not distinguish the Bush administration from other great powers, historically. What does distinguish it is the reckless determination to dispense with any project that would integrate others—whether rivals, dissidents, junior partners, or dependents—in a rule-based international order. Anatol Lieven, a senior associate at the Carnegie Endowment for International Peace in Washington, reminds us that the plan for "unilateral world domination through absolute military superiority" has been "consistently advocated and worked on by the group of intellectuals close to Dick Cheney and Richard Perle since the collapse of the Soviet Union in the early 1990s." Even Secretary of State Colin Powell, considered the in-house dove in the Bush administration, shares this basic goal with the rest of the security establishment. As early as 1992, when he was chairman of Joint Chiefs of Staff, Powell declared that the United States requires sufficient power "to deter any challenger of ever dreaming of challenging us on the world stage." The famous strategy document drawn up by Paul Wolfowitz in the last year of the senior Bush administration incorporated this very goal. His son proclaimed it as official policy in his West Point speech of June 2002: the guiding purpose of U.S. post–Cold War strategy should be to prevent the emergence of any "peer competitor" anywhere in the world. What distinguishes Powell from the hawks in the administration is not this basic goal but their commitment to preemptive war, now official American doctrine. Americans need to be aware of the logic of preemptive war. It is not accidental that most genocides have been carried out in times of war. The population is told: if you do not kill, you will be killed. You kill because you fear they may do to you what you are about to do to them. Preemptive war is the logic for genocide.

The current Bush administration is the ideological descendant of the Reagan administration. Prominent "bleeders" in the Reagan administration who shaped the ideological character of the Afghan War, like Richard Perle, are powerful influences in the shaping of defense policy in the current administration. The rhetoric about democratizing the Arab world, including the conviction that democracy must spread through American power, echoes Reagan, who heralded the contras and the mujahideen as "founding fathers" of democracy in Nicaragua and Afghanistan and the counterrevolution as a "democratic revolution." Just as "democracy" has become an imperial banner waved in the face of Third World nationalist regimes, as in the Reagan years, so has national security become an imperial project simultaneously eroding democracy at home and undercutting nationalist attempts to build a meaningful sovereignty in the era of globalization.

Israeli Power and Local Impunity

No one should be surprised that the United States is indeed considering a "solution" for the Palestinian National Authority in the Occupied Territories similar to that for Iraq: a regime change followed by a form of trusteeship. The resemblance between U.S. policy in Iraq and Israeli policy in the Occupied Territories has increased markedly since 9/11. As the United States was able to maintain in Iraq the combination of an intermittent air war with sanctions that have been shown to result in mass murder, Israel has effectively choked economic life in the Occupied Territories and reduced its inhabitants to bare-bones levels of poverty through a combination of regular punishment with extended curfews and restricted movement. On February 2, 2002, the *New York Times* reported the publication of a statement in Jerusalem, signed by more than one hundred Israeli reservists, saying they would refuse to continue serving in the West Bank and on the Gaza Strip because Israel's policies there involved "dominating, expelling, starving and humiliating an entire people." Like the United States in Iraq, Israel publicly refused to make a distinction between civilian and military targets in the Occupied Territories—justifying "our terror" either as a preemptive strike or as a response to "their terror." In the process, the Iraqi and the Palestinian people have suffered collective punishment, meted out with impunity.

Ever since Israel reoccupied Palestinian territories, the events at Jenin have become the metaphor for Israeli state terror. Like the United States, Israel, too, is convinced of the need to use massive power, totally out of proportion to the alleged provocation, so as to leave the outcome in no doubt. "By what inhuman calculus," asked Edward Said,

> did Israel's army, using dozens of tanks and armored personnel carriers, along with hundreds of missile strikes from US-supplied Apache helicopter gunships, besiege Jenin's refugee camp for over a week, a one-square-kilometer patch of shacks housing 15,000 refugees and a few dozen

men armed with automatic rifles and no missiles or tanks, and call it a response to terrorist violence and a threat to Israel's survival?

The use of disproportionate power can be sustained only in the absence of accountability and a guarantee of impunity. That guarantee can be provided only by American power. In the era when the United States had regularly insisted that the protection of human rights must trump any claim of state sovereignty, Israel remained the exception: it successfully refused to have its actions in Jenin investigated, when it did not even claim sovereignty over the city. Since no UN inquiry occurred, we may never know the full story of what happened in Jenin. But we can get some idea from individual accounts. Particularly illuminating is the story of Moshe Nissim, called "Kurdi Bear" over the military radio—"Kurdi" referring to his Kurdish origins and "Bear" to the sixty-ton D-9 demolition bulldozer he operated. He was given a few hours' training in driving the bulldozer and then left in charge of it. In the words of the Israeli newspaper that ran his story: "For 75 hours with no break, he sat on the huge bulldozer, charges exploding around him, and erased house after house. . . . There was not one soldier in Jenin that did not hear his name. Kurdi Bear was considered the most devoted, brave and probably the most destructive operator." How does a man work so long, with no break?

Do you know how I held out for 75 hours? I didn't get off the tractor. I had no problem of fatigue, because I drank whisky all the time. . . . For three days, I just destroyed and destroyed. The whole area. Any house that they fired from came down. And to knock it down, I tore down some more. . . . If I am sorry for anything, it is for not tearing the whole camp down.

If Kurdi Bear presented the face of a state terrorist, the Israeli army was not without those who resisted orders to target civilians. The right-wing Israeli newspaper *Hatzofeh* carried the story of "an Israeli helicopter gunship pilot" who "refused to fire a missile at a Palestinian house." *The Guardian* correspondent in Jerusalem cited this as "the latest sign of growing unease among some Israeli troops over the conduct of the fighting in Palestinian cities of the West Bank." The pilot refused the order to fire repeatedly: the first time when a regimental commander ordered the strike at the house "to 'liquidate' five alleged terrorists apparently hiding inside"; the second time when the commander assured the pilot "that the terrorists could be exactly pinpointed in the house and again ordered him to shoot"; and the third time when the commander told him "that the terrorists had disappeared, but ordered him to fire at the house nonetheless."

The destruction in Jenin was not mindless or just punitive. If Ariel Sharon claimed its purpose was to destroy "the infrastructure of terror," this made sense only if one understood him to mean by it the infrastructure of resistance, including the very capacity for organized civic life. That the operation went far beyond targeting armed guerrillas to destroying the civic life of Palestinians was a fact discussed far more critically in the Israeli than in the American press. Amira Hass wrote in *Ha'aretz:*

> Let's not deceive ourselves; this was not a mission to search and destroy the terrorist infrastructure. . . . If they thought incriminating evidence was hidden in the Education Ministry and the International Bank of Palestine and in a shop that rents prosthetics, the soldiers would have examined document after document, and not thrown the files on the floor without opening them. . . . There was a

decision made to vandalize the civic, administrative, cultural infrastructure developed by Palestinian society. . . . It's so easy and comforting to think of the entire Palestinian society as primitive, bloodthirsty terrorists, after the raw material and product of their intellectual, cultural, social and economic activity has been destroyed. That way, the Israeli public can continue to be deceived into believing that terror is a genetic problem and not a sociological and political mutation, horrific as it may be, derived from the horrors of the occupation.

The practice of collective punishment involves the denial of both individual responsibility and individual agency. Both are central to Culture Talk. The racial branding of Palestinians—and of Arabs in general—seems to be gaining a degree of respectability that would have been unthinkable before 9/11. In a recent interview with the Israeli historian Benny Morris, former Israeli prime minister Ehud Barak spoke of Palestinians in words that few American racists would dare utter in print: "They are products of a culture . . . in which to tell a lie creates no dissonance. They don't suffer from the problem of telling lies that exists in Judeo-Christian culture. Truth is seen as an irrelevant category. There is only that which serves your purpose and that which doesn't." In the next sentence, Barak applied this generalization to "Arab society": "The deputy director of the US Federal Bureau of Investigation once told me that there are societies in which lie detector tests don't work, societies in which lies do not create cognitive dissonance."

The tendency to brand Palestinians and Arabs racially has not been limited to the domain of politics. Take the following example from the American academic establishment. The 2001 issue of

Human Immunology, the journal of the American Society of Histocompatibility and Immunogenetics, contained an article by a team led by the Spanish geneticist Professor Antonio Arnaiz-Villena of Complutense University in Madrid titled "The Origin of Palestinians and Their Genetic Relatedness with Other Mediterranean Populations." It began with scientific evidence indicating that "Jews and Palestinians in the Middle East share a very similar gene pool and must be considered closely related and not genetically separate." The authors concluded that "rivalry between the two races is therefore based 'in cultural and religious, but not in genetic differences.' " A year after its publication, the article was removed from *Human Immunology*'s Web site, and "letters have been written to libraries and universities throughout the world asking them to ignore or 'preferably to physically remove the relevant pages.' " The journal's editor, Nicole Suciou-Foca of Columbia University, claims "the article provoked such a welter of complaints over its extreme political writing that she was forced to repudiate it." So as to remove any doubt about the journal's political position, Arnaiz-Villena was sacked from it's editorial board.

In the annals of the modern state, the practice of collective punishment is identified with colonialism and racism. It has involved abrogating notions of individual responsibility central to a rule of law in favor of collective responsibility for all political acts. In this vein, Alan M. Dershowitz, Frankfurter Professor of Law at Harvard, wrote in *The Jerusalem Post*, proposing the destruction of a Palestinian village in retaliation for every Palestinian act of resistance or terror: "It will be a morally acceptable trade-off even if the property of some innocent civilians must be sacrificed in the process." As a professor of law, Dershowitz could not have been unaware of how article 6(b) of the 1945 Nuremberg Charter for the Trial of the Major Nazi War Criminals defines war crimes:

"namely, violations of the laws or customs of war. Such violations shall include, but not be limited to, . . . wanton destruction of cities, towns or villages."

Unlike crime, political acts make sense only when linked to collective grievances. Whether we define them as acts of terror or of resistance, we need to recognize a feature common to political acts: they appeal for popular support and are difficult to sustain in the absence of it. If there is a logic behind the practice of collective punishment, it is the acknowledgment that collective punishment can only be a response to political acts, not criminal deeds. Take the debate around the September 3, 2002, decision by the Israeli Supreme Court that the army could expel from the West Bank the brother and sister of a Palestinian militant accused of organizing a suicide bombing and send them to the Gaza Strip. Amnesty International argued that the "unlawful forcible transfer" of Palestinians under Israeli occupation constituted a war crime under the Fourth Geneva Convention. More important than the legal reasoning by the nine-judge panel is the political rationale behind the decision. The *New York Times* recognized that this was part of a larger attempt to halt Palestinian suicide attacks.

Security trumps rights—in Israel when it comes to the rights of Palestinians, and in the United States when the rights in question are of groups stigmatized as terrorist. If the invasion of Afghanistan led to the internees in Guantánamo Bay, the invasion of Iraq has gone alongside a similar internment at Camp Cropper, on the outskirts of Baghdad International Airport. None of its Iraqi prisoners—3,000 in August 2003—were charged with any offence. They were listed as suspected "looters" or "rioters" or simply as "loyal to Saddam Hussein." The International Red Cross was allowed inside the camp, but its officials were barred from describing what they saw. However, some of the staff broke ranks to tell

Amnesty International of the conditions of daily life in Camp Cropper. Here is a composite description: "Each prisoner receives six pints of rank, tepid water a day. He uses it to wash and drink in summer noonday temperatures of 50 degrees Celsius. He is not allowed to wash his clothes. He is provided with a small cup of delousing powder to deal with the worst of his body infestation. For the slightest infringement of draconian rules he is forced to sit in painful positions. If he cries out in protest his head is covered with a sack for lengthy periods." Camp Cropper also held a growing number of "special prisoners," such as former deputy prime minister Tariq Aziz, the former speaker of the Iraqi Parliament, Saadium Hammadi, and Dr. Hudda Ammash, said to be a key member of Saddam's chemical and biological program. According to one of the few prisoners released, Adnan Jassim, "Tariq Aziz has aged very much in the past months in the camp. He shuffles and has a stoop. This may be because he has to dig his own toilet. It is forbidden for anyone to help him to do this. He is treated just like anyone else—an animal to be driven wherever the guards want him." Another former detainee, Qays Al Saiman, said, "The worst offenders had their hands tied behind their backs and were put face down on the ground in the sun for two hours." According to a Red Cross visitor, the women, like the men, "are not allowed to wash their underwear—and several have developed unsightly sores." Amnesty International said in June 2003 that the conditions in the camp "may amount to cruel, inhuman or degrading treatment or punishment, banned by international law." Such was daily life in America's shameful Gulag until it was closed in October 2003 and its inmates were transferred, presumably to another detention facility.

If we are to find a way out of the dialectic of collective punishment and group resistance—and out of the cycle of terror in its many forms, state and societal—we have no choice but to identify and address the politics that inform all sides of the debate.

The Settler and the Suicide Bomber

The violence of the settler and the suicide bomber, more than any other, has come to define the contemporary world of terrorism and counterterrorism. The debate on terrorism revolves around two poles, the cultural and the political. Culture Talk seeks the explanation for a deed in the culture of the doer. In contrast, Political Talk tends to explain the deed as a response to issues, to a political context of unaddressed grievances. Whereas I am more partial to political than to cultural explanations of political terror, I am also aware that both share a common predisposition: for both, political terror is an *inevitable* response, either in the grip of a premodern culture or in the face of terrible oppression. Neither point of view considers political terror an act of choice, and both lack a historical perspective. Cultural explanations ignore the specific issues that fuel conflict, while political explanations overlook the fact that the practice of terrorism over time leads to the development of an extremely short-term point of view and an amoral political culture that legitimizes the use of terror in the pursuit of worthy causes.

The debate on suicide bombing has brought out the cultural and political explanations of political terror. Stephen Schwartz's article "Ground Zero and the Saudi Connection" is still the best-known example of an argument that tries both to disassociate the roots of terror from the cultural tradition of Islam and to locate it in one particular tradition within Islam. He begins with a politically correct posture: "The attacks of 11 September are simply not compatible with orthodox Muslim theology, which cautions soldiers 'in the way of Allah' to fight their enemies face-to-face, without harming non-combatants, women or children." Schwartz seeks the cultural roots of terrorism in "a strain of Islam"—Wahhabi Islam—a form of "stripped-down Islam" that "hate[s] ostentatious spirituality," which emerged "less than two centuries ago" and is "violent," "intolerant," and "fanatical beyond measure." A single example—"the Wahhabis fell upon the city of Karbala in 1801 and killed 2,000 ordinary citizens in the streets and markets"—suffices to establish the claim that "from the beginning" this "cult was associated with the mass murder of all who opposed it." Then follows his own stripped-down conclusion: "all Muslim suicide bombers are Wahhabis," immediately followed by an afterthought: "except, perhaps, for some disciples of atheist leftists posing as Muslims in the interests of personal power, such as Yasser Arafat or Saddam Hussein." Undeterred, our author continues: "Bin Laden is a Wahhabi. So are the suicide bombers in Israel. So are his Egyptian allies. So are the Algerian Islamic terrorists. So are the Taleban-style guerrillas in Kashmir." One has the impression that Schwartz is here talking of terrorists as if they were victims of a premodern tradition that had seized hold of them almost as would a tropical or desert fever. To the extent that "culture" becomes a code word for describing certain peoples by ascribing to them a set of unchanging attributes, it functions as a latterday counterpart of race talk.

A more benign version of Culture Talk can be found in a piece by Sohail Hashmi, a professor of international relations at Mount Holyoke College in Massachusetts. Writing in the *Washington Post,* Hashmi is struck by how some Islamic scholars, such as the popular Sheikh Yusuf Qaradawi of Egypt, can strongly condemn some terrorist attacks (like those of 9/11) but not others (like the suicide bombings in Israel): "It is the religious scholars as much as the bomb makers who are responsible for sending young men and women—often impressionable teenagers—on their murderous missions with promises of a martyr's reward." Hashmi is disturbed because "suicide bombings challenge two fundamental principles of Islamic ethics: the prohibition against suicide and the deliberate killing of noncombatants." At the same time, they can also not be "reconciled with Islam's rejection of the idea of collective responsibility."

The point of view of the suicide bomber has best been brought out in an article in *The Times* (London) titled "Inside the World of the Palestinian Suicide Bomber." The reader is introduced to Yunis, a twenty-seven-year-old art school graduate "who was preparing for a suicide mission that might be days or weeks away." Yunis explains his decision as, first of all, a response to a very contemporary political reality, the occupation: "My aim is to prohibit settlers from enjoying their lives here. My aim is to force the Israeli checkpoint out of my country. If they leave in peace, I have no intention of following them into their areas. But if they remain here I shall use the methods at my disposal to force them out." His decision is also an acknowledgment of another aspect of reality, the simple fact of a technological imbalance between the Israeli state and Palestinian residents of the Occupied Territories: "I know I cannot stand in front of a tank that would wipe me out within seconds, so I will use myself as a weapon. They call it terrorism. I say it is self-defence." But he also intends the act as an ode to freedom. Life, he declares, is "precious," which is why "we have no choice but to fight": "Freedom is not handed as a gift. History is testimony to the fact that major sacrifices have to be made to attain it." Claiming that suicide bombers are "educated strugglers" and "not terrorists," Yunis delivers his final message: "At the moment of executing my mission, it will not be purely to kill

Israelis. The killing is not my ultimate goal, though it is part of the equation. My act will carry a message beyond to those responsible and the world at large that the ugliest thing is for a human being to be forced to live without freedom."

I have often wondered whether the label "suicide bombing" accurately captures either the practice or the motivation behind it. Clearly, the prime objective of the suicide bomber is not to terminate his or her own life but that of others defined as enemies. We need to recognize the suicide bomber, first and foremost, as a category of soldier. Does not the suicide bomber join both aspects of our humanity, particularly as it has been fashioned by political modernity, in that we are willing to subordinate life—both our own and that of others—to objectives we consider higher than life? Suicide bombing needs to be understood as a feature of modern political violence rather than stigmatized as a mark of barbarism. The danger of a moral discussion by itself (how can any culture condone suicide) is that it quickly turns into a replay of Culture Talk, stereotyping individuals and preventing any deliberation about alternative strategies. Thus the need to combine a moral discussion with a broad historical and political one.

Like the left-wing guerrilla, the right-wing settler, too, blurs the boundary between the civil and the military: a large proportion of the fighting force is often made up of civilian commandos, and all adult males, as in South Africa, or all adults, male or female, as in Israel, undergo compulsory military training and are drafted into reserve forces placed on short call. It is the spectacular expansion of Israeli settlements in the West Bank and Gaza after the Six-Day War of 1967, and particularly after the 1993 Oslo talks, that explains the context that produced the suicide bomber.

Israel occupied the West Bank and the Gaza Strip after the Six-Day War of 1967. The movement of settlers into the Occupied

Territories did not involve significant numbers until the Yom Kippur War of 1973–1974. In this period, a rapidly growing religious movement, led by the Kookists (followers of Rabbi Kook), gave religious sanction to a political program for settler conquest and supremacy. The Kookist movement took off when a group of rabbis, hawkish young secularists, Kookists, and other religious Zionists who had served in the Israel Defense Forces (IDF) and fought in Israel's wars formed a group they called Gush Emunim, the "Bloc of the Faithful." For Kookists, the victory of Israel in 1967 "was conclusive proof that Redemption was indeed under way and God was indeed pushing history forward to its final consummation." There was no question of withdrawing from any of the Occupied Territories, for "the return of every inch of the sacred land would be a victory for the forces of evil." Whereas labor Zionism tried to normalize Jewish life, the Gush tried to exceptionalize it, believing that "because Jews had been chosen by God, they were essentially different from all other nations and were not bound by the same rules," including UN resolutions forbidding Jewish settlement of conquered Palestinian territory.

After the Yom Kippur War, the Gush formed "a master plan for the settlement of the whole of the West Bank: the aim was to import hundreds of thousands of Jews into the area and to colonize all the strategic mountain strongholds." On Israeli Independence Day in 1976, nearly twenty thousand armed Jews attended a West Bank "picnic," marching from one part of Samaria to another. When the new right-wing Likud Party came to power in 1977, Menachem Begin "visited the aged Rabbi Kook at Merkav Harav, knelt at his feet, and bowed before him." The Likud government "began a massive settlement initiative in the occupied territories." Ariel Sharon, the new head of the Israeli Lands Commission, began by declaring "his intention of settling one million

Jews on the West Bank within twenty years." In 1978, each West Bank settlement became "responsible for security in its own area, and hundreds of settlers were released from regular army units to protect their community and police roads and fields. They were given a great deal of sophisticated arms and military equipment." In March 1979, "the government established five regional councils on the West Bank with the power to levy taxes, supply services, and employ workers." The Gush supplied 20 percent of the West Bank settlers, and "Gush members usually had key roles" in these councils.

Gush members generally agreed "that Palestinians had no rights to the land and that there was no place for them there." The movement of settlers into the Occupied Territories took place in phases, accelerating with each successive one. Settlers numbered an estimated forty-six thousand by 1984, the end of the decade that followed the Yom Kippur War. By the time the Oslo Accord was signed a little less than ten years later, in 1993, there were roughly 200,000 settlers in the Occupied Territories. The irony is that the flow increased after the Oslo Accord. In the third decade, by the end of 2002, the number of settlers had doubled, to nearly 400,000—including those in East Jerusalem, now claimed by Israel. A recent Israeli human-rights report notes that Israeli settlements now control almost 42 percent of the West Bank, not including Palestinian East Jerusalem.

The reach of settlers goes beyond the land they directly control to shaping the conditions in which Palestinians eke out a living. Settlers in the Gaza Strip, for example, form 0.5 percent of its residents but control 20 percent of the land. According to Amira Hass in *Ha'aretz*, even after the so-called 1993 peace process, "settlers continued to dictate how the Palestinians would live—where a water pipe would not be, where a refugee camp would not expand, where cars would not drive and where a sewage treatment plant would not be built. . . . It is an 'axiom' now that 'state lands' are only for Jews; that Palestinians need less land and water per head than Jews; that they do not deserve or require the same infrastructure or conveniences as Jews; that Palestinians live here because we allow them, not because it is their right. . . . That is the discrimination practiced every day, and every minute of every day. It is an alienating, burning insult, the same one familiar to the blacks of South Africa, the blacks of the United States, and the Jews of Eastern Europe."

The Occupied Territories do not include East Jerusalem in official Israeli pronouncements. But life for Palestinians in Jerusalem is not very different. Though Palestinians make up more than a third of the population of "Israeli" Jerusalem, they "have access to only 6% of its land for all their residential, communal and commercial needs." Palestinian homes in East Jerusalem are regularly demolished; Jeff Halper of the Israeli Committee Against House Demolitions has documented "more than 300 in the past decade, with hundreds of demolition orders outstanding." Even after the signing of the U.S.-designed road map, the Israeli government issued "dozens of demolition orders" in just a few weeks. According to Halper, "Israel argues that 'East Jerusalem' is not covered by the Road Map since it has been formally annexed to Israel."

Without understanding this context, it is difficult to grasp the sense of hopelessness and despair that marked the beginning of the second intifada and the spate of suicide bombings. To one who came to political maturity at the height of the antiapartheid struggle, the contemporary debate on suicide bombing recalls an earlier antiapartheid debate around necklacing, a practice whereby township vigilante youths would dip a used tire in gasoline, place it around the neck of a suspected apartheid informer, and set it alight. As with suicide bombing, the debate on necklacing also had two sides to it. Its moral side often sounded less like a critique of necklacing than a settler discourse on the lack of civilization among natives: What kind of society would countenance such a practice? In contrast, the debate among natives—in the ranks of liberation movements—was more often than not about the political effectiveness of necklacing in checking the proliferation of informers.

We can draw four lessons from that period. First, the more the moral debate gained the upper hand, the more the political debate was stifled. Second, the spread of necklacing was testimony to two closely related developments: on the one hand, the penetration of the antiapartheid resistance by agencies of the apartheid state, and, on the other, the spread of a militaristic culture of street gangs that in turn fueled a rough-and-ready vigilante culture among natives. Third, the political debate on necklacing had to distinguish between its immediate and long-term effectiveness. Immediately, it was difficult to argue that necklacing was not effective. To the contrary—just as with suicide bombing—necklacing, too, seemed to give public evidence that the oppressed were capable of mustering a force to counter the spreading tentacles of settler occupation. Many nodded in agreement when Winnie Mandela, fire in her eyes, declared at Munsieville, near Johannesburg, on April 13, 1985: "We have no guns—we have only stones, boxes of matches and petrol. Together, hand in hand, with our boxes of matches and our necklaces we shall liberate this country." Even the African National Congress (ANC) leadership was reluctant to criticize the speech publicly. ANC president Oliver Tambo said as much to a summit meeting of nonaligned nations in Harare: "We are not happy with the necklace but we will not condemn people who have been driven to adopt such extremes." Eventually, however, the political debate had to go beyond the question of the immediate effectiveness of necklacing to probe its longer-run political costs: alienating allies, both at home and abroad, both when the wrong person was necklaced and when not, in which case it raised anxiety about growing militarism in the culture of resistance. The final lesson is of course that so long as there was no effective political alternative, it was difficult to discredit necklacing politically. Once a nonviolent way of ending apartheid did appear as an alternative, it was as if the sun had come up, the fog lifted, and there was a new dawn; in a land where few had dared even to whisper criticism only yesterday, hardly anyone could be found to champion necklacing the day after.

The South African debate on necklacing turned out to be part of a broader political debate on questions such as: Who is a settler and who a native? Who is the enemy and who are we? This debate pointed up the differences between settlers and natives and between three political views. The first to be formulated were two variants of nationalism, conservative and radical. For conservative nationalism, the answer was relatively simple: every immigrant was a settler. The point of the struggle against settler nationalism was to restore the situation that existed before settler conquest: native freedom guaranteed by a native state. Radical nationalism, however, made a distinction between immigrants and settlers. The settler was a person whose privilege was inscribed in law; alternately, immigrants were of different types, whites with privilege, nonwhites without. Whereas immigrants and natives could coexist in a single polity, settlers and natives could not. The point then was to rid the land of settlers who sought political power to undergird a privileged position in the economy and society. The radical-nationalist Pan African Congress summed up this point of view neatly, if rather crudely, in its motto: "One settler, one bullet." Of greater relevance in shaping the future for a postapartheid

South Africa was the third point of view, which transcended both forms of nationalism. Here the problem was not the settler but the settler state, the legal setup that guaranteed settler privilege. Without a state that legally discriminated between settler and native, there would be no settler privilege and, thus, no settler, since all settlers would become as immigrants whose historical origins would cease to have significance in law. The enemy from this point of view was everyone who defended the power of the settler state. Instead of embracing a mirror image of settler ideology—by turning the identity "native" from a racial stigma into a badge of racial pride—the promise of postapartheid South Africa was to let go of both "settler" and "native" as twin political identities generated by the settler state. As the ANC put it so subversively in its Freedom Charter, South Africa belongs to all those who live in it. From a postapartheid point of view, the real issue in Palestine and Israel is not whether there should be one, two, or ten states but how to base any state on equal citizenship for all those who live in it.

Conclusion

BEYOND IMPUNITY
AND COLLECTIVE
PUNISHMENT

Should terrorism be dealt with like a criminal act, as several critics of American bombing of Afghanistan have argued? It sounds appealing, but if terrorism were simply a crime, it would not be a political problem. The distinction between political terror and crime is that the former makes an open bid for public support. Unlike the criminal, the political terrorist is not easily deterred by punishment. Whatever we may think of their methods, terrorists have not only a need to be heard but, more often than not, a cause to champion. Notwithstanding Salman Rushdie's claim in an article in the *New York Times* that terrorists are nihilists who wrap themselves in objectives but have none—and so we must remorselessly attack them—one needs to recognize that terrorism has no military solution. Even a successful military confrontation with terrorists requires their political isolation, precisely by addressing the issues they raise. That is why official

America's bombing campaign in Afghanistan is more likely to be remembered as a combination of blood revenge and medieval-type exorcism than as a search for a solution to terrorism.

Few would fail to notice the growing common ground between the perpetrators of 9/11 and the official response to it called "the war on terror." Both sides deny the possibility of a middle ground, calling for a war to the finish. Both rally forces in the name of justice but understand justice as revenge. If the perpetrators of 9/11 refuse to distinguish between official America and the American people, target and victim, "the war on terror" has proceeded by dishing out collective punishment, with callous disregard for either "collateral damage" or legitimate grievances. Both practices are likely to nurture the spirit of revenge. I have written this book with the conviction that the response to injury does not have to be vengeance and that we need to distinguish between revenge and justice. A response other than revenge is possible and desirable. For that to happen, however, we need to turn the moment of injury into a moment of freedom, of choice. For Americans, that means turning 9/11 into an opportunity to reflect on America's place in the world. Grief for victims should not obscure the fact that there is no choice without a debate and no democracy without choice.

The post-Afghanistan debate in the United States and globally has been preoccupied with a second question: What, if any, is the connection between the war on terror and the war on Iraq? If 9/11 shattered the sense of immunity—nowadays called security—held by ordinary Americans, it also eroded the confidence shared by successive administrations that America could continue to exercise power with impunity. To some in the establishment, this was reason to question the legacy of the Cold War, to move beyond it to forge a rule of law and a regime of international accountability.

But for the Bush administration, 9/11 offered a rare historical opportunity to turn a widespread social concern for security in the face of terrorism into an opportunity to pursue a factional neo-Reaganite agenda—to settle unfinished business from the Cold War. It is this agenda that provides a clue both to the self-righteous and punitive conduct of the war on terror and to its shading into a new war, that against "the axis of evil." It illuminates the bridge between the invasion of Afghanistan and that of Iraq. To what extent is the axis of evil but a post–Cold War edition of the evil empire? Does not the Bush administration's promise to "democratize" the axis recall Reagan's repudiation of détente so as to roll back the evil empire, heralding a "democratic revolution"?

Privatizing Terror During the Late Cold War

Political terror comes out of a government's or guerrilla movement's failure to win civilian support. The most obvious link is with the practice of counterinsurgency that the British pioneered in their Malaysian colony during the Second World War and that Samuel Huntington advised America to emulate during the Vietnam War. Huntington called for the creation of strategic hamlets, to which to relocate the population sympathetic to the Viet Cong, so as to detach guerrillas from the population on which they had come to depend for support. Counterinsurgency turned the theory of guerrilla struggle on its head. If guerrillas claimed to be waging a political struggle with arms, moving through the population with the ease of fish in water, to use Mao's metaphor—and not a conventional war in which one could easily separate soldiers from civilians—then the point of counterinsurgency was first to drain the water so as to isolate the fish. Counterinsurgency, however, did not work as long as guerrillas actually enjoyed the political support of the civilian population. So civilians had to be targeted militarily and intimidated into submission.

The difference between counterinsurgency and a strategy of terror was that the latter deliberately hit soft targets, a lesson perversely learned from guerrilla warfare, which also blurred the line between the military and the civil. Not only did guerrillas claim to be civilians who had taken up arms in defense of civil and political rights, but the core of their strategy was to identify targets that were soft and political, that is, civilians, rather than military. As if taking a cue from left-wing guerrillas fighting right-wing dictatorships, right-wing terrorist groups confronting militant Third World nationalist governments began by eliminating civilian leaders—ranging from the political leaders of local councils to civic leaders and technical cadres in cooperatives, health centers, state farms; in short, in any government-connected production facility or social service.

Not for the first time did adversaries learn from one another. Had not Jerry Falwell, faced with the phenomenal success of black churches in the civil-rights movement in the United States, concluded that the way forward lay in breaching the line between the religious and the secular? When it came to learning from left-wing guerrillas, the political intellectuals in the apartheid military did the pioneering work. Take the example of the apartheid minister of defense, Magnus Malan, who made it compulsory for all antiguerrilla units to study Mao Zedong's essential writings on guerrilla war. Under his leadership, the South African Defense Forces began to emulate Soviet intelligence methods, going beyond using torture to extract information from captured guerrillas to developing methods to "convert" former guerrillas into apartheid agents before reinserting them into guerrilla ranks as informers—as at Vlakplaas, apartheid's well-known conversion camp.

The difference between left-wing "guerrillas" and right-wing "terrorists" lay in the following: as a rule, guerrillas operated in contexts where they could muster substantial civilian political support, whereas terrorists were substantially isolated from the civilian population. In practice, the distinction was blurred in several cases. The first was when guerrillas failed to win political support, as with the Revolutionary United Front (RUF) leadership and cadres in Sierra Leone—antigovernment guerrillas who turned to violence to coerce support from civilians they had failed to persuade in the first place. The second was when they lost popular support, as in the case of the Sendero Luminoso (Shining Path) in Peru who called for armed strikes, and resorted to violence against all those who would not join them, even if they were not with the government. Though they commanded significant support from the Ameri-Indian population in the region where they first organized, the Sendero Luminoso failed to win support in the rest of the country. And the third was when guerrillas ceased to make a distinction between civilian agents of unpopular dictatorship and their beneficiaries or supporters in the civilian population, turning the latter into soft targets. This last applies to movements that have resorted to terror as a tactic—rather than as a strategy—at different points in their history, from the Weathermen in the mass antiwar movement in the United States of the sixties to sections of the Palestinian and South African resistance, which resorted to violence against civilian targets when the future looked gloomy. The temptation and pitfalls of a liberation movement resorting to political terror for tactical purposes were depicted brilliantly in the film *The Battle of Algiers* (1967).

Cost to the United States

The U.S. flirtation with terror was part of the executive branch's effort to break free of legislative constraints on foreign policy in the post-Vietnam era. This constraint was formally introduced in legislation, first as the Clark Amendment of 1976, which forbade any covert assistance to parties in the Angolan civil war, and then as the Boland Amendment of 1984, at the time of the contra war in Nicaragua. The first cost America has paid for embracing terror is a growing erosion of democracy at home. The will to separate foreign from domestic policy is characteristic of imperial democracies and was one of the key legacies of the Cold War. The less accountable the executive branch was to legislative organs, the more official America came to see foreign policy in purely instrumentalist terms. Time and again, this was justified as a vulgar pragmatism: it is right because it works.

The second cost of the Afghan War arose because the United States and its allies created, trained, and sustained an infrastructure of terror, international in scope, free of any effective state control, and wrapped up in the language of religious war. Official America learned to distinguish between two types of terrorism—"theirs" and "ours"—and cultivated an increasingly benign attitude to ours. But then it turned out that their terrorism was born of ours.

The best-known CIA-trained terrorist was, of course, Osama bin Laden; in Arundhati Roy's illuminating phrase, "bin Laden has the distinction of being created by the CIA and wanted by the FBI." Bin Laden was not the only distinguished CIA creation—the others, as discussed, included Abdullah Azzam, a founder of Hamas, and Sheikh Omar Abdel Rahman, the blind Egyptian prayer leader. All CIA inventions, all were on the FBI list of those most wanted. The co-conspirators in the 1993 World Trade Center bombing included two other veterans of the Afghan jihad: Ramzi Ahmed Yousef and Mahmud Abouhalima. The World Trade Center bomb exploded underground, leaving a crater two hundred feet wide and several stories deep. The bomb was made of ammonium nitrate and fuel oil—according to Cooley, a formula "taught in CIA manuals."

The third cost of the Afghan jihad was the development of a parallel infrastructure of criminality connected with the international development of an illicit drug trade. The simple fact the government had to face was that if you decide to wage war without legislative consent, then you are likely to be short of funds. Time and again, the agencies pursuing covert wars seemed to arrive at the same solution to their financial problems: collude with drug lords. In 1995, the former CIA director of the Afghan operation, Charles Cogan, admitted the CIA had indeed sacrificed the drug war to fight the Cold War but added:

> Our main mission was to do as much damage as possible to the Soviets. We didn't really have the resources or the time to devote to an investigation of the drug trade, . . . I don't think that we need to apologize for this. Every situation has its fallout. . . . There was fallout in terms of drugs, yes. But the main objective was accomplished. The Soviets left Afghanistan.

But the fallout was not unanticipated; the consequences were known. It is a matter of debate as to whether the fallout would have been considered justifiable had executive agencies been effectively subjected to democratic accountability. This much is clear from Alfred McCoy's study of the global drug trade since the Vietnam War. The sudden spread of high-grade number 4 heroin among GIs in Vietnam came in 1970. The U.S. Army provost marshal ruled out any possibility that the heroin was coming from the north. By mid-1971, U.S. Army medical officers estimated that 10 to 15 percent of its low-rank soldiers were using heroin on a regular basis.

During the Afghan jihad, as Afghanistan became the world's "top heroin producer," it supplied "60% of U.S. demand." As heroin from Afghanistan and Pakistan poured into America, notes David Musto, the Yale University psychiatrist and former White House adviser on drug policy, "the number of drug-related deaths in New York City rose by 77 percent."

When it came to the contra war and CIA involvement in the cocaine trade, the consequences were direct. Between 1982 and 1985, the number of cocaine users in the United States rose by 38 percent to 5.8 million, more than ten times the number of heroin addicts. On August 18, 1996, *The Mercury News* of San Jose, California, published a lead story with the headline "America's Crack Plague Has Roots in Nicaraguan War" and the main theme: "For the better part of a decade, a San Francisco Bay Area drug ring sold tons of cocaine to the Crips and Bloods street gangs of Los Angeles and funneled millions in drug profits to a Latin American guerrilla army run by the CIA." The story detailed "how a group of Nicaraguan exiles set up a cocaine ring in California, establishing ties with the black street gangs of South Central Los Angeles who manufactured crack out of shipments of powder cocaine" and "how much of the profit made by the Nicaraguan exiles had been funneled back to the contra army." On October 4, the *Washington Post* went to town on *The Mercury News* and its reporter, Gary Webb, denying that there was evidence of a "contra-tied plot." But the outrage that followed *The Mercury News* series could not be ignored; CIA Director John Deutsch ordered his agency's inspector general, Frederick Hitz, to launch an investigation. It took seventeen investigators eighteen months to review a quarter million pages of documents and conduct 365 interviews to produce a two-volume report.

The result was nothing less than remarkable. The inspector general flatly denied any direct CIA involvement. In introducing his report to Congress in March 1998, he said he found "absolutely no evidence to indicate that the CIA as an organization or its employees were involved in any conspiracy to bring drugs into the United States." But he closed the same introduction with an important admission: "Let me be frank. There are instances where CIA did not, in any expeditious or consistent fashion, cut off relationships with individuals supporting the contra program who were alleged to have engaged in drug trafficking or take action to resolve the allegations." The inspector general admitted that none was investigated for drug dealing "as expeditiously as they should have been." The CIA finally posted a heavily censored version of volume two of the Hitz report on its Web site. The report revealed that the CIA had worked with fifty-eight contras implicated in cocaine trafficking but had concealed their criminal activities from Congress. Alfred McCoy, whose example I have followed in reading the fine print of the report, comments:

> Starting at paragraph 913, Hitz explores, with unprecedented frankness, the Agency's alliance with the notorious Alan Hyde, providing a revealing case study of the operational pressures that led the CIA into a compromised relationship with a criminal who was, quite possibly, the leading smuggler of cocaine across the Caribbean into the United States. Over the space of 48 dense, detailed paragraphs, the inspector general quotes classified correspondence up to the level of Deputy Director to provide extraordinary documentation about the dynamics of a CIA alliance with drug lords—a story that the national press somehow overlooked even though the controversy over the "dark alliance" case still raged.

The fourth cost of the Afghan jihad was an increasing incoherence in state agencies meant to enforce U.S. policy, a fact that came to light dramatically on 9/11, the day the terror produced by the Afghan jihad crossed U.S. national borders and took on truly global dimensions. This incoherence was dramatically illustrated in relations between the CIA and two other agencies of the federal government: the FBI and the Drug Enforcement Administration (DEA). Cooley cites the case of Robert Fox, New York's regional FBI director, who "had mentioned the CIA training of several of the World Trade Center bombers on a 1993 television broadcast— and was transferred, 'by coincidence,' several weeks later."

From the time the CIA got involved in drug trafficking as a way of financing covert operations, there was a similar incoherence in the coordination between the CIA and the DEA. It reached truly blatant proportions in the Reagan administration. In 1982, the attorney general announced that the FBI, not the DEA, would henceforth control antidrug campaigns inside the United States. The 1998 report of the CIA inspector general revealed that only two months after Reagan had authorized covert CIA support for the contras, CIA Director William Casey was able to conclude a secret "Memorandum of Understanding" with Attorney General William French Smith. Dated February 11, 1982, this memorandum exempted the CIA from reporting drug trafficking by its assets who were not formally CIA employees, such as "pilots who ferried supplies to the contras, as well as contra officials and others." The agreement was modified four years later to require more reporting, but the CIA continued to work with these assets. Even more remarkable, the waiver remained in effect until scrapped by the Clinton administration in 1995.

The Way Out

Modern Western empires are different from empires of old as well as the Soviet empire of yesterday in one important respect: they combine a democratic political system at home with despotism abroad. Even in the German case, as Sheldon Wolin reminds us, Nazi terror was not applied to the population generally. So long as democracy is a living reality at home, democratic empires are potentially self-correcting. Anyone who lived through the antiwar movement in the Vietnam era would recognize the significance of this fact. A key lesson of the Vietnam War is that the antiwar and anti-imperialist movement inside the United States restrained American military power from being fully unleashed on the people of Vietnam.

Successive U.S. administrations have held the American press responsible for defeat in Vietnam. Their argument has been simple if self-serving: by concentrating on "our" atrocities and remaining silent about "their" atrocities, the press aided a popular movement against the war. After the killing fields of Cambodia, the accusation had a ring of credibility. From then on, right through to Iraq, the press has tended to turn to official America for accounts of "their" atrocities. In doing so, it has contributed to removing foreign policy from processes of democratic accountability—a process that seems to have reached its "patriotic" conclusion with the arrival of "embedded" reporters in the recent Iraq war.

The self-censorship of the press has been reinforced by developments in the marketplace. With the changing ownership of media giants, several have been taken over by corporations based in the defense or entertainment industry, reinforcing the tendency to treat news as marketable entertainment. Yet another reason for the continuing erosion of press freedom arises from the common sense that the press shares with those in power. When it comes to the Middle East, Israel is the Achilles' heel of American liberalism, the blind spot that is part of its "common sense." The domestic importance of Israel became dramatically clear during the second Reagan administration. As the Iran-contra scandal unraveled, it became clear that the executive branch had been guilty of such gross disregard of legislative restraint that the consequences were likely to be no less severe than those after the Watergate scandal. But this did not happen, for one reason: liberals in Congress and in the press hesitated. An important part of the reason was that Israel was involved.

America and Israel: The Heart of the Matter

If critics of U.S. policy in the Middle East see it as oil driven, its proponents see defense of Israel at the heart of the policy. The more central the Middle East has come to be in U.S. foreign policy, as it indeed has after 9/11, the larger Israel has loomed in the imagination of advocates and critics alike. The higher the cost of America's Israel policy, the more its motivation seems obscure and difficult to fathom. Could this be no more than a replay of official America's constructive engagement with apartheid South Africa? Or does the absence of even the hint of a critique in America's Israel policy indicate a more special relationship, the grounding of which must be located in more than just state interest?

In the search for credible answers, many have turned to the influence of civil society–based groups, first to the extraordinary power of the Israel lobby in Washington and more recently to the growing weight of the Christian right in the Republican party. The Israeli lobby is "a loose network of individuals and organizations," of which the most important are the American Israel Public Affairs Committee (AIPAC) and the Conference of Presidents of Major American Jewish Organizations. Rather than "a traditional ethnic voter machine" that would organize the Jewish vote behind particular candidates, the Israeli lobby functions more as "an ethnic donor machine," which has emulated the ways of issue-based interest groups such as the National Rifle Association or the pro- and antiabortion groups. Its power is exercised through campaign contributions and government appointments. The most notable appointments in the current Bush administration are those of Richard Perle, a member (and until his recent resignation the chair) of the quasi-official but highly influential Defense Advisory Board, and Douglas J. Feith, undersecretary of defense. Both straddle the U.S. and Israeli defense and foreign-policy establishments. In 1996, they coauthored a paper advising Israeli prime minister Benyamin Netanyahu to make "a clean break from the peace process." In 1997, Feith wrote a paper called "A Strategy for Israel," calling on Israel to reoccupy "the areas under Palestinian Authority control," even though "the price in blood would be high."

Neither state reasons such as geopolitics nor the weight of special interests in the state or civil society quite explain why there is not even the trace of a public debate in America when it comes to Israel. Internationally, there is one state that stands in defiance of practically every UN resolution that affects it: Israel. In the international community, Israel stands for the exercise of power with impunity. Israel defies the international community consistently—not because it is the world's sole superpower but because it is backed up by the world's sole superpower. At the same time, within America, it is easier to criticize the government than it is to criticize Israel. The same American liberal who will uphold your democratic right to criticize any government in the world, including that of the United States, will consider criticism of the state of Israel as potentially anti-Semitic, in the words of the current president of Harvard, in effect if not in intent. Why do American liberals not use the same standard for the state of Israel that they would not hesitate using for every other state in the world, including the United States? What explains the enduring nature of the special relationship between the United States and Israel? To understand that enduring motivation, I think it necessary to focus away from special interests to the American mainstream, so as to understand the ways in which the political project called Israel has come to resonate with American historical sensibilities.

To be sure, U.S.-Israeli relations have gone through different phases since the founding of the state of Israel in 1948. Relations were the most stretched during the 1956 Suez Crisis when Israel, along with Britain and France, was forced to acknowledge America's rise as the hegemonic Western power. It is only after 1967, and more so 1973, that we can speak of the building of a strategic alliance between the United States and Israel. The makers of the strategic alliance have been able to tap into an American sensibility, a reservoir of support, to enshrine this alliance with a halo.

To make sense of that historical sensibility, one can look at the relationship between the United States and Israel through the historical experience of postapartheid Africa. If you look at America from the southern tip of the African continent, gazing from Cape Town across the Atlantic, "Africa" and "America" do not appear as just two names of two different continents but also as names that signify two radically different historical trajectories. With the end of apartheid, the African experience stands for the end of settler colonialism—unlike the American experience, which signifies the triumph of settler colonialism.

This triumph is written in the history of citizenship in the United States. That history comes to light if one asks, Who is an American? The answer has been shaped by two major struggles, the Civil War and the civil rights struggle. The Civil War began a few years after the 1857 *Dred Scott* decision. This is how Chief Justice Roger Taney put the question as he placed the locus of American citizenship in the individual states rather than the union:

> The question is simply this: Can a Negro, whose ancestors were imported into this country, and sold as slaves, become a member of the political community formed and brought into existence by the Constitution of the United States, and as such become entitled to all the rights, and privileges, and immunities, guaranteed by that instrument to the citizen?

As Paul Finkelman sums up, Justice Taney's response left no doubt: "Free blacks could never be citizens of the United States and have standing to sue in federal courts." The Civil War both shifted the locus of American citizenship from individual states to the union, thereby reversing the legacy of *Dred Scott*, and changed the basis of state citizenship from ancestry to residence; but it did not create an equal citizenship for black and white Americans. The American nation after the Civil War was still a nation of white settlers. The redefinition of the nation, from a white to a settler nation, *regardless of color*, was the fruit of the civil rights movement that followed the Second World War.

The postwar period represented a double shift, on grounds of both race and religion. Before the war, it was presumed that whites were Christians; more often than not, the heritage of Christianity was defined in opposition to that of Judaism. The idea of a single

Judeo-Christian tradition is mainly a post-Holocaust idea with weak historical depth. It is post-Holocaust America's antidote to anti-Semitism. Contemporary America is a multicultural and multireligious political community that has yet to come to grips with its settler origins.

I came face-to-face with the common sense born of this history during antiwar teach-ins after 9/11, and more specifically in September 2002 when Columbia University organized a conference called "A South African Conversation on Israel and Palestine." Even among many of the antiwar American youth, the suggestion that Israel is a settler colony aroused strong opposition: Israelis were not settlers, but returning natives. The passion and the conviction reminded me of when I was a lecturer at the University of Dar-es-Salaam in the 1970s, and we listened to representatives of a group that championed the rights of native Liberians. When they claimed that Liberia was a settler-colonial state, no different from apartheid South Africa, the Tanzanian and East African audience was noticeably uncomfortable. We all knew that Liberia, like Sierra Leone, had been founded as a colony for freed slaves in the nineteenth century: Liberia was to be a settlement of freed American slaves, and Sierra Leone for freed British slaves—meaning those American slaves who had cast their lot with Britain in the American War of Independence and subsequently moved to the British Isles. Our reluctance to accept the analogy with apartheid South Africa was grounded in this historical fact: we saw Americo-Liberians as returning natives, even if returning after centuries, and not as settlers. It was then, in the heat of debate in the post–9/11 American academy, that I understood why it was important to acknowledge the American historical sensibility if one was interested in changing the American point of view, which itself recognizes the subjectivity of the Jew who "returns" to Israel.

From this point of view, Israeli Jews see themselves not as settlers but as returning natives, even if returning after millennia. Such an analogy might yield more fruitful insights into the relationship between America and Israel.

The Liberian analogy points up the insensitivity to native interests born of the settler experience. Comparing Liberia and Israel, it is clear both united the victims and perpetrators of the catastrophe in question—even if at the expense of a new set of native victims. Liberia was an experiment championed enthusiastically by both former slaves and former slave owners. With the cause of Israel, there are the most ardent Zionists alongside the most anti-Semitic sections of the Christian right, led by Jerry Falwell and Pat Robertson. Here, for example, is the text of a full-page ad in the *New York Times* of December 3, 2002:

Dear Dr. Pat Robertson: As activist leaders of the Jewish community joined by people of goodwill everywhere, we thank you and other Christian leaders who have shown unwavering support for Israel. At a time when Israel is under such mortal threat, enemies of terror must speak out. For standing up to evil, we say Todah Rabbah. Signed: Coalition for Jewish Concerns—AMCHA [The Coalition for Jewish Concerns, based in Riverdale, New York].

This unity has been forged around commitment to a shared civilizing mission, with civilization understood as a settler product that must be brought to natives. The Americo-Liberians thought it their God-given right to civilize native Liberians who had never left home. Not only that, their notion of "civilization" was forged in the land of slavery; it was punctuated by the very artifacts of the civilization into which they had been denied entry—artifacts ranging all the way from the top hat to the green dollar to the White House. Zionists who return to Israel see Palestinians as interlopers, squatters; without a right grounded in a biblically sanctioned "civilized" history, they must now clear the way for the rightful owners of the land.

America's response to major catastrophes—first slavery, then the Holocaust—has crystallized a tendency among Americans to see overseas settlements as a solution, not a problem. In both cases, the American solution was a return home, but a return so marked by a callous disregard for the rights of those who were already home, who had never left home, that in each instance the project turned into one of settler colonialism. How does one explain the insensitivity to native interests that seems to be a special feature of American political history? Could it be that America, both official and unofficial, both privileged and not, which has never dared look its original crime, the expropriation and genocide of Native Americans, in the face, has historically tended to see settler projects as effective ways to cope with major internal dislocations, at the same time projecting them as so many civilizing missions to the world at large?

The African experience shows that the claim of a civilizing mission can take many forms. Who can forget that apartheid South Africa claimed to be "the only democracy in Africa," just as Israel today claims to be "the only democracy in the Middle East"? This is not entirely a hoax, but in neither case does it reflect the whole truth. True, many natives in Dar-es-Salaam or Kampala had lesser rights than some natives in Johannesburg or Durban, and Palestinians in Israel have greater rights than do many natives in the Arab world. The larger truth, however, is that the "civilizing mission" was never meant to include all the natives. It was never meant to generalize the regime of rights or democracy to natives. The whole truth is that, just as the colony of Liberia and apartheid South Africa, Zionist Israel, too, reflects a contradictory unity, a democratic despotism, in a single space. At a more general level, it is no different from the civilizing mission that Western powers brought to the colonies in an earlier era. To begin with, that mission shut out the vast majority of the colonized from the project of modernity and democracy. But when natives resisted this exclusion, it turned around to stigmatize them as antimodern and thus unworthy of democracy.

The state of Israel is a state. It is not a religion or a people. The Israeli state should be submitted to the same scrutiny as any other state, not only for the sake of the Palestinian people or the Israeli people, but, now more than ever, for the sake of humanity. The scale of Israeli atrocities—"our terror"—has ballooned since 9/11. It has been packaged in the American media as an inevitable response to "their terror" and has shown the way for the Bush Administration's "war on terror." A case in point is the building, after 9/11, of what the Israeli government calls "the fence," the European media has described as "the wall," and the mainstream American media has chosen not to describe at all. Only *Ha'aretz,* has had the courage to describe this atrocity:

> Israelis still use the convenient and misleading term "fence" to describe the system of fortifications that is currently being erected on Palestinian lands in the West Bank. Even "wall," the term more commonly used in foreign-language reports, is insufficient to describe what is really being built at this very moment: A concrete wall eight meters high, wire fences and electronic sensors, ditches four meters deep on either side, a dirt path to reveal footprints, an area into which entry is forbidden, a two-lane road for

army patrols, and watchtowers and firing posts every 200 meters along the entire length. These are the components of the "fence."

The estimated cost to Israel is $2 billion. The cost to Palestinians is in livelihood: "Thousands of Palestinians have lost their lands, their livelihood and their savings, which had been invested in green houses or reservoirs or houses for their children, because of these fortifications. According to the World Bank, the number of Palestinians who will eventually be directly hurt by the fence is between 95,000 and 200,000." This is an atrocity comparable to the mass explusions of 1948 and the occupation of 1967. Even if the road map pushed by the Bush administration is followed, concludes Amira Hass in the same article, the borders of the Palestinian state will be defined by "these facts on the ground": "three enclaves, completely cut off from each other, without the Jordan Valley, without the fertile agricultural lands between Jenin and Qalqilyah, without 'metropolitan Jerusalem,' which includes the land between the settlements of Givat Ze'ev to the northwest, Betar to the southwest and Ma'aleh Adumin to the east." Not an innocuous neighborhood fence meant to keep out trespassers, and far more ambitious than a wall—as in the Berlin Wall, which was meant to imprison the city's population within an enforced political boundary, this fortification is meant both to fragment and to imprison, as it undercuts the livelihood of thousands. If realized, it will turn the Occupied Territories into a series of halfway houses between apartheid-style Bantustans and Nazi-style concentration camps.

There is more than a passing resemblance between the Zionist project in Israel and the Occupied Territories and the Islamist political project in central Asia. Both have unfolded under the political and ideological umbrella of the United States. In both cases, American patronage has been key to turning religious identities into political ones. In both cases, righteousness in politics has had nihilistic consequences. We have seen that the impact of the Afghan jihad was central both to the Islamization of the Pakistani state under the Zia regime and to the privatization and internationalization of terror during the Reagan administration. On both counts, we can see disturbing parallels in the Middle East. To begin with, Israel—like Pakistan—is dedicated to the notion that a religious community must also be a nation possessing its own state, thereby rendering those of its citizens who do not belong to the state religion as not only a political minority but also second-class citizens with lesser rights. At the same time, the founders of Israel considered themselves secular Jews, as the founders of Pakistan were self-declared secular Muslims. The shift from a secular to a religious Zionism in Israel under Begin, just as the Islamization of the Pakistani state, under Zia, occurred under the protective American umbrella during the Cold War. At the same time, the settler occupation of Palestinian territories has been internationalized as a political project of both the Christian and the Zionist right. Both cases confirm that righteousness—or fundamentalism—in religion does not automatically translate into political terrorism. Rather, only when a righteous perspective—religious or secular—is integrated into a ruthless and ideologically intolerant political project does it provide the language that fuels terrorism.

Historical Responsibility

To understand who bears responsibility for 9/11, it will help to contrast two situations, after the Second World War and after the

Cold War. The Second World War was fought in Europe and Asia, not in the United States. Europe and Asia thus faced physical and civic destruction at the end of the war that America did not face. The question of responsibility for postwar reconstruction arose as a political rather than a moral question. Its urgency in Europe was underscored by the changing political situations in Yugoslavia, Albania, and Greece in particular. Faced with the possibility of enhanced Communist influence, the United States accepted responsibility for restoring conditions for decent civic life in non-Communist Europe. The result was the Marshall Plan.

The Cold War was largely not fought in Europe but in what came to be called the Third World, through wars that were mostly covert. Should we, ordinary humanity, hold official America responsible for its actions during the Cold War? Should official America be held responsible for napalm bombing and spraying Agent Orange in Vietnam, Cambodia, and Laos? Should it be held responsible for the environment of impunity that nurtured terrorist movements in southern Africa, central Africa, and central Asia? Official America's embrace of terrorism did not end with the Cold War. Right up to September 10, 2001, the United States and Britain compelled African countries to reconcile with terrorist movements. Take the example of Sierra Leone, where civilian government was restored in 1998. On January 6, 1999, rebel gunmen killed, maimed, and raped their way across the capital city, Freetown. The unspeakable acts of terror took the lives of more than five thousand civilians. The British and American response was to call for reconciliation between victims and purveyors of terror, between government and rebels, in the July 1999 Lome Agreement. Sierra Leone is but one example of the benign gaze with which western governments have condoned terror—"black-on-black" violence—in Africa before 9/11. Before that, there was the

Rwanda genocide, in which 800,000 civilians were killed in ninety days, and the war in Congo, where upward of 3 million have been killed. The demand was always that governments must share power with the purveyors of terror in the name of reconciliation—in Mozambique, Sierra Leone, and Angola. Reconciliation was turned into a code word for impunity and became part of a Cold War political strategy designed to undermine hard-won state independence.

We need to recognize diverse routes to terrorism. At least three come to mind. I have traced the main route: an imperial search for effective ways of undermining the political support of leftist nationalist governments (such as Frelimo in Mozambique and the Sandinistas in Nicaragua) or simply governments it considered as belonging to a hostile camp (such as the Amin government in Afghanistan). I consider this the main route for one reason: without the strategic embrace of terror by a superpower, there would not have been the global political environment of impunity, which was critical for the development of terrorism by other routes. The second route, its mirror opposite, involved the internal degeneration of guerrilla movements, as with the RUF in Sierra Leone and Shining Path in Peru. The third route has been the result of a profound social—rather than narrowly political—crisis. Instead of terror being espoused by groups with clear ideological agendas, whether of the left or the right, and instead of an unadulterated quest for power, we have in this case the use of political violence by nonideological groups that have neither expounded a cause openly nor attempted to organize support in civilian strata. The best example of this kind of nonideological group is the Lord's Resistance Army (LRA) in northern Uganda, a largely homegrown Renamo-style group that kidnaps children and turns them into recruits.

Rather than argue whether terrorism is a foreign import or a homegrown product, I have tried to point up the relationship between the two: the homegrown product could not have flourished except in a global environment where at least one superpower turned a blind eye to "its" terror. This, after all, was a logical extension of the Kirkpatrick thesis that distinguished "right" from "left" dictatorships: excusing "our" dictators as both useful and temporary. I have argued that whereas political terror was an import in such cases as Mozambique, and later Nicaragua, the strategic embrace of terror in Liberia and Sierra Leone was more the result of a process of internal degeneration combined with learning by example from other Cold War contexts. Even if terrorism was a Cold War brew, it turned into a local potion as the Cold War progressed. Whose responsibility is it? Like Afghanistan, were these countries hosting terrorism, or were they also hostage to terrorism? I think both.

Perhaps no other society paid a higher price for the defeat of the Soviet Union than did Afghanistan. Out of a population of roughly 20 million, 1 million died, another million and a half were maimed, another 5 million became refugees, and just about everyone was internally displaced. UN agencies estimate that nearly a million and a half went clinically insane as a consequence of decades of continuous war. Those who survived lived in the most mined country in the world. Afghanistan was a brutalized society even before the American bombing began.

Unlike Afghanistan, which hosted the last great Cold War confrontation between the United States and the Soviet Union, Iraq was the first to face a low-intensity barrage through the multilateral proxy of the UN. Supposedly the beneficiary of a humanitarian oil-for-food program, Iraq paid with the lives of hundreds of thousands of children under the tender age of five.

Beyond Impunity and Collective Punishment

America has a habit of not taking responsibility for its own actions. Instead, it habitually looks for a high moral pretext for inaction. I was in Durban at the 2001 World Conference Against Racism when the United States walked out of it. The Durban conference was about major crimes of the past, such as racism and xenophobia. I returned from Durban to New York City to hear Condoleezza Rice—President Bush's national security advisor—talk about the need to forget slavery because, she said, the pursuit of civilized life requires that we forget the past. It is true that unless we learn to forget, life will turn into revenge seeking. Each of us will compile a catalog of wrongs done to a long line of ancestors and nurse these as grievances. But civilization cannot be built just on forgetting. Not only must we learn to forget, we must also not forget to learn. We must also memorialize crimes that are monumental. America was built on two monumental crimes: the genocide of Native Americans and the enslavement of African Americans. The United States tends to memorialize other peoples' crimes, not its own—to seek a high moral ground as a pretext to ignore real issues.

The events that are 9/11 present the world with a particularly difficult political challenge, even if this challenge appears the most immediate for Muslims. Both the American establishment led by President Bush and militants of political Islam insist that Islam is a political, and not simply a religious or cultural, identity. Both are determined to distinguish between "good Muslims" and "bad Muslims," so as to cultivate the former and target the latter. Should 9/11 and its aftermath caution us against reading a person's politics from his or her culture and religion?

I know of no one inspired by Osama bin Laden for religious

reasons. Bin Laden is a politician, not a theologian. Those who embrace him do so politically. Both Bush and bin Laden employ a religious language, the language of good and evil, the language of no compromise: you are either with us or against us. Both deny the possibility of a third response. For both, political loyalty comes before political independence. The danger of bringing notions of good and evil into politics cannot be underestimated. The consequence of bringing home—wherever home may be—the language of the war on terror should be clear: it will create a license to demonize adversaries as terrorists, clearing the ground for a fight to the finish, for with terrorists there can be no compromise. The result will be to displace attention from issues to loyalties, to criminalize dissent, and to invite domestic ruin. Worse still, if the struggle against political enemies is defined as a struggle against evil, it will turn into a holy war. And in holy war, there can be no compromise. Evil cannot be converted; it must be eliminated.

During the Cold War, small countries were tempted to line up for protection behind one or another international bully. Some in the Third World then tried to pioneer an alternative international order, one dedicated to two goals: to hold every bully accountable to minimal norms and to guarantee a share of justice to every historical victim. That initiative became identified with Bandung, the Indonesian town that hosted the friendship meeting of nonaligned states in the Cold War. With the Cold War over and the United States triumphantly walking the ring, thumping its chest, our most urgent need is to build on this legacy. If there is one lesson the Third World drew from its colonial past and defended during the Cold War, it was that there can be no independence without independent thought. In the weeks and months and years ahead, the first priority must be to defend that right to independent thought.

Beyond Impunity and Collective Punishment

America promoted two different religious wars over the past quarter century, one in the course of the Cold War and the other after, one in Afghanistan and the other in Israel, one Islamist and the other Zionist. Today, both projects have been unleashed on a broader scale, one boomeranging on America, the other unfolding as part of official America's global war on terror. Had the United States ended the Cold War with demilitarization and a peace dividend, 9/11 would not have happened. But the United States did not dismantle the global apparatus of empire at the end of the Cold War; instead, it concentrated on ensuring that hostile states—branded "rogue states"—did not acquire weapons of mass destruction that it already possessed, thereby raising the suspicion that its opposition was not to weapons of mass destruction but to their proliferation in hands it could neither control nor trust. Similarly, the United States did not accept responsibility for the militarization of civilian and state life in regions where the Cold War was waged with devastating consequences—as in Southeast Asia, southern Africa, Central America, and Central Asia. Instead, it walked away from responsibility. The Cold War came to an end with the subduing of one protagonist, the Soviet Union. Humanity is now left with a challenge: how to subdue and hold accountable the awesome power that the United States built up during the Cold War.

If state terror claims to be an exercise in maintaining law and order, societal terror presents itself as a fight for justice. I have stressed the importance of grasping the relation between the two: no Chinese wall divides "our" terrorism from "their" terrorism. Each tends to feed on the other. Whether domestic or international, terror has a political dimension. On April 19, 1995, a much-decorated American infantry soldier named Timothy McVeigh blew up a federal building in Oklahoma City, killing 168 innocent men, women, and children. In letters from jail, McVeigh indicated "that he had acted in retaliation for what had happened at Waco" two years earlier, when FBI agents had helped kill more than eighty members of a conservative Christian cult, of whom twenty-seven were children. Noting that Waco was "the largest massacre of Americans by their own government since 1890, when a number of Native Americans were slaughtered at Wounded Knee, South Dakota," Gore Vidal, the American essayist, pointed out that McVeigh "even picked the second anniversary of the slaughter, April 19, for his act of retribution." McVeigh remained silent throughout his trial, except for one statement when invited by the judge to speak before being sentenced to death. This is what he said: "I wish to use the words of Justice [Louis] Brandeis dissenting in *Olmstead* to speak for me. He wrote: 'Our government is the potent, the omnipresent teacher. For good or for ill, it teaches the whole people by its example.' "

Rather than explain away forms of societal terrorism as a racial or cultural affliction, "black-on-black" violence in Africa or "Islamic terrorism" globally, we need to understand that both forms of contemporary terror were forged in an environment of impunity created by state terror during the late Cold War. Rather than split "our" terrorism from "theirs"—only to excuse the former and demonize the latter, as with "good" and "bad" Muslims—we need to locate and understand both as part of a single historical process.

Before 9/11, the United States called for reconciliation in the face of societal terror. After 9/11, this stance was reversed. Instead of reconciliation, there is now a policy of zero tolerance and a demand for justice. When accompanied by a blanket refusal to deal with issues, the call for justice turns into a vendetta, the pursuit of revenge. In such a context, it is worth reflecting on the difference between law and violence. Against whom do we use the law and against whom violence? What is the point of distinguishing between two kinds of terrorists, Americans and non-Americans at some point, westerners and nonwesterners at other times? What is the point being made by the U.S. government when it ensures due process for Americans accused of terrorism, whether Timothy McVeigh or John Walker Lindh (the so-called American Taliban), but denies non-Americans and nonwesterners interned at Guantánamo Bay even the basic elements of due process, such as the right of habeas corpus and review by courts? The American government has invented a legal fiction for the purpose, calling the non-Americans "illegal combatants"; indeed, if they were to be considered prisoners of war, of the war on terror, then the relevant Geneva conventions would apply, making it a war crime for their captors to interrogate them or even to go beyond asking for identification. If to live by the rule of law is to belong to a common political community, then does not the selective application of the rule of law confirm a determination to relegate entire sections of humanity as conscripts of a civilization fit for collective punishment?

Finally, it is worth reflecting on the two adversaries in the war on terror: the United States and al-Qaeda. Both are veterans of the Cold War, in fact on the same side, and both have been marked indelibly by it. Both see the world through lenses of power. Both are informed by highly ideological worldviews, which each articulates in a highly religious political language, one that is self-righteous. The righteousness of self goes alongside the demonization of the other as evil. The point about ideological language, whether its idiom is religious or secular, is that it justifies the use of power with impunity. In the contest for power, each has eyes for none but the other. There is an eerie similarity between the

American bombing of Iraq and Afghanistan and the al-Qaeda bombing of embassies in Nairobi and Dar-es-Salaam and of the Twin Towers on 9/11: both testify that, when it comes to the contest for power, the rest of the world exists only as collateral.

This, however, is where the comparison must end, for the *moral* equivalence between the two does not translate into a *political* equivalence. There is no denying the global character of American power, before which the network known as al-Qaeda can only be described in the diminutive.

Caught in a situation where both adversaries in the war on terror claim to be fighting terror with weapons of terror, nothing less than a global movement for peace will save humanity. If we are to go by the lesson of the last global struggle for peace—that to end the war in Vietnam—this struggle, too, will have to be waged as a mass movement inside each country, particularly the democratic countries, and especially in the United States and Israel.

The era of proxy wars that began with America's defeat in Vietnam closed with the invasion of Iraq. The open and unabashed invasion was based on two assumptions. Domestically, the Bush administration presented the invasion as a defensive move, a preemptive strike against an imminent threat to national security, a necessity in the post–9/11 era. At the same time, the neoconservative strategists of the Iraq invasion assured America and the world that the long-suffering people of Iraq would welcome American soldiers as a liberating force.

But the expected warm Iraqi embrace has not materialized. Instead of being hailed as an army of liberation, American soldiers have been treated as an occupation force. Faced with resistance, official America is already looking for allies—and proxies—in Iraq. Already, a new kind of proxy has been deployed in Iraq. *The Guardian* (London) reported that "while the official coalition figures list the British as the second largest contingent with around 9,900 troops, they are narrowly outnumbered by the 10,000 private military contractors now on the ground." As a result, it calculated that "the proportion of contracted security personnel in the firing line is ten times greater than during the first Gulf War. In 1991, for every private contractor, there were 100 servicemen and women; now there are 10." Of the $87 billion earmarked for the Iraqi campaign this year, the U.S. Army estimates that a third, nearly $30 billion, will be spent on contracts to private companies. To understand the kind of interests that drive this campaign, one needs to keep in mind a key advantage of privatizing war: it allows deployment to proceed "without the kind of congressional and media oversight to which conventional deployments are subject."

At home, too, there is growing anxiety that the promised war on terror, a defensive national war, has metamorphosed into an offensive imperial war. The war agenda of the coalition of neo-conservatives and Christian fundamentalists in the Bush administration, dubbed a fight against "the axis of evil," echoes the old Reaganite offensive against Third World nationalism. The neo-Reaganites defend this imperial endeavor as a disinterested global quest for democracy, for good against evil, for the time being reinforcing good Iraqis against bad, and good Muslims against bad. Like the Islamist radicals who would forever close "the gates of ijtihad," the neo-Reaganite talk of "good" and "evil" closes the door to political reform. From a post–Cold War perspective, we can see how self-serving Jeanne Kirkpatrick's two claims were: that there was a distinction between left-wing "totalitarian" and right-wing "authoritarian" regimes, and that whereas the latter could be reformed from within, the former would have to be forcibly overthrown from without. The fact is that left-wing regimes—from the Soviet Union to China—successfully reformed from within. The prerequisite was a defense of sovereignty and, in that context, the right to reform. In contrast, Iraq was not allowed to reform from within. If North Korea has escaped that same fate, could it be because it possesses weapons of mass destruction, which Iraq did not, and which provide the final guarantee of its right to reform?

But if the same Iraqis who yesterday welcomed the overthrow of Saddam Hussein today see American troops as an occupying force, is it not time to question the simplifying assumption that the problem lies with bad as opposed to good Iraqis? If good and bad Iraqis—and good and bad Muslims—are really quasi-official names for those who support and oppose American policies, is it not time to go beyond the name-calling and review policies that consistently seem to erode support and generate opposition? Whether in America, Iraq, or elsewhere, the revitalization of democracy in the era of globalized American power requires no less.

Herein lies the continuing relevance of Vietnam. The lesson of Vietnam was that the battle against nationalism could not be won as a military confrontation: America would need to recognize the legitimacy of nationalism in the era of imperialism and learn to live with it. Just as America learned to distinguish between nationalism and Communism in Vietnam, so it will need to learn the difference between nationalism and terrorism in the post–9/11 world. To win the fight against terrorism requires accepting that the world has changed, that the old colonialism is no more and will not return, and that to occupy foreign places will be expensive, in lives and money. America cannot occupy the world. It has to learn to live in it.

Notes

Introduction: Modernity and Violence

4 On a world scale: The phrase is Bernard Lewis's, but it was popularized following Samuel Huntington, *The Clash of Civilizations and the Remaking of World Order* (New York: Simon and Schuster, 1996).

4 The violence of the Holocaust: For a discussion of group violence as evil, see Ervin Staub, *The Roots of Evil: The Origins of Genocide and Other Group Violence* (Cambridge: Cambridge University Press, 1989). On the relationship between evil and historical time, see Paul Ricoeur, *The Symbolism of Evil* (Boston: Beacon Press, 1969); Alain Badiou, *Ethics: An Essay on the Understanding of Evil* (London: Verso, 2001); Georges Bataille, *Literature and Evil,* tr. by Alastair Hamilton (London & New York: Boyars, 1997); Malcolm Bull, ed., *Apocalypse Theory and the Ends of the World* (Oxford: Blackwell, 1995); and Alenka Zupancic, *Ethic of the Real: Kant, Lacan* (London: Verso, 2000). I am thankful to Robert Meister of the University of California, Santa Cruz, for suggesting this latter set of readings.

5 In 1499, seven years: Karen Armstrong, *The Battle for God: A*

History of Fundamentalism (New York: Alfred A. Knopf, 2000), pp. 3–8.

6 "Of the two main": Hannah Arendt, *The Origins of Totalitarianism* (New York: Harcourt Brace, 1975), p. 207.

6 The idea that "imperialism": Herbert Spencer wrote in *Social Statics* (1850), "The forces which are working out the great scheme of perfect happiness, taking no account of incidental suffering, exterminate such sections of mankind as stand in their way." This is a train of thought Charles Lyell had pursued twenty years earlier in *Principles of Geology:* if "the most significant and dimunitive of species . . . have each slaughtered their thousands, why should not we, the lords of creation, do the same?" His student, Charles Darwin, confirmed in *The Descent of Man* (1871) that "at some future period not very distant as measured in centuries, the civilized races of man will almost certainly exterminate and replace throughout the world the savage races." "After Darwin," comments Sven Lindqvist in his survey of European thought on genocide, "it became accepted to shrug your shoulders at genocide. If you were upset, you were just showing your lack of education." See Sven Lindqvist, *"Exterminate All the Brutes": One Man's Odyssey into the Heart of Darkness and the Origins of European Genocide* (New York: New Press, 1996), pp. 117, 107, 130.

6 Similar fates awaited: Except where indicated, all quotations are from Lindqvist, *"Exterminate All the Brutes,"* pp. 141, 119, 149–51, 158, 160.

7 The first systematic: Sven Lindqvist, *A History of Bombing* (New York: New Press, 2001), pp. 1–2.

7 The gassings of Russians: Arno J. Mayer, *Why Did the Heavens Not Darken? The Final Solution in History* (New York: Pantheon, 1988).

8 In his *Discours:* Aimé Césaire, *Discours sur le colonialisme* (Paris: Présence Africaine, 1995), p. 12.

8 "Not so long ago,": Frantz Fanon, *The Wretched of the Earth* (London: Penguin, 1967), p. 75; for a discussion, see David Macey, *Frantz Fanon, A Biography* (New York: Picador, 2000), pp. 471, 111.

8 The first genocide: See Mahmood Mamdani, *When Victims Become Killers: Colonialism, Nativism, and Genocide in Rwanda* (Princeton: Princeton University Press, 2001), pp. 10–13.

8 The revolutionary theorist: Fanon, *Wretched of the Earth;* also see Macey, *Frantz Fanon,* p. 22.

9 Fanon has come to be regarded: Hannah Arendt, *On Violence* (New York: Harcourt Brace, 1970).

9 "He of whom": Fanon, *Wretched of the Earth,* pp. 33, 66, 68, 73.

10 Anyone familiar with: For a journalistic account of the specter of genocide in the white South African imagination, read Rian Malan, *My Traitor's Heart: A South African Exile Returns to Face His Country, His Tribe, and His Conscience* (New York: Atlantic Monthly Press, 1990).

Chapter One: Culture Talk; or, How Not to Talk about Islam and Politics

17 During the Cold War: Reinhard Schulze, *A Modern History of the Islamic World* (New York: New York University Press, 2002), p. xiii.

19 In a rare but significant example: Aryeh Neier, "Warring Against Modernity," *The Washington Post*, October 9, 2001.

20 "It is my hypothesis,": Samuel Huntington, "The Clash of Civilizations?" *Foreign Affairs* 72, no. 3, summer 1993, p. 22.

21 Huntington's argument was built: "The Velvet Curtain of culture has replaced the Iron Curtain of ideology as the most significant dividing line in Europe." Samuel Huntington, "The Clash of Civilizations?" p. 31.

21 For William Lind: William Lind, "Defending Western Culture," *Foreign Policy* 84, fall 1991, pp. 43–44.

21 Régis Debray, himself: Régis Debray, *Tous azimuts* (Paris: Odile Jacob, Foundations pour les études de defense nationale, 1990), pp. 44–45, cited in Roxanne L. Euben, *Enemy in the Mirror: Islamic Fundamentalism and the Limits of Western Rationalism, a Work of Comparative Political Theory* (Princeton: Princeton University Press, 1999), p. 6.

22 Edward W. Said: Edward Said, "The Clash of Definitions," in *Reflections on Exile and Other Essays* (Cambridge, Mass.: Harvard University Press, 2000), p. 581.

22 "There is something": Bernard Lewis, "The Roots of Muslim Rage," *The Atlantic,* September 1990. Available at www.theatlantic.com/issues/90Sep/rage.htm.

23 To this, he added the absence: The proprietary equation of secularism with Western modernity—and thus the presumption so dear to Bernard Lewis that there can be no secularization without Westernization—has been critiqued recently by Amartya Sen. See Amartya Sen, "Exclusion and Inclusion," *Mainstream* (New Delhi), November 28, 2001; also see Amartya Sen, "A World Not Neatly Divided," *New York Times,* November 23, 2001. Also see Bernard

Lewis, *What Went Wrong? Western Impact and Middle Eastern Response* (New York: Oxford University Press, 2002), pp. 103, 159.

23 Warning the policy establishment: Lewis, "Roots of Muslim Rage," available at www.theatlantic.com/issues/90sep/rage.htm.

24 Democracy lags: "While more than three-quarters of 145 non-Muslim nations around the world are now democracies, most countries with an Islamic majority continue to defy the trend, according to a survey by Freedom House, an independent monitor of political rights and civil liberties based in New York." Barbara Crossette, "As Democracy Spreads Islamic World Hesitates," *International Herald Tribune,* December 23, 2001.

24 As if taking a cue: Stephen Schwartz, "Ground Zero and the Saudi Connection," *The Spectator* (London), September 22, 2001.

24 Even the pages of the *New York Times:* For an account of bad Muslims, see Blaine Harden, "Saudis Seek to Add U.S. Muslims to Their Sect," *New York Times,* October 20, 2001; Susan Sachs, "Anti-Semitism Is Deepening Among Muslims," *New York Times,* April 27, 2002. For a portrayal of good Muslims, see Laurie Goodstein, "Stereotyping Rankles Silent, Secular Majority of American Muslims, *New York Times,* December 23, 2001, p. A20.

24 Lewis opens: Lewis, *What Went Wrong?* p. 4

25 One of the best studies: Tomaž Mastnak, *Crusading Peace: Christendom, the Muslim World, and Western Political Order* (Berkeley and Los Angeles: University of California Press, 2002), pp. 95–125.

26 The Israeli cultural historian: Gil Anidjar, *"Our Place in al-Andalus": Kabbalah, Philosophy, Literature in Arab Jewish Letters* (Stanford: Stanford University Press, 2002), pp. 1, 6, 15, 22, 172.

27 Orientalist histories of Islam: I am thankful to Tim Mitchell for gently persuading me to explore the debate around Orientalism.

28 Based on the Mercator projection: Marshall G. S. Hodgson, "In the Center of the Map," in *Rethinking World History: Essays on Europe, Islam and World History* (edited with an introduction and conclusion by Edmund Burke III), (Cambridge: Cambridge University Press, 1993), pp. 29–34; Edmund Burke III, "Introduction," in ibid., p. xvii.

29 Hodgson should have added: Christopher Miller, *Blank Darkness: Africanist Discourse in French* (Chicago: University of Chicago Press), 1985).

29 "The West" referred: Marshall G. S. Hodgson, *The Venture of Islam: Conscience and History in a World Civilization,* vol. 1: *The Classical Age of Islam* (Chicago: University of Chicago Press, 1974), p. 53.

30 With the advantage of accumulated findings: Noel Swerdlow and

Otto Neugebauer, *Mathematical Astronomy in Copernicus's De Revolutionibus* (New York: Springer-Verlag, 1984), pp. 42–43, 295. For an elaborated discussion, see George Saliba, *Rethinking the Roots of Modern Science: Arabic Manuscripts in European Libraries,* occasional papers, Center for Contemporary Arab Studies (Edmund A. Walsh School of Foreign Service, Georgetown University, 1999), pp. 6–7.

30 The contemporary history of science: Saliba, *Rethinking the Roots of Modern Science,* p. 13. It is well known that the European Renaissance was nourished by sources as diverse as Greece, China, India, Arabia, and Africa. The long list of inventions developed elsewhere and then diffused into Europe included gunpowder, firearms, the compass, the sternpost rudder, decimal notation, and the university, among others. Francis Robinson notes that at least sixty Greek authors in fields including philosophy, medicine, mathematics, physics, astronomy, geography, and the occult sciences were translated into Arabic during the 'Abbasid Caliphate alone. Rather than just a passageway through which a literary global heritage poured, fertilizing Europe's post-Renaissance modernity, could it be that Andalusian Spain and classical Islam were the crucibles in which that early modernity was nurtured? See Burke, "Introduction," in Hodgson, *Rethinking World History,* p. xix; Francis Robinson, "Modern Islam and the Green Menace," *The Times Literary Supplement,* January 21, 1994, quoted in Euben, *Enemy in the Mirror,* pp. 12, 173.

31 The reconsideration of African history: Cheikh Anta Diop, *The African Roots of Civilization* (Chicago: Lawrence Hill Books, 1974).

31 Diop questioned: Today, Diop has been turned into an icon of North America–based Afrocentric scholarship, which seems preoccupied with proposing African identity as an "identity of color" and with incorporating ancient Egypt into a historically continuous notion of "black civilization," not only parallel to but also longer than "western civilization." Of greater significance, in my view, is Diop's pioneering critique of dominant nationalist scholarship of "the West."

31 In the study of classics: An important strand in nationalist African scholarship has been concerned with historicizing—and thus relativizing—the divide between North Africa and sub-Saharan Africa. Samir Amin showed that the Sahara was more a bridge than a barrier prior to the initiation of the Atlantic slave trade. Abdallah Laroui demonstrated the problem with isolating the history of Africa from that of the Mediterranean. Barry Boubacar wrote a history of Senegambia, a region that lies on both sides of the geographic divide. See Samir Amin, *Unequal Development: An Essay on*

Social Formations of Peripheral Capitalism (New York: Monthly Review Press, 1976); Abdalla Laroui, *The History of the Maghreb: An Interpretive Essay* (Princeton: Princeton University Press, 1977); Barry Boubacar, *Senegambia and the Atlantic Slave Trade* (Cambridge: Cambridge University Press, 1998).

31 Diop's work provided: Martin Bernal, *Black Athena: The Afroasiatic Roots of Classical Civilizations* (New Brunswick, N.J.: Rutgers University Press, 1987).

32 The first dogma: Edward Said, *Orientalism* (London: Penguin, 1985), pp. 300–301.

33 Here, too, the tendency: Nationalist politicization of cultured identities was often a response to Orientalist history writing. It is this simple historical insight that is missing in the post-9/11 warning contained in a piece on Occidentalism: "But one thing is clear in this murky war, it is that we should not counter Occidentalism with a nasty form of Orientalism. Once we fall for that temptation, the virus has infected us too." The problem, of course, is that a history of the disease shows that its course has been the reverse, from Orientalism to Occidentalism! See Ian Buruma and Avishai Margalit, "Occidentalism," *The New York Review of Books,* January 17, 2002, p. 7.

33 The nationalist response: David Crawford, "Morocco's Invisible *Imazighen*," *The Journal of North African Studies* 7, no. 1, spring 2002, pp. 59, 66.

33 How else are we to understand: All three estimates are cited in Crawford, "Morocco's Invisible *Imazighen*," p. 61.

34 Arabic-speaking: For a historical account, see Boubacar, *Senegambia and the Atlantic Slave Trade,* pp. 10, 15, 53.

35 "Afro-Arab integration": The book was intended to act as a beacon, bringing a fresh and healing perspective to civil conflicts then rife across the African continent. See Ministry of Foreign Affairs, Sudan, *Peace and Unity in the Sudan: An African Achievement* (Khartoum: Khartoum University Press, 1973), pp. 58–59.

35 "One sees that in all things": Ernest Renan, cited in Said, *Orientalism,* p. 149.

38 Karen Armstrong has located: Armstrong, *Battle for God,* pp. 175–77.

40 "The modern point of view": Susan Friend Harding, *The Book of Jerry Falwell: Fundamentalist Language and Politics* (Princeton: Princeton University Press, 2000), pp. 62–63.

41 The founder, Bob Jones: Armstrong, *Battle for God,* pp. 215, 268.

41 The first wave followed: Ibid., pp. 268–75.

42 Televangelists started the national: Harding, *Book of Jerry Falwell*, p. 77.

42 Speaking on the "Nebraska tragedy": Ibid., p. 23.

42 When Falwell founded: Ibid., pp. 17, 22, 79, 158, 161, 162, 190.

43 Though thirty of thirty-two: Phyllis Schlafly, *The Power of the Christian Woman* (Cincinnati: Standard, 1981), p. 117, cited in Armstrong, *Battle for God*, p. 311.

44 In his speech at the opening: Sara Diamond, *Roads to Dominion: Right-Wing Movements and Political Power in the United States* (New York: Guilford Press, 1995), pp. 1, 237; Harding, *Book of Jerry Falwell*, pp. 19–20.

45 When Renan published: Nikki Keddie, *An Islamic Response to Imperialism: Political and Religious Writings of Sayyid Jamal al-Din 'al-Afghani* (Berkeley: University of California Press, 1983), pp. 87–97.

46 On the other, this very necessity: Bassam Tibi, *The Crisis of Modern Islam: A Preindustrial Culture in the Scientific-Technological Age* (Salt Lake City: University of Utah, 1988), p. 70; cited in Armstrong, *Battle for God*, pp. 156–58.

46 There is a major debate: Schulze has pointed out that "in Islam there was no religious power that had to be separated from worldly power, since Islam had no clergy and no priesthood . . . so it would be senseless to burden Islam with a problem of Christian dogmatics." Schulze, *Modern History of the Islamic World*, p. 3. Whereas Schulze's insight illuminates mainstream Islam, I shall later point out that it needs to be modified in light of developments in contemporary Shi'a Islam.

46 However, Schulze points out: I am thankful to Tim Mitchell for driving this point home over and over again.

47 This is why it makes: Samir Amin has made the point succinctly: "These movements are commonly designated 'Islamic fundamentalism' in the West, but I prefer the phrase used in the Arab world: 'Political Islam.' We do not have religious movements, *per se,* here—the various groups are all quite close to one another—but something much more banal: political organization whose aim is the conquest of state power, nothing more, nothing less." Samir Amin, "Political Islam," *CovertAction Quarterly,* winter 2001, p. 3.

47 The split between: For a political analysis of Indian Islam, see Ayesha Jalal, *Self and Sovereignty, Individual and Community in South Asian Islam Since 1850* (New York: Routledge, 2001).

47 Contrary to what: Writing of Sayyid Ahmed Khan, Ayesha Jalal observes:

> The Aligarh movement which he fathered was to be seen as

the purveyor of modernist and rational thinking among the Muslim elite and, ironically enough, also the harbinger of latter-day Muslim political "separatism" and "communalism." By contrast, his more culturally exclusive Muslim opponents, harbouring anti-colonial feelings and sentiments of Islamic universalism, steeped themselves in religious structures at *madrasas* and *maktabs* only to end up squarely on the side of an inclusionary and "secular" Indian nationalism.

See Jalal, *Self and Sovereignty,* pp. 77–78.

48 He called for the institution:

He had never thought much of the Turkish khilafat and still less of Gandhian non-cooperation. In his opinion, "no sincere Muslim could join [the khilafat movement] for a single minute. In November 1922, Iqbal was among the few who acclaimed the Turkish Grand National Assembly's decision to abolish the sultanate and appoint a new khalifa stripped of any temporal authority. Seeing it as the correct exercise of collective as opposed to individual ijtihad, Iqbal later declared that among the Muslim countries of the world "Turkey alone ha[d] shaken off its dogmatic slumber, and attained . . . self-consciousness" through the exercise of "her right to intellectual freedom." Muslims in the rest of the world, including India, were "mechanically repeating old values, whereas the Turk . . . [was] on the way to creating new values."

Jalal, *Self and Sovereignty,* pp. 244–45.

49 The six-point program: The program included: (1) the interpretation of the Koran in the spirit of the age; (2) the unity of Islamic nations; (3) raising the standard of living and achievement of social justice and order; (4) a struggle against illiteracy and poverty; (5) the emancipation of Muslim lands from foreign dominance; and (6) the promotion of Islamic peace and fraternity throughout the world. See Armstrong, *Battle for God,* pp. 218–26. On disavowing violence, see Richard Mitchell, *The Society of the Muslim Brothers* (Oxford: Oxford University Press, 1969); cited in Talal Asad, "Comments (Yet Again) on Political Islam in the Middle East" (Graduate Center, City University of New York, October 11, 2002, mimeographed).

49 But the society soon split: Schulze, *Modern History of the Islamic World,* pp. 134–35.

50 This demands a jihad: A Muslim thus seeks unity between the personal and the political. Any attempt to fence off any area from this overall religious effort would be a violation of a cardinal Islamic

principle, *tawhid* (unification). It is the principle of tawhid that Bernard Lewis cites as the basis of his claim that Islam has no doctrinal room for a secular accommodation. In doing so, he not only turns his back on historical Islam but also identifies Islam doctrinally with one particular interpretation.

50 The lesser jihad: Farish A. Noor, "The Evolution of Jihad in Islamist Political Discourse: How a Plastic Concept Became Harder," Social Science Research Council, available at http://www.ssrc.org/sept11/essays/noor.htm. Ayatollah Khomeini wrote an article titled "The Greater Jihad" in 1972. The title referred to one of his favorite hadiths, whereby the Prophet says after returning home from a battle, "We are returning from the lesser jihad to the greater jihad." It is from this perspective that politics is the lesser struggle and the spiritual transformation of self and society the larger struggle.

50 Tomaž Mastnak: Mastnak, *Crusading Peace,* pp. 64–65.

51 Among the Berbers: For a historical account, see Boubacar, *Senegambia and the Atlantic Slave Trade,* pp. 25, 46, 51–52, 58, 81, 94–95.

52 The third time jihad: Tariq Ali, *The Clash of Fundamentalisms: Crusades, Jihads, and Modernity* (London: Verso, 2002), pp. 41–42, 73–74.

53 It is estimated: Francis M. Deng, *War of Visions: Conflict of Identities in the Sudan* (Washington, D.C.: The Brookings Institution, 1995), pp. 49–52.

54 To realize that end: Schulze, *Modern History of the Islamic World,* pp. 116–117.

54 He defined "the ultimate": Sayyid Abul A'la Mawdudi, *Let Us Be Muslims,* ed. Khurram Murad (London: Islamic Foundation, 1985), pp. 285, 288.

54 With both eyes focused: Ibid., p. 295.

54 He also secularized: Ibid., p. 297.

55 Mawdudi was the first: Euben, *Enemy in the Mirror,* p. 74; Armstrong, *Battle for God,* pp. 236–38.

55 Even if Qutb: Schulze, *Modern History of the Islamic World,* p. 176.

55 His first book: For a short biographical sketch, see Hamid Algar, "Introduction," to Sayyid Qutb, *Social Justice in Islam,* trans. John B. Hardie, rev. with an introduction by Hamid Algar (Oneonta, N.Y.: Islamic Publications, 2000), pp. 1–17.

55 Qutb explained his objective: Qutb, *Social Justice in Islam,* p. 19.

57 Modernization through the natural: Sayyid Qutb, *Milestones,* rev. trans. with a foreword by Ahmed Zaki Hammad (Indianapolis: American Trust, 1990), pp. 91–94.

57 "Islam is a declaration": Ibid., pp. 49–50, 46.

58 Here, Qutb echoed: Ibid., p. 9.
58 Acting as a trustee: Schulze, *Modern History of the Islamic World.* On Ali Shariati, see p. 178; on Ayatollah Khomeini, see p. 223.
60 "Mankind today is": Qutb, *Milestones,* pp. 5–6.

Chapter Two: The Cold War After Indochina

64 A joint resolution: Ignacio Ramonet, "State-Sponsored Lies," *Le Monde Diplomatique,* available at http://mondediplo.com/2003/07/01ramonet.
65 After Tet: Charles Mechling, Jr., "Counterinsurgency: The First Ordeal by Fire," in *Low-Intensity Warfare: Counter-Insurgency, Proinsurgency, and Antiterrorism in the Eighties,* ed. Michael T. Klare and Peter Kornbluh (New York: Pantheon, 1988), pp. 41–45.
66 Even at the end: Alfred W. McCoy, " 'Fallout': The Interplay of CIA Cover Warfare and the Global Narcotics Traffic," paper presented to the conference the Civil War and Cold War, 1975–1990: A Comparative Analysis of Southern Africa, Central America, and Central Asia (Institute of African Studies, Columbia University, New York, N.Y., November 14–15, 2002, mimeographed), pp. 2–3.
66 To defend the freedom: *The Opium War* The Compilation Group of the History of Modern China Series (Peking: Foreign Language Press, 1976).
66 In a monumental historical study: The material on the growth of the opium and heroin trade in Southeast Asia's Golden Triangle is based on Alfred W. McCoy, *The Politics of Heroin: CIA Complicity in the Global Drug Trade* (New York: Lawrence Hill Books, 1991), pp. 18–19, 162–63, 222–23, 290–91, 349, 376–77.
68 In 1967, the CIA: Alexander Cockburn and Jeffrey St. Clair, *Whiteout: The CIA, Drugs, and the Press* (London: Verso, 1998), pp. 245, 247.
71 It is this plan: Georges Nzongola-Ntalaja, *The Congo: From Leopold to Kabila: A People's History* (London: Zed Books, 2002), pp. 106–12.
72 Piero Gleijeses, professor: Piero Gleijeses, *Conflicting Missions: Havana, Washington, and Africa, 1959–1976* (Chapel Hill: University of North Carolina Press, 2002), pp. 61–66.
73 Gleijesis concludes: Ibid., pp. 69–70; on the Simba rebellion, see Nzongola-Ntalaja, *The Congo,* pp. 131–35.
74 The Simba responded: Gleijeses, *Conflicting Missions,* pp. 70–71, 73–75, 97, 126–28, 386.
75 Piero Gleijeses gives: Ibid., pp. 72–73, 129–32.

76 Whereas their Congolese auxiliaries: Ibid., pp. 157–58.

77 In pursuit of this goal: Ibid., pp. 330–46.

78 One of the sharpest: Ibid., p. 354.

80 In the years that followed: Lucas Khamisi, *Imperialism Today* (Dar-es-Salaam: Tanzania Publishing, 1981), pp. 167–68.

81 "The lesson of Vietnam": Michael T. Klare and Peter Kornbluh, "The New Interventionism: Low-Intensity Warfare in the 1980s and Beyond," in Klare and Kornbluh, *Low-Intensity Warfare*, p. 13.

82 Before the fiscal year: Senate Resolution 152, introduced on December 15, 1975.

82 Not since the start: See K. C. Johnson, "The Clark Amendment," Department of History, City University of New York, available at http://academic.brooklyn.cuny.edu/history/johnson/clark.htm.

83 Clark was convinced: Ibid.

84 Heikal came upon: Mohamed Heikal, *Iran: The Untold Story* (New York: Pantheon, 1982), pp. 112–16.

85 "When Itzhak Rabin": Ibid., p. 116.

86 As eighteen thousand Cuban: Gleijeses, *Conflicting Missions,* p. 392.

87 "Kissinger," Heikal noted: Kissinger was, of course, not the only one happy about this arrangement: "Also aware of the existence of the new alliance, and happy that it should exist, were David Rockefeller and the Chase Manhattan Bank, with its heavy African investments." See, Heikal, *Iran,* p. 112–13.

87 CIA chief William J. Casey: Renamo derived from an acronym for the Mozambique National Resistance, a covert armed group set up by white Rhodesian officers to overthrow the government of newly independent Mozambique.

88 Malan's tenure: Truth and Reconciliation Commission of South Africa, *Report* (Cape Town: CTP Book Printers, 1998), vol. 2, para. 120, pp. 28–29.

89 The partnership between: On Angola and Mozambique, see William Minter, *Apartheid's Contras: An Inquiry into the Roots of War in Angola and Mozambique* (Atlantic Highlands, N.J.: Zed Books, 1994), pp. 2–5, 142–49, 152–68; Alex Vines, *RENAMO: Terrorism in Mozambique* (Bloomington: Indiana University Press, 1991), pp. 24, 39; Victoria Brittain, *Death of Dignity: Angola's Civil War* (London: Pluto Press, 1998), p. 65.

89 But this did not rule out: Thomas Bodenheimer and Robert Gould, *Rollback: Right-Wing Power in U.S. Foreign Policy* (Boston: South End Press, 1989), available at http://www.thirdworldtraveler.com/Ronald_Reagan/ReaganDoctrine_TWRollback.html, October 3, 2002, p. 7.

90 In a candid remark: Quoted in Minter, *Apartheid's Contras,* p. 152.

91 And the UN estimated: See Ibid., pp. 4–5.

92 As a curtain-raiser: Ibid., p. 149.

93 Muldergate included: Karen Rothmyer, "The South Africa Lobby," *The Nation,* April 19, 1980, pp. 455–58.

93 No less a personality: Sara Diamond, *Roads to Dominion: Right-Wing Movements and Political Power in the United States* (New York: Guilford Press, 1995), pp. 222–23.

93 Less than a year after: Vines, *RENAMO,* p. 24.

94 "South Africa, in search": Gleijeses, *Conflicting Missions,* p. 274.

94 The militarization of the apartheid: Truth and Reconciliation Commission, *Report.*

95 "Given the proposition": John D. Waghelstein, "Post-Vietnam Counterinsurgency Doctrine," *Military Review,* May 1985, p. 46, quoted in Klare and Kornbluh, "The New Interventionism," in Klare and Kornbluh, *Low-Intensity Warfare,* p. 5.

96 Observing that "containment": Bodenheimer and Gould, *Rollback,* pp. 1–2.

96 When reelected in 1984: Cited in Klare and Kornbluh, "New Interventionism," in *Low-Intensity Warfare,* pp. 6, 9.

97 SOF funds had: Bodenheimer and Gould, *Rollback,* pp. 8–9.

97 That same year, 1986: Cited in Klare and Kornbluh, "New Interventionism," in *Low-Intensity Warfare,* pp. 4–5.

98 These forces, Secretary of State: Cited in Michael T. Klare, "The Interventionist Impulse: U.S. Military Doctrine for Low-Intensity Warfare," in Klare and Kornbluh, *Low-Intensity Warfare,* p. 63.

98 When he signed: See Ronald Reagan, "Statement on Signing the International Security and Development Cooperation Act of 1985," available at http://www.reagan.utexas.edu/resource/speeches/1985/80885d.htm.

99 Deadpan and matter of fact: Oliver North, Neil Livingstone, J. Michael Kelly, and Senator Rudman, cited in Klare and Kornbluh, "New Interventionism," in *Low-Intensity Warfare,* pp. 14–16, 19.

101 Declaring that contra leaders: Bodenheimer and Gould, *Rollback,* p. 6.

102 By mid-1982: See Defense Intelligence Agency, weekly intelligence summary, July 16, 1982, p. 21; Clarridge's testimony is in *The Miami Herald,* October 20, 1984; Americas Watch, "Human Rights in Nicaragua: Reagan, Rhetoric and Reality," July 1985, p. 16; David Siegel, M.D., "Nicaraguan Health: An Update," *LASA Forum,* winter 1986, p. 30. All quotes cited in Peter Kornbluh, "Nicaragua: U.S. Proinsurgency Warfare Against the Sandinistas," in *Low-Intensity Warfare,* pp. 140–41, 142.

102 The U.S.-based Nicaraguan Association: Bodenheimer and Gould, *Rollback*, p. 7.

103 Even in these instances: This information is from Kornbluh, "Nicaragua," in *Low-Intensity Warfare*, pp. 142–46.

104 In response, Congress: See Public Law 98-215 (H.R. 2968), December 9, 1983, Intelligence Authorization Act for Fiscal Year 1984.

105 Soon after, Robert McFarlane: Cockburn and St. Clair, *Whiteout*, p. 9.

105 As in the Golden Triangle: McCoy, *Politics of Heroin*, p. 24. All other information on this here and below is from pp. 478–84.

107 In 1990, after another: Cockburn and St. Clair, *Whiteout*, p. 14.

107 Both groups specialize: Alfred McCoy gives several examples of this affinity over the course of the Cold War: thus, "when the CIA needed a legion of thugs to break the 1950 communist dock strike in Marseille, it turned to that city's Corsican milieu"; when it wanted to assassinate Fidel Castro in the 1960s, "it retained American Mafia syndicates who could not only kill on contract but also ensure confidentiality—something no official U.S. agency, except the CIA itself, could do"; in the mountains of Asia, the CIA was allied "with the heroin merchants in Laos" and "Chinese opium dealers in Burma." See McCoy, *Politics of Heroin*, p. 15.

107 The NSA released: See Peter Kornbluh's "Crack, the Contras and the CIA: The Storm over 'Dark Alliance,'" available at http://www.gwu.edu/~nsarchiv/NSAEBB/NSAEBB2/storm.htm.

109 One enthusiastic pastor: Diamond, *Roads to Dominion*, pp. 214–15, 221, 228, 237–38.

110 Appearing at its 1987: Ibid., pp. 238–39, 243.

111 As "a quid pro quo": Jane Hunter, *Israeli Foreign Policy: South Africa and Central America* (Boston: South End Press, 1987); *Time*, March 28, 1983; SIPRI Yearbook, 1980, p. 96; all cited in Jonathan Marshall, Peter Dale Scott, and Jane Hunter, *The Iran-Contra Connection: Secret Teams and Covert Operations in the Reagan Era* (Boston: South End Press, 1987), pp. 89–90.

111 *Time* magazine: *Washington Post*, December 16, 1984, and June 16, 1984; *The Middle East*, September 1981; *NACLA Report*, May/June 1983; *Time*, May 7, 1984; Benjamin Beit–Hallahmi, "U.S.-Israeli-Central American Connection," *The Link*, vol. xviii, November 1985; all cited in Marshall et al., *The Iran-Contra Connection*, p. 14.

111 As Israeli defense: *The Washington Post*, September 15, 1984; *U.S. News & World Report*, December 15, 1986; *New York Times*, March 8, 1982, and November 23, 1986; *Aerospace Daily*, August 18, 1982; *Newsweek*, December 8, 1986; all cited in Marshall et al., *The Iran-Contra Connection*, pp. 173–74.

113 After a White House: *New York Times,* November 26, 1986; *Ha'aretz,* November 18, 1986; all cited in Marshall et al., *The Iran-Contra Connection,* pp. 114, 121, 168, 174, 183.

114 *The Sunday Telegraph: The Sunday Telegraph* (London), March 5, 1989; quoted in *Israeli Foreign Affairs,* April 1989, p. 5; cited in Jonathan Marshall, "Israel, the Contras and the North Trial," *Middle East Report,* September/October 1989.

115 Few outside of official Washington: Kornbluh, "Nicaragua," pp. 136, 137, 140.

115 The scandal was: Cockburn and St. Clair, *Whiteout,* p. 9.

115 How far CIA thinking: The manual has been translated and published: Tayacán, *Psychological Operations in Guerrilla Warfare* (New York: Vintage, 1985); for citations, see Kornbluh, "Nicaragua," pp. 140–42.

117 Testifying before the World Court: David MacMichael, testimony before the World Court, September 8, 1985, p. 8 of the transcript, cited in Kornbluh, "Nicaragua," p. 138.

Chapter Three: Afghanistan: The High Point in the Cold War

119 "These gentlemen are": Cited in Eqbal Ahmad, "Genesis of International Terrorism," *Dawn* (Karachi), October 5, 2001 (speech originally given in October 1998).

120 Thus, the United States supported: Tariq Ali, *The Clash of Fundamentalisms,* p. 275.

121 Israeli intelligence allowed: A former Israeli military commander of the Gaza Strip was quoted in 1986 to the effect that "we extend some financial aid to Islamic groups via mosques and religious schools in order to help create a force that would stand against the leftist forces which support the PLO." Quoted in Graham Usher, "The Rise of Political Islam in the Occupied Territories," *Middle East International* (London), no. 453, June 25, 1993, p. 19. The Israeli experts on defense policy Ze'ev Schiff and Ehud Ya'ari give a short account of Israeli policies toward Hamas so far as bank transfers and other margins of maneuver are concerned. See Ze'ev Schiff and Ehud Ya'ari, *Intifada* (New York: Simon & Schuster, 1991), pp. 233–34. Finally, Khaled Hroub acknowledges that the Israelis used Hamas and the PLO against each other but discounts any deliberate Israeli role in aiding Hamas. See Khaled Hroub, *Hamas: Political Thought and Practice* (Washington, D.C.: Institute for Palestinian Studies, 2000),

pp. 200–203. I am thankful to Joseph Massad for pointing out these sources.

121 Between 1971 and 1975, Sadat: Karen Armstrong, *The Battle for God: A History of Fundamentalism* (New York: Alfred A. Knopf, 2000), pp. 290–91.

123 CIA and State Department documents: Steve Galster, "Afghanistan: The Making of U.S. Policy, 1973–1990," p. 11, in the National Security Archive, September 11th Sourcebooks, "Volume II: Afghanistan: Lessons from the Last War," available at http://www.gwu.edu/~nsarchiv/NSAEBB/NSAEBB57/essay.html.

123 This much was confirmed: Cited in Ali, *Clash of Fundamentalisms,* pp. 207–8.

123 The CIA was determined: Barnett R. Rubin, *The Fragmentation of Afghanistan: State Formation and Collapse in the International System,* 2d ed. (New Haven: Yale University Press, 1995), p. 223.

124 Among the more influential: Pervez Hoodbhoy, "The Genesis of Global Jihad in Afghanistan" (Quaid-e-Azam University, Islamabad, Pakistan, mimeographed) p. 5.

126 The coup and the Soviet invasion: Galster, "Afghanistan," p. 15.

126 They flocked to ISI-run: Hamid Hussein, "Forgotten Ties: CIA, ISI & Taliban," *CovertAction Quarterly* 72, spring 2002, p. 3.

126 There is the well-known example: Cited in Lawrence Wright, "The Man Behind Bin Laden: How an Egyptian Doctor Became a Master of Terror," *The New Yorker,* September 16, 2002, p. 72.

127 A CIA asset: John K. Cooley, *Unholy Wars: Afghanistan, America, and International Terrorism* (London: Pluto Press, 1999), pp. 87–88.

128 In March 1985, Reagan: Steve Coll, *Washington Post,* July 19, 1992; quoted in Michel Chossudovsky, "Who Is Osama Bin Laden?" Montreal, Centre for Research on Globalisation, available at http://globalresearch.ca/articles/CHO109C.html, posted September 12, 2001, see n. 4.

129 The redefined war: Ahmed Rashid, *Taliban: Militant Islam, Oil, and Fundamentalism in Central Asia* (New Haven: Yale University Press, 2000), pp. 129–30.

130 While ISI was the main: John Cooley, a former Middle East correspondent for *The Christian Science Monitor* and ABC-TV, writes of Israeli involvement:

> As for Israel, the evidence is much sketchier. At least half a dozen knowledgeable individuals insisted to the author, without citing proof, that Israel was indeed involved in both training and supply; . . . Several Americans and Britons who took part in the training program have assured

the author that Israelis did indeed take part, though no one will own to actually having seen, or spoken with, Israeli instructors or intelligence operatives in Afghanistan or Pakistan. What is certain is that of all the anti-Soviet coalition, the Israelis have been the most successful in concealing the details and even the broad traces of a training role. (Cooley, *Unholy Wars,* p. 101).

Tariq Ali, the Pakistani-born British political commentator, also agrees that Israel's role "remains one of the best-kept secrets of the War" and then recounts a significant detail: "In 1985, Ahmed Mansur, a young Pakistani journalist working for *The Muslim,* accidentally stumbled across a group of Israeli 'advisors' at the bar of the Intercontinental Hotel in Peshawar. Aware that the news would be explosive for the Zia dictatorship, he informed his editor, some friends and a visiting WTN correspondent. A few days later, the mujahidin, alerted by Pakistan's Inter-Services Intelligence, captured and killed him." (Ali, *Clash of Fundamentalisms,* p. 209).

132 Martin Stone writes: Martin Stone, *The Agony of Algeria* (New York: Columbia University Press, 1997), pp. 182–83.

132 Fighters in the Peshawar-based: Ibid., p. 183.

132 Bin Laden was recruited: Robin Blackburn, *Terror and Empire,* chap. 3, "The U.S. Alliance with Militant Islam," available at http://www.counterpunch.org/robin3.html.

132 In 1986, bin Laden worked: Rashid, *Taliban,* p. 132.

133 That organization was al-Qaeda: Wright, "Man Behind Bin Laden," p. 75. Rashid's account confirms 1989 as the year of its founding. Cooley gives the improbable date of 1985. See Rashid, *Taliban,* p. 132, and Cooley, *Unholy Wars,* pp. 120, 220–21.

134 To get an idea: Cooley, *Unholy Wars,* pp. 83, 86.

135 He had "sent his sons": Ibid., pp. 87–88.

136 Cooley's list includes: Ibid., pp. 188–89.

136 The London-based Indian journalist: Quoted in Chossudovsky, "Who Is Osama Bin Laden?" at http://globalresearch.ca/articles/CHO109C.html.

136 By the late 1980s: Ahmed Rashid, *Jihad: The Rise of Militant Islam in Central Asia* (New Haven: Yale University Press, 2002), p. 44.

137 Pervez Hoodbhoy gives: Pervez Hoodbhoy, "The Genesis of Global Jihad in Afghanistan," revised version, paper presented to the conference Civil War and Cold War, 1975–1990: A Comparative Analysis of Southern Africa, Central America, and Central Asia (Institute of African Studies, Columbia University, New York, N.Y., November 14–15, 2002, mimeographed) pp. 7–8.

137 In spite of their proliferation: Barnett Rubin, private communication, February 10, 2004.

137 Brigadier Muhammad Yusuf: Hussein, "Forgotten Ties," p. 3.

137 United States authorities: *Los Angeles Times,* August 4 and 5, 1996.

138 Eventually, Rashid concludes: Rashid, *Taliban,* p. 44. These numbers are reproduced in several articles, often without a distinction between those trained in the madrassahs and those who actually fought in the war. This is why one can find a wide a range of figures—ranging from 35,000 to more than 100,000—when it comes to estimates of how many were trained or fought in the Afghan War. Arundhati Roy, for example, says that the CIA recruited "almost 100,000" "soldiers for America's proxy war." Cooley gives a figure of 40,000 to 50,000 non-Afghan fighters who "either trained or fought in Afghanistan." See Arundhati Roy, "The Algebra of Infinite Justice," *The Guardian* (London), September 29, 2001; Cooley, *Unholy Wars,* p. 232.

138 Tariq Ali gives: Ali, *Clash of Fundamentalisms,* p. 196.

138 Cooley notes that: Cooley, *Unholy Wars,* 2000 edition, p. 90.

140 "Your government": John-Thor Dahlburg, "Legacy of Fear: Afghanistan's Mix of Faith, Terror—A Global Scourge," *Los Angeles Times,* August 4, 5, and 6, 1996.

141 Years later, Musto: Alfred W. McCoy, *The Politics of Heroin: CIA Complicity in the Global Drug Trades* (New York: Lawrence Hill Books, 1991), pp. 436–37.

141 As early as February 1980: Cooley, *Unholy Wars,* p. 60.

141 In fiscal year 1987 alone: Eqbal Ahmad and Richard J. Barnet, "Bloody Games," *The New Yorker,* April 11, 1988, pp. 44–86.

141 Noting that this sum: Galster, "Afghanistan," p. 18.

142 As the Mujahideen: Alfred McCoy, "Drug Fallout: The CIA's Forty-Year Complicity in the Narcotics Trade," *The Progressive,* August 1, 1997, pp. 24–27.

142 Writing in *The Nation:* Lawrence Lifschultz, "Bush, Drugs and Pakistan: Inside the Kingdom of Heroin," *The Nation,* November 14, 1988, pp. 477, 492–96.

142 *The Herald* of Pakistan: Cited in McCoy, *Politics of Heroin,* p. 454.

142 Finally, the CIA provided: McCoy, "Drug Fallout," pp. 24–27.

143 Accounting for less than: The United Nations International Drug Control Program Report (part of the United Nations Office on Drugs and Crimes) is cited in "Drug Prohibition and Political Violence: Making the Connection," in *The Week Online with DRCNet,* Issue 203, September 21, 2001 available at http://stopthedrugwar.org/chronicle/203/politicalviolence.shtml. Similar information can be

found in "The Opium Economy in Afghanistan: An International Problem," a study published by The United Nations Office on Drugs and Crimes in January 2003, available online at http://www.unodc.org/pdf/publications/afg_opium_economy_www.pdf.

143 "Just as CIA support": McCoy, *Politics of Heroin*, pp. 440–41.

143 The worst example: Ibid., p. 451.

144 The *New York Times* reported: John F. Burns, "Afghans: How They Blame America," February 4, 1990; cited in McCoy, *Politics of Heroin*, p. 450.

144 Mullah Nasim: *New York Times*, June 18, 1986; cited in McCoy, *Politics of Heroin*, p. 458.

145 In the end, Mullah Nasim: The information on the turf war is from Barnett Rubin, testimony before the House Subcommittee on Europe and the Middle East, pp. 18–20, 35, cited in McCoy, *Politics of Heroin*, pp. 454, 458, 450.

145 From the start of: McCoy, *Politics of Heroin*, p. 452.

146 With fourteen thousand employees: Canal Walsh, "Spies Hide as Bank Faces BCCI Charges," *The Observer* (London), January 19, 2003.

146 The New York prosecutor: Cooley, *Unholy Wars*, p. 114.

147 The subcommittee complained: For the report of the congressional subcommittee, see "The BCCI Affair," available at http://www.fas.org/irp/congress/1992_rpt/bcci/index.html.

149 The Saudi-BCCI link: Cooley, *Unholy Wars*, p. 113. The BCCI question is discussed on pp. 112–16.

149 Zia ul-Haq: Cited in Tariq Ali, *Clash of Fundamentalisms*, p. 156.

150 The harvest came: Ahmed Rashid, "The Taliban: Exporting Extremism," *Foreign Affairs* 78, no. 6, November–December 1999, p. 22.

151 When declared a "terrorist": Tariq Ali, *Clash of Fundamentalisms*, p. 199.

151 "The sole child": Dahlburg, "Legacy of Fear," *Los Angeles Times*, August 5, 1996.

152 Both major religious sects: Tariq Ali, *Clash of Fundamentalisms*, p. 198.

152 The number of officially registered: The official figures are from Tariq Ali, *Clash of Fundamentalisms*, p. 195. The UN estimates below are from McCoy, *Politics of Heroin*, pp. 454–55.

155 Thus, Ahmed Rashid: Rashid, *Jihad*, p. 210.

155 As early as 1985: Cooley, *Unholy Wars*, p. 62.

156 Barnett Rubin: Rubin, *Fragmentation of Afghanistan*, pp. 83, 203, 210–21, 272, 279.

158 It led to a brief alliance: Eqbal Ahmad, "In a Land Without Music," *Dawn* (Karachi), July 23, 1995.

159 Rebel leaders had admitted: Galster, "Afghanistan," p. 23.

159 When the international press: Rubin, *Fragmentation of Afghanistan,* pp. 250–51, 257.

160 On October 4, 1996: John-Thor Dahlburg, "Conspiracy Theory Links U.S. with Afghan Militia," *Los Angeles Times,* October 4, 1996.

160 After a State Department meeting: Rashid, *Taliban,* p. 179.

161 An old man in a mosque: Ahmad, "In a Land Without Music."

161 Ahmed Rashid noted: Rashid, *Jihad,* p. 210.

162 In Ahmed Rashid's words: Ibid., p. 211.

162 When I asked two colleagues: Ahmed Rashid explains that the Taliban did not only ban women from public life; they also banned numerous male-centered activities, such as any game with a ball or music (except for drums), lest any of these entice members of either sex. See Eqbal Ahmad, "In a Land Without Music," *Dawn* (Karachi), July 23, 1995.

162 First, the experience of: Barnett Rubin and Ashraf Ghani, conversation with author, November 16, 2001.

163 "The ideologies of war": Eqbal Ahmad, "In Afghanistan, A Ceasefire Please," *Dawn* (Karachi), April 7, 1991.

165 The Algerian sociologist: Quoted in Cooley, *Unholy Wars,* p. 203.

165 Cooley estimates: Ibid., pp. 203–5.

165 In the 1990s: Dahlburg, "Legacy of Fear," especially for the three biographies. I have also relied on Stone, *Agony of Algeria,* p. 183, for my account of Kamerredin Kherbane.

168 Al-Zawahri wrote in his memoir: Cited in Wright, "Man Behind Bin Laden," p. 67.

168 The Luxor attack: Cooley, *Unholy Wars,* pp. 185–86.

169 "Time and again,": Ibid., pp. 88–91, 185, 195, 203–6.

170 This is why it is necessary: In an essay on September 11, Olivier Roy has usefully—even if too neatly—contrasted radical political Islam with conservative "neo-fundamentalism," casting the former as social movements from below and the latter as vehicles of state agendas, driven from above. But the distinction is not particularly useful in understanding the dynamic that led to 9/11, mainly because Roy gives only marginal importance to the encounter with Western power during the Cold War. See Olivier Roy, "Neo-Fundamentalism," Social Science Research Council, available at http://www.ssrc.org/sept11/essays/roy.htm.

171 The first, the military resistance: My understanding of Hizbullah re-

lies heavily on Nizar Hamzeh, "Lebanon's Hizbullah: From Islamic Revolution to Parliamentary Accommodation," *Third World Quarterly* 14, no. 2, 1993; also published as an electronic document at Al Mashriq in collaboration with the American University of Beirut. See http://almashriq.hiof.no/ddc/projects/pspa/hamzeh2.html.

173 Predicated on a notion: Talal Asad, "Introduction: Thinking About Secularism," in *Formations of the Secular: Christianity, Islam, Modernity* (Stanford: Stanford University Press, 2003).

174 "The revolutionary regime": Richard Bulliet, "Twenty Years of Islamic Politics," *The Middle East Journal* 53, no. 2, spring 1999, pp. 7–9.

174 Islamist politics are driven: Olivier Roy describes as "neo-fundamentalist" all Islamist movements that share an explicit political agenda. See Roy, "Neo-Fundamentalism," at http://ssrc.org/sept11/essays/roy/htm.

176 Eqbal Ahmad observed: Eqbal Ahmad, "The Afghan Lessons," *Dawn* (Karachi), May 3, 1992.

176 Precisely when they were ready: Eqbal Ahmad, "Stalemate at Jalalabad," *The Nation*, October 9, 1989; "The Afghan Lessons," *Dawn*, May 3, 1992; "The War Without End," *Dawn*, August 20, 1992.

177 John Cooley gives the example: Cooley, *Unholy Wars*, pp. 83, 86.

Chapter Four: From Proxy War to Open Aggression

181 Nicholas D. Kristof: Nicholas D. Kristof, "Cheney Didn't Mind Saddam," *International Herald Tribune*, October 12–13, 2002, p. 8.

181 An official army letter: Both the U.S. Army letter and Meselson cited in David Ruppe, "Army Gave Chem-Bio Warfare Training to Iraqis," Global Security Newswire, http://www.govexec.com/dailyfed/0103/012803gsn.htm.

181 Further, a report: John J. Mearsheimer and Stephen M. Walt, "An Unnecessary War," *Foreign Policy*, no. 134, January/February 2003.

181 A central figure in Reagan's effort: Charles Glass, "Iraq Must Go!" *London Review of Books*, October 3, 2002, p. 13.

182 In spite of public revelations: Samantha Power, *"A Problem from Hell": America and the Age of Genocide* (New York: Basic Books, 2002); for details on U.S. loans and credits, see pp. 173, 176–77, 236; for details on U.S. diplomatic protection to the Iraqi regime during the time of the first and the second chemical-gas attacks, see pp. 191, 195, 200–201, 210, 230–31, 234.

182 Matters came to: Available at http://www.gulfwarvets.com/victims.htm

and Heather Wokusch, "Lawsuit for Gulf War Veterans Targets WMD Businesses," available at http://heatherwokusch.com/columns/columns50.html.

183 In his introduction: For a discussion, see Alfred W. McCoy, " 'Fallout': The Interplay of CIA Cover Warfare and the Global Narcotics Traffic," paper presented to the conference on the Cold War and the Civil War, Institute of African Studies, Columbia University (New York, N.Y., November 14–15, 2002, mimeographed), p. 3.

184 Former attorney general: Ramsey Clark, interview with Rasha Saad in *Al–Ahram* (Cairo), December 26, 2002.

184 Eric Hoskins, a Canadian: Cited in David Edwards and David Cromwell, "The British Liberal Press Target Iraq," Third World Network Features, *Sunday News* (Dar-es-Salaam), July 14, 2002.

184 Thomas Friedman: Thomas Friedman, "A Rising Sense that Saddam Hussein Must Go," *New York Times,* July 7, 1991.

184 In the worst-case: Linda Rothstein, "Editor's Note: Loyal to a Fault," *Bulletin of Atomic Scientists,* 59, no. 4, p. 2.

185 In October 1998: Cited in Tariq Ali, *The Clash of Fundamentalisms,* p. 145; also see Anthony Arnove, ed., *Iraq Under Siege: The Deadly Impact of Sanctions and War* (Cambridge, Mass.: South End Press, 2002), pp. 9–20. Also see Alex de Waal, "US War Crimes in Somalia," *New Left Review* 1, no. 230, July/August 1998.

185 Round-the-clock: This information is available on the Department of Defense Web site at http://www.dod.gov/news/Dec1998/t12201998_t1219coh.html. The numbers of missiles and strike sorties is at http://www.dod.gov/news/Dec1998_t1219coh.html.

186 A further set of resolutions: Marc Bossuyt, "The Adverse Consequences of Economic Sanctions on the Enjoyment of Human Rights," working paper for UN Sub-Commission on the Promotion and Protection of Human Rights, available at http://www.scn.org/ccpi/UNreport-excerpt.html. I am thankful to Adam Branch for bringing this report to my attention.

187 But as a working paper: Ibid., para. 62, p. 2. For further information on how the oil-for-food program operated, see Denis J. Halliday (former head of the program), "Iraq and the UN's Weapon of Mass Destruction," *Current History* 98, no. 625, February 1999, pp. 65–68; interview with Hans von Sponeck and Denis Haliday in *The Guardian,* November 29, 2001; Hans Von Sponeck, "Too Much Collateral Damage: 'Smart Sanctions' Hurt Innocent Iraqis," *The Globe and Mail* (Toronto), July 2, 2002.

187 Whereas child mortality: Not only did the north receive 22 percent more per capita in dollar-value goods from the oil-for-food program

than did the center and the south, 10 percent of the value going into the northern autonomous region was in the form of cash—allowing for greater local participation—whereas only goods went into the center and the south.

189 UNICEF data "showed": Cited in Von Sponeck, "Too Much Collateral Damage."

189 Writing in the summer: Richard Garfield, "The Public Health Impact of Sanctions: Contrasting Responses of Iraq and Cuba," *Middle East Report* 215, summer 2000, pp. 16–17.

189 Noting that "even": Richard Garfield, "Changes in Health and Well-Being in Iraq During the 1990s," in *Sanctions on Iraq: Background, Consequences, Strategies,* proceedings of the conference hosted by the Campaign Against Sanctions on Iraq, November 13–14, 1999, Cambridge, England, pp. 36, 50–51; Garfield, "Public Health Impact of Sanctions," pp. 16–17.

189 By 2000, there was: Bossuyt, "Adverse Consequences of Economic Sanctions on the Enjoyment of Human Rights," para. 63, p. 2.

190 The moral indefensibility: Ibid., p. 5, n. 59.

190 She described both her research: Joy Gordon, "Cool War: Economic Sanctions as a Weapon of Mass Destruction," *Harper's Magazine,* November 2002, pp. 43–49.

190 Gordon found that: Ibid., p. 47.

191 The only time: Ibid.

191 In a 1999 interview: Hans Von Sponeck, interview recorded by Grant Wakefield and Miriam Ryle, the UN building, Baghdad, April 5, 1999, available at http://www.firethistime.org/sponeckinterview.htm.

191 Forced to take: Bossuyt, "Adverse Consequences of Economic Sanctions on the Enjoyment of Human Rights," para. 68, p. 3; Halliday, "Iraq and the UN's Weapon of Mass Destruction," p. 67; for Hans Von Sponeck's remarks, see Agence France-Presse, "UN Aid Coordinator Quits Under US Pressure Over Iraqi Sanctions," February 14, 2000, available at http://www.commondreams.org/headlines/021400-01.htm.

192 Human Rights Watch wrote: Cited in Edwards and Cromwell, "British Liberal Press Target Iraq," p. 3.

195 The Pentagon's response: Ben Cubby, "New, Improved and More Lethal: Son of Napalm," available at http://www.smh.com.au/articles/2003/08/08/1060145828249.html, August 8, 2003; James W. Crawley, "Officials Confirm Dropping Firebombs on Iraqi Troops, Results Are 'Remarkably Similar' to Using Napalm," *The San Diego Union Tribune,* available at http://www/signonsandiego.com/news/military/20030805-9999_1n5bomb.html.

195 According to Damacio: Damacio A. Lopez, Executive Director, International Depleted Uranium Study Team, testimony before the European Parliament, Brussels, Belgium, June 10, 2003, available at http://www.idust.net.

197 When the war ended: *El Pais* (Madrid), May 7, 2003; John Kampfner, "Saving Private Lynch Story 'Flawed'," BBC, London, May 18, 2003; *Los Angeles Times,* May 20, 2003; *New York Times,* June 3, 2003.

197 "She had lost": *El Pais,* May 7, 2003.

198 "It was like": Kampfner, "Saving Private Lynch Story 'Flawed.' "

198 Robert Scheer: Robert Scheer, "Pentagon Aims Guns at Lynch Reports," *The Nation,* posted online on May 30, 2003, http://www.thenation.com/doc.mhtml?!=20030616&s=scheer20030529; and "Saving Private Lynch: Take 2," posted online on May 20, 2003, http://www.thenation.com/doc.mhtml?i=20030602&s=scheer20030520.

198 The OSP was: Seymour M. Hersh, "Selective Intelligence," *The New Yorker,* May 12, 2003.

199 OSP's main: Shaun Waterman, "9/11 Report: No Iraq Link to al-Qaeda," Washington, United Press International, July 23, 2003.

200 "It is clear that": David Corn, "Did Bush Mislead US into War," *The Nation,* June 26, 2003.

201 Perhaps anticipating: David Usborne, "WMD Just a Convenient Excuse for War, Admits Wolfowitz," *The Independent,* May 30, 2003.

201 Writing in April: Cited in Anatol Lieven, "A Trap of Their Own Making," *London Review of Books,* May 8, 2003.

204 His differences with: Eric Rouleau, "The US and World Hegemony, Why Washington Wants Rid of Mr. Boutros-Ghali," *Le Monde Diplomatique,* November 1996; also see Paul Lewis, "Boutros-Ghali's book Says Albright and Clinton Betrayed Him," *New York Times,* May 24, 1999.

205 Kofi Annan's rise: Alexander Cockburn, "Counterpunch Diary—Handmaid in Babylon: Annan, Vierira de Mello and the UN's Decline and Fall," available at http://www.counterpunch.org/cockburn08302003.html.

205 The significance of oil: Cited in Tom Barry, "The U.S. Power Complex: What's New," Interhemispheric Resource Centre, http://www.fpif.org/papers/02power/index.html.

206 *The Guardian* credited: George Monbiot, "Chemical Coup d'etat," *The Guardian* (London), April 16, 2002. Subsequent examples and quotes are taken from Ian Williams, "The US Hit List at the United Nations," April 30, 2002, circulated by Women's Caucus for Gender

Justice, May 7, 2002. Williams is a writer for *Foreign Policy in Focus* and author of *The UN for Beginners* (New York: Writers and Readers Publishing, 1995).

207 When Robin Cook: Cited in Michael J. Glennon, "How War Left the Law Behind," *New York Times*, November 21, 2002.

209 Outraged by the move: Evelyn Leopold, "Bitter Fight with US Leads to Compromises on Court," *Sunday News* (Dar-es-Salaam), July 14, 2002.

209 An Amnesty International: "Amnesty Criticizes US, S. Leone Impunity Deal," *The Monitor* (Kampala, Uganda), May 10, 2003, p. 6.

210 When it came to drafting: Chalmers Johnson, *Blowback: The Costs and Consequences of American Empire* (New York: Henry Holt, 2000), pp. 12–13.

210 Anatol Lieven: Anatol Lieven, "The Push for War," *London Review of Books*, October 3, 2002, pp. 8–11.

212 On February 2, 2002: Joel Greenberg, "Protesting Tactics in West Bank, Israeli Reservists Refuse to Serve," *New York Times*, February 2, 2002.

212 "By what inhuman calculus,": See Edward Said, "What Israel Has Done," *The Nation*, May 6, 2002, pps. 20–23.

213 Particularly illuminating: Told in his own words in the Israeli paper *Yediot Aharonot*, it was subsequently circulated on the Web by the well-known Israeli peace activist Uri Avineri. See Tsadok Yeheskeli, "I made them a stadium in the middle of the camp," *Yediot Aharonot*, May 31, 2002, available at http://www.gush-shalom.org/archives/kurdi_eng.html.

213 In the words of the newspaper: Ibid.

214 The right-wing Israeli newspaper: Peter Beaumont, "Helicopter Pilot 'Refused Order to Blast Palestinian House,' " *The Guardian* (London), April 18, 2002.

214 Amira Hass: Amira Hass, "Vandalnacht: Operation Destroy the Data," *Ha'aretz*, April 24, 2002.

215 In a recent interview: Benny Morris, "Camp David and After: An Exchange (An Interview with Ehud Barak)," *The New York Review of Books* 49, no. 10, June 13, 2002, p. 42.

216 It began with scientific: A. Arnaiz-Villena, N. Elaiwa, C. Silvera, A. Rostom, J. Moscoso, E. Gomez-Casado, L. Allende, P. Varela, and J. Martinez-Laso, "The Origin of Palestinians and Their Genetic Relatedness with Other Mediterranean Populations," *Human Immunology* 62, 2001, pp. 889–900; for the full story, see Robin McKie "Journal axes gene research on Jews and Palestinians," *The Observer* (London), November 25, 2001 and online at http://observer.guardian.co.uk/international/story/0,6903,605798,00.html.

216 In this vein, Alan M. Dershowitz: David Villareal, "Dershowitz Editorial Draws Fire," *The Harvard Crimson* (Cambridge, Mass.), March 18, 2002.

217 The *New York Times* recognized: Joel Greenberg, "Court Says Israel Can Expel 2 of Militant's Kin to Gaza," *New York Times,* September 4, 2002.

218 Here is a composite: Gordon Thomas, "America's Gulag for Iraq's VIP Prisoners," available at http://www.yourmailinglistprovider.com/pubarchive_show_message.php?globeintel+141; "U.S. Closes Notorious Baghdad Prison Camp," *Agence France-Presse,* October 6, 2003 available at http://quickstart.clari.net/qs_se/webnews/wed/dg/Qiraqprison.RADy_DO6.html.

219 Stephen Schwartz's article: Stephen Schwartz, "Ground Zero and the Saudi Connection," *The Spectator,* September 22, 2001.

220 Writing in the *Washington Post:* Sohail H. Hashmi, "Not What the Prophet Would Want: How Can Islamic Scholars Sanction Suicidal Tactics?" *Washington Post,* June 9, 2002.

221 The point of view: Hala Jaber, "Inside the World of the Palestinian Suicide Bomber," *The Times* (London), March 24, 2002.

222 We need to recognize: As a secondary-school student in colonial Uganda, I remember having to memorize Tennyson's poem "The Charge of the Light Brigade." This is what I remember of Tennyson's tribute to the heroism of British soldiers who knowingly went "into the jaws of death": "Cannon to right of them, / Cannon to left of them, / Cannon behind them / Volley'd and thunder'd; . . . Into the jaws of Death, / Into the mouth of Hell / Rode the six hundred."

223 The Kookist movement: This section draws from Armstrong, *The Battle for God,* pp. 261–63, 281–87, 345–49. My conclusion, though, differs from that of Armstrong, who tends to equate the religious right with religious fundamentalism and all forms of the religious right with political terrorism.

224 The Gush supplied 20 percent: Every possibility of peace pits the Gush against secularists in government. The first such possibility followed Anwar Sadat's historic journey to Jerusalem in 1977 and the signing of the Camp David Accords between Begin and Sadat the following year. To comply with the accords, Israel decided to evacuate the settlement of Yamit in Sinai. Moshe Levinger declared that Zionism had been infected by the "virus of peace" and led thousands of settlers back to Yamit. Levinger "reminded the settlers of the Jewish wars against Rome during which 960 men, women and children had committed suicide in the fortress of Masada rather than submit to the Roman army. But when consulted by Gush

rabbis, Israel's two chief rabbis 'ruled against martyrdom.' " Lev-inger tore his garments in mourning. See Armstrong, *Battle for God,* pp. 66–72, 287. The second possibility for peace followed the first Palestinian intifada (1987) and the signing of a second accord at Camp David, in which Israel promised to evacuate part of the West Bank; the Gush were enraged.

224 A recent Israeli human-rights: For figures on the number of settlers over the decades, see Saeb Erekat, "Saving the Two-State Solution," *The New York Times,* December 20, 2002. There are two contrast-ing figures for the number of settlers in the West Bank: 220,000 as against roughly 400,000. The lower count excludes Israeli settlers in Palestinian East Jerusalem, on grounds that since it has been legally incorporated into the state of Israel, the Israelis who move into it cannot be counted as settlers. The result is a restricted count of Is-raelis settled in *the rest of the West Bank,* that which is *forcibly oc-cupied* by Israel, but excluding Palestinian East Jerusalem which is *forcibly incorporated* into Israel.

224 According to Amira: Amira Hass, "No End to the Growing Settle-ments Insult," *Ha'aretz,* July 2, 2003.

225 Palestinian Homes: Jeff Halper, coordinator, Israeli Committee against House Demolitions, "A Test of the Road Map," July 29, 2003 available at http://www.icahd.org/eng/articles.asp?menu=6&submenu =2&article=125. Like any rogue state, Israel, too, claims that sover-eignty is a limitless license to trample on citizens' rights.

226 Second, the spread: There is a parallel with the Palestinian situation, in which not only has Arafat been able to build nine different security agencies with American help—as, indeed, have other Arab autocracies—but that the very helplessness of these agencies in the face of the Israeli onslaught has given rise to a militarism from below, in the form of street gangs. Hanan Ashrawi's comments on this are illuminating: "Of course, there have been different cultures at work here. There is a culture of militarisation, a culture of revolu-tion." Ashrawi contrasts the history of prewar Palestine, long before Israel was conceived, as "a center of enlightenment" in the region and argues that militarism has been fueled from two sources: from "among the people who came back from exile to set up a govern-ment" and from among those on the street who found this govern-ment unable to protect them against settler encroachment. See Avi Machlis and James Drummond, "Colliding Cultures Hamper the Palestinian Road to Democracy," *Financial Times* (Johannesburg), June 28, 2002.

226 ANC president Oliver Tambo: Anthony Sampson, *Mandela, The Authorized Biography* (New York: Alfred A. Knopf, 1999), p. 350.

227 The final lesson: From this point of view, it is instructive to recall the short history of suicide bombing in Lebanon and the conditions that led to its cessation. Hizbullah pioneered suicide bombings in Lebanon following the 1983 Israeli occupation. Islamic Resistance (al-Muqawamah al-Islamiyyah), created by Hizbullah in 1983—and comprising members who were combatants in time of need, returning to normal occupations when not required—claimed responsibility for numerous suicide bombings against the U.S. embassy and the U.S. and French military compounds and was credited with prompting the withdrawal of the Multi-National Forces (MNF) in 1984. At the same time, it was the Israeli withdrawal in 1985 that created the political conditions for an end to suicide bombing in Lebanon. See Nizar Hamzeh, "Lebanon's Hezbullah: From Islamic Revolution to Parliamentary Accommodation," *Third World Quarterly* 14, no. 2, 1993, pp. 2, 8.

Conclusion: Beyond Impunity and Collective Punishment

229 Notwithstanding: Salman Rushdie, "This is About Islam," *New York Times,* November 2, 2001.

232 Under his leadership: See Truth and Reconciliation Commission of South Africa, *Report,* vol. 2, p. 30, para. 124.

233 The first was when guerrillas: Deborah Poole and Gerardo Rénique, "Terror and the Privatized State: A Peruvian Parable," *Radical History Review* (winter 2003), pp. 150–63.

234 The best-known CIA-trained terrorist: Arundhati Roy, "The Algebra of Infinite Justice," *The Guardian* (London), September 27, 2001.

234 Bin Laden was not the only: Three days after 9/11, the Revolutionary Association of the Women of Afghanistan (RAWA) issued a public statement expressing "sorrow and condemnation for this barbaric act of violence and terror" and then added:

> But unfortunately we must say that it was the government of the United States who supported Pakistani dictator Gen. Zia ul-Haq in creating thousands of religious schools from which the germs of Taliban emerged. In the similar way, as is clear to all, Osama Bin Laden has been the blue-eyed boy of [the] CIA. But what is more painful is that American politicians have not drawn a lesson from their pro-fundamentalist policies in our country and are still supporting this or that fundamentalist band or leader. "RAWA Statement on the Terrorist Attacks in the US,"

September 14, 2001, available at http://www.globalresearch
.ca/articles/RAW109A.html.

235 The bomb was made of: Cooley, *Unholy Wars,* pp. 223, 236–37, 243, 245.

235 In 1995, the former CIA director: Alfred McCoy, "Drug Fallout: The CIA's Forty Year Complicity in the Narcotics Trade," *The Progressive,* August 1, 1997.

235 By mid-1971, U.S. army: McCoy, *The Politics of Heroin,* pp. 222–23.

236 During the Afghan jihad: McCoy, "Drug Fallout."

236 As heroin from Afghanistan: McCoy, *Politics of Heroin,* p. 437.

236 Between 1982 and 1985: Ibid., p. 478.

236 On October 4: Alexander Cockburn and Jeffrey St. Clair, *Whiteout: The CIA, Drugs, and the Press* (London: Verso, 1998), pp. 1–2, 37.

237 Alfred McCoy, whose example: U.S. Central Intelligence Agency, Office of the Inspector General, "Allegations of Connections Between CIA and Contras in Cocaine Trafficking in the United States" (1) (96-0143-IG). All quotations cited in Alfred W. McCoy, " 'Fallout': The Interplay of CIA Covert Warfare and the Global Narcotics Traffic," paper presented to the conference Civil War and Cold War, 1975–1990: A Comparative Analysis of Southern Africa, Central America, and Central Asia (Institute of African Studies, Columbia University, New York, N.Y., November 13–15, 2002, mimeograph), pp. 24–25.

238 Cooley cites the case: Cooley, *Unholy Wars,* p. 134.

239 Even in the German case: Sheldon Wolin, "Inverted Totalitarianism," *The Nation,* May 19, 2003.

241 In 1997, Feith wrote: For more on the lobby, see "The Israeli Lobby," *Prospect Magazine* (Britain), no. 73, April 2002, p. 3.

243 As Paul Finkelman: Paul Finkelman, *Dred Scott v. Sandford: A Brief History with Documents* (Boston: Bedford Books, 1997), p. 34. Also see Don E. Fehrenbacher, *The Dred Scott Case: Its Significance in American Law and Practice* (New York: Oxford University Press, 1978).

243 The idea of a single Judeo-Christian: It is worth recalling that the identification of the state and the nation with white settlers provoked two different kinds of movements: one called for a looser definition of the notion of whites so that Jews, Asians, and so on could become white; the other called for an end to white privilege, however defined.

245 Here, for example: *New York Times,* December 3, 2002.

247 Only Har'aretz, has had: Amira Hass, "The Misleading Term 'Fence,' " *Ha'aretz,* July 16, 2003.

250 The British and American response: David Keen, "Blair's Good Guys in Sierra Leone," *The Guardian* (London), November 7, 2001.

252 Those who survived: See "Afghanistan" in *Landmine Monitor Report, 2001,* available at http://www.icbl.org/lm/2001/afghanistan/.

256 In letters from: Quoted in Gore Vidal, *Perpetual War for Perpetual Peace: How We Got to Be So Hated* (New York: Nation Books, 2002), pp. ix, 81, 84–85.

258 *The Guardian* (London) reported: Ian Traynor, "The Privatization of War $30 Billion Goes to Private Military; Fears Over 'Hired Guns' Policy," *The Guardian,* December 10, 2003.

Index

Abedi, Agha Hassan, 146, 147, 148–9
Abouhalima, Mahmud, 139, 234
Abourezk, James, 83
Abrams, Elliott, 108
Abu Nidal group, 147
Adham, Kamal, 149
Afghanistan, 91, 100; Communist takeover in 1978, 125; invasion of 2001, 133, 183, 229–30; Taliban's rise to power, 159–63, 176–7
Afghan jihad (Afghan War): BCCI and, 146–9; beginning of U.S. support for mujahideen, 123–4; bin Laden's role, 132–3; costs to Afghanistan, 252; cost to United States for its embrace of terror, 234–6, 238; drug trade and, 140–6, 235–6; financing of, 140–9; Islamist terror, connection to, 131, 138–40, 163–9, 177; Israeli role, 275–6n; jihad status, 127–8; 9/11 terrorist attacks and, 131; number of Islamic radicals in, 137–8, 277n; Pakistan, effect on, 149–53; political differences among Islamists, 153–63; recruitment of radical Islamists for, 126–7, 131–5; refugee camps, 145; revolutions of 1979 and, 120–3; right-wing Islamism fostered by, 129–30; "rollback" policy and, 119–20, 124; scope of, 120; training of Islamic fighters, 136–8; U.S. blueprint for, 130–1; U.S. objectives, 124, 128–9; U.S.-Pakistani relations and, 125–6

Index

Afghan National Liberation Front, 156
Africa in Eurocentric history, 31
African National Congress (ANC), 226, 228
African Origin of Civilization, The (Diop), 31
Africa Watch, 91
Aguado, Marcos, 107
Ahmad, Eqbal, 119, 161, 162–3, 176
Akhundzada, Mullah Nasim, 144–5, 156
al-Afghani, Jamal al-Din, 45–6, 48–9, 56
al-Banna, Hassan, 48–9, 56, 167
Albright, Madeleine, 190, 203, 207
al-Fadl, Jamal, 133
al-Faisal, Prince Turk, 132
Algeria, 126, 132, 172–3; Islamist terror in, 164–6
al-Hamidi, Sheikh Muhammed, 135
Ali, Tariq, 138, 276n
al-Kifah Afghan Refugee Center, 135
al-Mahdi (Muhammad Ahmed), 52–3
Al-Moravid movement, 51
al-Qaeda, 13, 147, 168, 177; creation of, 133; Iraq, alleged link to, 198, 199–200; Taliban and, 162; United States, similarity to, 257–8
al-Zawahri, Ayman, 167–8
Amal, 172
Americas Watch, 102
Amidror, Gen. Ya'akov, 201
Amin, Samir, 27, 265n, 267n
Ammash, Hudda, 218
Amnesty International, 209, 217, 218

Angola, 13, 100, 251; civil war, 70, 77–80, 83, 89–90, 91
Anidjar, Gil, 26
Annan, Kofi, 205
Arab civilizational history, 33–4
Arendt, Hannah, 6, 9
Armed Islamic Group, 165, 166
Armstrong, Karen, 38, 39, 61
Arnaiz-Villena, Antonio, 216
Ashrawi, Hanan, 286n
Aziz, Tariq, 181, 218
Azzam, Sheikh Abdullah, 126–7, 133, 135, 234

Bank of Credit and Commerce International (BCCI), 146–9
Bank of England, 147, 148
Barak, Ehud, 215
Battle of Algiers, The (film), 233
Bazargan, Mehdi, 121
Begin, Menachem, 223, 249
Beit-Hallahmi, Benjamin, 111
Belgium, 70, 71, 73
Bendjedid, Chadli, 165
Bennoune, Mahfoud, 140, 165
Berbers, 33–4, 51
Bernal, Martin, 27, 31–2
Bernard, St., 26
Bhutto, Benazir, 139, 150
Bhutto, Zulfiqar Ali, 121, 126
bin Laden, Osama, 127, 151, 166, 167, 220, 234, 253–4, 287n; Afghan jihad, 132–3; al-Qaeda, 133; Taliban and, 162
bin Laden family, 132
Black Athena (Bernal), 31–2
Blair, Tony, 24
Blix, Hans, 193
Bob Jones University, 41
Boland Amendment, 104–5, 115, 234
bombing, 7; in Afghanistan,

229–30; in Gulf War, 183–4; peacetime bombing of Iraq, 185
Bonner, Arthur, 144
Book of Jerry Falwell, The (Harding), 40–1
Boubacar, Barry, 265–6n
Boutros-Ghali, Boutros, 203–5
Brandeis, Louis, 256
Brazil, 188, 206
Brezhnev, Leonid, 80
Bryan, William Jennings, 39–40
Brzezinski, Zbigniew, 123–4, 141
Buchanan, Patrick, 44
Buckley, William, 113
Bulliet, Richard, 173–4
Burghardt, Jutta, 192
Burma, 67, 143
Bush I administration, 184
Bush II administration, 12, 15, 24, 44, 124, 179, 253; international rule of law, dispensing with, 202–3, 209, 210–11; Iraq/Middle East policy, 196–202; Israeli lobby and, 241; religious language in political discourse, 254. *see also* war on terror
Bustani, Jose Mauricio, 204, 206–7

Cambodia, 91, 100, 209–10
Camp Cropper, 217–18
Canada, 188, 209
Carter administration, 44, 86, 111, 123–4, 125–6, 140–1
Casey, William J., 87, 100, 129, 149, 238
Castle Bank, 147
Central Intelligence Agency (CIA), 199; Afghan jihad, 123–48 *passim,* 155, 157, 158, 163, 235; Angolan civil war, 90;

BCCI and, 147–9; Congolese civil wars, 71, 72, 74, 76; contra war, 100–1, 102, 103, 105, 106, 111, 116, 117, 236–7; coordination problems with U.S. agencies, 238; drug trade and, 67–9, 105, 106, 107, 141–4, 145–6, 235, 236–7, 238, 273n; Islamist terror, role in initiating, 163, 169; Laos proxy war, 65, 68–9; Pakistan and, 150–1; terrorism training for proxy forces, 116; Vietnam War, 65
Césaire, Aimé, 8
CFB company, 80
Chaker, Salem, 34
Chalabi, Ahmad, 199
chemical weapons, 122, 181, 182
Cheney, Dick, 210
China, 66, 67, 130
Christianity: fundamentalism in, 36, 38–44; Islam as enemy of, 25–6. *see also* political Christianity
Christian Voice, 42, 109
Church, Frank, 71
Clark, Dick, 82–3, 98
Clark, Ramsey, 184, 207–8
Clark Amendment, 63, 70, 80, 81–4, 87, 90, 234
Clarridge, Duane, 102
"Clash of Civilizations?, The" (Huntington), 20–1
Cleland, Max, 199–200
Clinton administration, 133, 160, 185, 203, 238
Coalition for Jewish Concerns, 245
Cockburn, Alexander, 205
Cogan, Charles, 235
Colby, William, 78–9

Cold War: defined, 12; nationalism equated with Soviet expansion, 70; 9/11 terrorist attacks and, 13; political Islam and, 14; "rollback" policy, 12–13, 95–7, 100; "United States held responsible for its actions" issue, 250–3, 255. *see also* proxy wars

collateral damage, 88, 91, 183, 184

collective punishment: Iraq sanctions regime as, 179, 180–1, 185–94; logic behind, 217; of Palestinians by Israel, 212–17

colonialism, *see* imperialism

Committee of Santa Fe, 96

Concerned Women for America, 110

Congolese civil wars, 70–6, 85, 251

Congress, U.S., 65, 77–8; proxy wars, legislation regarding, 77, 80, 81–4, 87, 90, 104–5

constructive engagement, 13, 92–5, 96

contra war, 13, 98; CIA command of, 100–1; cost to United States for its embrace of terror, 236–7; drug trade and, 105–9, 236–7; financing of, 101, 104–5, 110, 112–13, 115; formation of contra force, 100–1; Iran-contra scandal, 99, 112–15; Israeli involvement, 111, 114; lessons for U.S. policymakers, 123; Noriega's involvement, 108–9; political Christianity and, 109–10; public-relations effort on behalf of contras, 102–3, 115; sabotage operations, 103–4; terrorism in, 101–2,

116–18; U.S. "rollback" policy and, 100

Cook, Robin, 207

Cooley, John, 134, 135, 136, 138, 165, 169, 177, 235, 238, 275–6*n*, 277*n*

Copernicus, 30

counterinsurgency, 88, 97, 231–2

crime/terrorism distinction, 229–30

Crocker, Chester, 92

Crusades, 25–6, 50, 51

Cruz, Arturo, 101

Cuba, 78, 79, 86, 100

Culture Talk, 11; clash of civilizations, 4, 20–2, 24–7, 61; good Muslim/bad Muslim concept, 15–16, 22–4, 260; Islam and, 18–19, 20–7; politicization of culture, 17–18, 27–36; premodern peoples and, 18–20; racial branding of Arabs, 215–16; terrorism and, 219–21; two versions of, 20

Dahlburg, John-Thor, 165, 166

Daily, Col. Mike, 195

Dallaire, Gen. Romeo, 205

Darrow, Clarence, 39–40

Darwin, Charles, 262*n*

Daud, Mohammad, 125

Dayan, Gen. Moshe, 85

Deaver, Michael K., 196

Debray, Régis, 21

Defense Intelligence Agency (DIA), 102, 199

democracy: imperialism and, 239; international rule of law and, 202–3, 211; political Islam and, 172–5

democratic despotism, 246–7

depleted uranium (DU) weapons, 195–6
Dershowitz, Alan M., 216
Deutsch, John, 236
Diamond, Sara, 110
dictatorships, 96, 259–60
"Dictatorships and Double Standards" (Kirkpatrick), 96
Diop, Cheikh Anta, 27, 31, 265n
Discourse on Colonialism (Césaire), 8
Dole, Robert, 90
Drug Enforcement Administration (DEA), 106, 142, 238
Drugs, Law Enforcement, and *Foreign Policy* (report), 106–7
drug trade: Afghan jihad and, 140–6, 235–6; CIA and, 67–9, 105, 106, 107, 141–4, 145–6, 235, 236–7, 238, 273n; contra war and, 105–9, 236–7; imperialism and, 66; Pakistan and, 142–3, 152–3; proxy wars and, 66–9
Dulles, Allen, 71

Eagleton, Thomas, 83
Educational Center for Afghanistan, 136–7
Egypt, 48–9, 56, 121, 126, 130, 132, 209; Eurocentric history and, 31–2; Islamist terror in, 167–9; Safari Club, 84, 85
Egyptian Islamic Group, 135
Eisenhower administration, 71
El Salvador, 104, 110–11
Escobar, Pablo, 105
Ethiopia, 86, 100
Eurocentric history, 28–33, 35–6
European Union, 209
evangelical movement, 41–2
Exxon-Mobil, 206

Fadlallah, Sheikh, 172
Falwell, Jerry, 42–3, 44, 47, 93, 232, 245
Fanon, Frantz, 8, 9–10
Federal Bureau of Investigation (FBI), 238
Feith, Douglas J., 196, 241
feminism, 43, 173–4
Fiers, Alan, 108
Finkelman, Paul, 243
Fischer, Eugen, 8
Ford administration, 77, 78–9, 80
Fox, Robert, 238
France, 33, 66, 73, 80, 139, 164, 242; Safari Club, 84, 85
French Revolution, 3, 36
Friedman, Thomas, 184
Front for National Liberation of Angola (FNLA), 77, 78
Front for the Liberation of Mozambique (Frelimo), 89
fundamentalism: in Christianity, 36, 38–44; Islam and, 36–7; modernity and, 39, 40–1; as political category, 37

Galster, Steve, 141
Garfield, Richard, 188, 189
Gates, Robert, 123
genocide, 10; Crusades and, 25–6; imperialism and, 6–8, 262n; Iraq sanctions regime as, 180–1, 186–92; preemptive war and, 211; terrorism and, 11
Ghorbanifar, Manucher, 149
Gleijeses, Piero, 72, 73, 75, 76, 77, 78
global movement for peace, need for, 258
Gonzalez, Sebastian, 108
good Muslim/bad Muslim concept, 15–16, 22–4, 260

Index

Gordon, Gen. Charles, 53
Gordon, Joy, 190, 194
Gospel Outreach church, 109–10
Gottlieb, Sidney, 71
Graham, Billy, 42
Great Britain, 52–3, 66, 80, 130, 185, 187, 242, 250
Greek civilization, 32
Grenada, 100
"Ground Zero and the Saudi Connection" (Schwartz), 219–20
Guatemala, 109–10, 111
guerrilla/terrorist distinction, 233
Guide of the Perplexed, The (Maimonides), 26
Gulf Oil Cabinda, 80
Gulf War, 167, 179, 180, 182, 183–4, 194–6, 204
Gulf War Syndrome, 182
Gush Emunim, 223, 224

Haider, Iftikar, 151–2
Haig, Alexander, 96
Halliday, Denis, 192
Halper, Jeff, 225
Hamas, 121, 127, 171, 274–5n
Hammadi, Saadium, 218
Hammoud, Muhammad, 148
Hampton-el, Claments Rodney, 139
Haq, Gen. Fazle, 142
Harding, Susan, 40–1
Harkat ul-Ansar, 151
Hashmi, Sohail, 220–1
Hass, Amira, 214–15, 224–5, 248
Hassan II, king of Morocco, 85
Hegel, G. W. F., 3
Heikal, Mohamed, 84, 87
Helms, Richard, 149
Herero people, 6, 8
Heritage Foundation, 90, 100

Herman, Jane, 200
Hersh, Seymour M., 198–9
Hikmatyar, Gulbuddin, 143–4, 145–6, 155–6, 157, 158, 159
Hiro, Dilip, 136
History of Bombing, A (Lindqvist), 7
history writing, 27–8
Hitz, Frederick, 236–7
Hizb-i-Islami, 144, 156, 157–8
Hizbullah, 171–2, 174, 175, 287n
Hoare, Col. Mike, 75
Hodgson, Marshall, 27, 29, 30
Holbrooke, Richard, 205
Holocaust, 4, 6, 7–8, 10
Hoodbhoy, Pervez, 137
Hoskins, Eric, 184
Hughes, Harold, 83
Hughes-Ryan Amendment, 77
Hull, John, 106–7
Human Rights Watch, 192
Hunter, Jane, 113
Huntington, Samuel, 20–1, 22, 24, 27, 231
Hussein, Saddam, 122, 179, 180, 181, 182, 183, 220
Hyde, Alan, 237

ijtihad, 48, 60–1, 175
illegal combatants, 257
Ilyas, Maulana Mohammad, 134
imperialism: civilizing mission, 245–7; colonial wars, 7; democracy and, 239; drug trade and, 66; genocide and, 6–8, 262n; international rule of law and, 202; native violence in response to, 8–10; political Islam and, 45–6, 47–8. see also settler colonialism
independent thought, right to, 254
India, 47–8, 53, 151–2, 209

Indonesia, 121, 126, 131
International Court of Justice, 196
International Criminal Court
  (ICC), 208–9
international rule of law, U.S.
  disregard for, 202–11, 256–7
international tribunals, 208–10
Inter Services Intelligence (ISI),
  126, 130, 142, 144, 145–6, 148,
  150–1, 154, 158, 159
Iqbal, Muhammad, 47, 48, 53, 54,
  59, 61, 171, 268*n*
Iran, 47, 100; Hizbullah and, 171,
  172; Israel, relations with,
  111–12; political process in,
  173–4; religious government,
  58; Safari Club, 84, 86. *see also*
  Iraq-Iran War
Iran-contra scandal, 99, 112–15
Iranian Revolution, 12, 120, 121–2
Iraq, 252; al-Qaeda, alleged link
  to, 198, 199–200; Gulf War,
  179, 180, 182, 183–4, 194–6;
  humanitarian crisis of 1990s,
  180–1, 186–92; invasion of
  2003, 24, 180, 196–202, 207,
  217–18, 258–60; peacetime
  bombing of, 185; propaganda
  war against, 196–201; sanctions
  against, 179, 180–1, 185–94,
  281*n*; U.S. alliance with, 122,
  180, 181–3; weapons of mass
  destruction program, 181, 182,
  184–5, 186, 193–4, 198–201,
  206; weapons of mass
  destruction used against, 194–6.
  see also Iraq-Iran War
Iraqi National Congress, 199
Iraq-Iran War, 111–12, 122, 180,
  181, 182–3
Iraq Survey Group, 201
Islam: as Christianity's enemy,

25–6; Culture Talk and, 18–19,
  20–7; fundamentalism and,
  36–7; modernity and, 19. *see
  also* Islamist terror; jihad;
  political Islam
Islamic Jihad, 172
Islamic Rescue Organization, 166
Islamic Resistance, 171–2, 287*n*
Islamic Salvation Front (FIS), 164,
  165, 166, 174
Islamist terror: Afghan jihad,
  connection to, 131, 138–40,
  163–9, 177; in Algeria, 164–6;
  CIA's role in initiating, 163, 169;
  as cultural concept, 17–18; in
  Egypt, 167–9; ideological,
  organizational, and political
  elements, 169–70; political
  Islam and, 38, 170–1; rule of
  law's breakdown and, 176–7;
  suicide bombings, 219–22, 225,
  285*n*, 286–7*n*; terrorist profile,
  177, 221–2; theoretical roots of,
  61; war on terror, common
  ground with, 230. *see also* 9/11
  terrorist attacks
Israel, 49, 85, 109, 121, 130, 205,
  209; Afghan jihad, 275–6*n*;
  Central American proxy wars,
  involvement in, 110–11, 114;
  democratic despotism, 246–7;
  genocide fears, 10; Hamas and,
  121, 274*n*; Iran, relations with,
  111–12; Iran-contra scandal,
  112–13, 114–15; political
  Christianity and, 245; religious
  Zionism, rise of, 248–9;
  returning Jews/settlers issue,
  244–5; state terrorism by,
  212–15, 222–5, 247–8; United
  States, special relationship
  with, 240–6

Israeli-Palestinian conflict: collective punishment of Palestinians, 212–17; equal citizenship issue, 228; Hizbullah and, 171–2; intifadas, 121, 225; militarism among Palestinians and, 286n; political Islam and, 121; settler movement, 222–5, 285–6n; suicide bombings, 221–2, 225; U.S. policy regarding, 211–12, 213; wall constructed by Israel, 247–8

Jalal, Ayesha, 267–8n
Jamaat-e-Ulema-Islam (JUI), 150
Jamaat-i-Islami, 54, 121
Jamiat-i-Islami (Afghanistan), 156, 157
Jam'iyat-i-Ulama-i-Hind, 53
Jassim, Adnan, 218
Javits, Jacob, 82
Jenin, Israeli assault on, 212–15
Jews, 5, 15; Arab culture and, 26–7; Holocaust, 4, 6, 7–8, 10; post-Holocaust history and, 35–6. *see also* Israel
jihad: Communism and, 57–8; history of armed jihad, 51–3; Mawdudi's views on, 53–5; political Islam and, 50–8; profiles of fighters, 139, 151–2; Qutb's views on, 55–8; two traditions of, 50, 127–8, 269n. *see also* Afghan jihad
Jinnah, Mohammed Ali, 47, 48, 59
Johnson administration, 64–6
Jones, Bob, 41
Judeo-Christian tradition, 35–6, 243–4

Kampfner, John, 198
Kashmir, 151, 152

Katzenbach, Nicholas, 76
Kelly, J. Michael, 99
Kennedy, Edward, 81
Kennedy administration, 71–2
Kerry, John, 106, 148
Khalil, Abdul Raouf, 149
Khalis faction, 157, 158
Khan, Sayyid Ahmed, 267–8n
Khashoggi, Adnan, 149
Kherbane, Kamerredin, 166
Khomeini, Ayatollah, 47, 58, 121, 122, 269n
Kirkpatrick, Jeanne, 96, 100, 252, 259
Kissinger, Henry, 70, 78, 79, 80, 84, 87, 115, 178
Kookist movement, 223
Korea, North, 260
Kosovo War, 183, 207
Kristof, Nicholas D., 181
Kuhn, Thomas, 30
Kurds, 184, 187

land mines, 91
Lang, W. Patrick, 199
Laos, 100, 101; bombing of, 183; proxy war in, 64, 65–6, 68–9
Laroui, Abdallah, 27, 265n
Lashkar-i-Tayyaba, 151
Laws, Curtis Lee, 38
Lebanon, 171–2, 286–7n
Levinger, Moshe, 285–6n
Lewis, Bernard, 20, 22–5, 26, 27, 46, 169
Liberia, 244, 245–6
Libya, 100
Lieven, Anatol, 210
Lifschultz, Lawrence, 142
Lind, William, 21
Lindh, John Walker, 257
Lindqvist, Sven, 7, 262n
Livingstone, Neil, 99

Lopez, Damacio, 195
Lord's Resistance Army (LRA), 251
low-intensity conflict (LIC), 12, 88, 95, 97–100, 178, 186–7
Lumumba, Patrice, 71
Luti, William, 199
Lyell, Charles, 262n
Lynch, Pvt. Jessica, 197–8

MacMichael, David, 117
madrassahs, 136–8, 151
Mahdist revolt, 52–3
Maimonides, Moses, 26
Malan, Gen. Magnus, 88, 232
Mandela, Winnie, 226
Mansur, Ahmed, 276n
maps, 28
marabout, 51–2
Marcus, Yo'el, 113
Marenches, Claude Alexandre de, 84
Mark-77 firebombs, 194–5
Markaz-ud-Daawa-Wal-Irshad, 152
Marshall, Jonathan, 113
Marshall Plan, 250
Massoud, Ahmed Shah, 157, 159
Mastnak, Tomaž, 25–6, 50
Mawdudi, Abdul A'la, 47, 53–5, 59, 61, 163, 167
McCoy, Alfred, 66–7, 69, 101, 105, 141, 142, 143, 235, 237, 273n
McFarlane, Robert, 105
McVeigh, Timothy, 255–6, 257
Medellín cartel, 105
Meese, Edwin, 114
Menses, Norman, 107
Meselson, Matthew, 181
Messaoudi, Aisa, 166
Milestones (Qutb), 56, 58, 59–60
Miller, Christopher, 29

Minter, William, 92
Miranda, Enrique, 107
Mobutu, Joseph, 71, 72, 76, 77, 78, 85
modernity: fundamentalism and, 39, 40–1; Islam and, 19; violence and, 4–8
Montt, Gen. Efrain Ríos, 109–10
Moon, Sun Myung, 110
Morales, George, 106
Moral Majority, 42–3, 109
Morgenthau, Robert, 148
Morocco, 33–4, 84, 90
Morris, Benny, 215
Mossad, 111
Mourad, Si Ahmad, 166
Movement of the Islamic Revolution, 156
Mozambique, 13, 251; civil war, 89–90, 91, 93–4
Muldergate scandal, 92–3
Mulele, Pierre, 72
Musil, Robert, 194–5
Musto, David, 140–1, 236

Nasser, Gamal Abdel, 49, 56, 121
National Association of Evangelicals (NAE), 41–2
National Islamic Front of Afghanistan, 156
National Logistics Cell (NLC), 142
Native Americans, 6, 246, 256
native violence, 8–10
Nazism, 7–8, 239
necklacing, 225–7
Neier, Aryeh, 19
Netanyahu, Benyamin, 241
Neugebauer, Otto, 30
Nicaragua, 12, 111. *see also* contra war

Nicaraguan Association for Human Rights, 102
Nicaraguan Freedom Fund, 110
Nicaraguan Humanitarian Aid Office (NHAO), 108
9/11 terrorist attacks, 11, 15, 230, 255; Afghan jihad and, 131; Cold War and, 13
Nissim, Moshe, 213
Nixon Doctrine, 63, 64, 69–70, 178
Noriega, Manuel, 108–9
Nortex company, 108
North, Col. Oliver, 99, 100, 103, 105, 106, 107–9, 110, 113–14
Nzongola-Ntalaja, Georges, 71

Ochoa, Jorge, 105
Office of Special Plans, 198–9
Office of Strategic Influence, 196–7
oil industry, 160, 205–6
Oklahoma City bombing, 255–6
Organization for the Prohibition of Chemical Weapons (OPCW), 204, 206–7
Orientalism (Said), 32
Owen, Robert, 108

Pakistan, 122, 129, 138, 176, 249, 287n; Afghan jihad and, 125–6, 149–53, 154–5, 158–9; Communist takeover in Afghanistan and, 125; drug trade and, 142–3, 152–3; formation of, 47–8, 53–4; jihadi culture, 149–53; Taliban and, 159, 161; United States, relations with, 125–6. *see also* Inter Services Intelligence
Palestine Liberation Organization (PLO), 121, 171

Palestinians, *see* Israeli-Palestinian conflict
Palmer, Michael, 108
Pan African Congress, 227
Panama, 108–9
Pao, Gen. Vang, 68, 69
Pastora, Eden, 106
Peay, Gen. J. H. Binford, 140
Peres, Shimon, 113
Perle, Richard, 124, 199, 210, 211, 241
Peru, 233
Philippines, 104, 130, 209
Pillsbury, Michael, 148
Poindexter, John, 108, 114
political Christianity, 36, 47; contra war and, 109–10; evangelical movement, 41–2; fundamentalists' initial avoidance of politics, 39–41; influence of, 43–4; Israel and, 245; new Christian right, birth of, 42–3; South Africa and, 93
political Islam, 37; Afghan jihad's fostering of right-wing Islamism, 129–30; Cold War and, 14; democracy and, 172–5; European imperialism, reaction to, 45–6, 47–8; Islamist terror and, 38, 170–1; jihad and, 50–8; as modern phenomenon, 175; multiple directions of, 37–8, 59, 170; pioneers of, 47; radicalization of, 48–50, 58–9; religious orientation, 58; secular orientation, 46–8, 267n; seizure of state power, focus on, 53–5, 59–60; sharia law and, 60–1, 174–5; society-centered and state-centered movements, 38, 122, 170, 176, 279n; U.S.

change in attitude toward,
120–2
Political Talk, 219
politicization of culture, 17–18,
27–36
Politics of Heroin, The (McCoy),
66–7
Popular Movement for the
Liberation of Angola (MPLA),
70, 77, 78
Powell, Colin, 206, 207, 210, 211
preemptive war, 211
premodern peoples, 18–20
press freedom, erosion of,
239–40
*Principle of Human Heredity and
Race Hygiene, The* (Fischer), 8
propaganda programs, 196–201
proxy wars, 12–13; Angolan civil
war, 70, 77–80, 83, 89–90, 91;
Congolese civil wars, 70–6, 85;
constructive engagement and,
92–5; counterinsurgency and,
88, 97; drug trade and, 66–9;
"ethical" defense of, 98;
financing of, 66–9; Gulf War,
179, 180; Iraq invasion of 2003,
258–9; in Laos, 64, 65–6, 68–9;
legislation regarding, 77, 80,
81–4, 87, 90, 104–5; low-
intensity conflict and, 12, 88,
95, 97–100, 178; Mozambican
civil war, 89–90, 91, 93–4;
origin of U.S. policy, 64, 65–6,
69–70, 81; Reagan policy of, 98;
Safari Club and, 84–7; Somalia-
Ethiopia War, 85–6; South
African role in U.S. policy, 87–8;
terrorism and, 87, 88; U.S. civil
institutions undermined by
proxy-war policy, 99–100. *see
also* Afghan jihad; contra war

Qaradawi, Sheikh Yusuf, 220
Qutb, Sayyid, 47, 49, 50, 53,
55–60, 61, 163, 167

Rabbani, Burhaneddin, 157, 159
Rabin, Yitzhak, 85
racial branding of Arabs, 215–16
Rahman, Sheikh Omar Abdel,
135, 234
Rashid, Ahmed, 132, 137, 138,
155, 161, 162
Rasul, Mohammed, 145
Razak, Saad Abdul, 197
Reagan, John Joseph, 145
Reagan administration, 178; CIA
involvement in drug trade, 238;
constructive-engagement policy,
92–5, 96; Iraq and, 181; legacy
of, 211; political Christianity
and, 44; proxy-war policy, 98;
"rollback" policy, 12–13, 95–7,
100, 119–20, 124. *see also*
Afghan jihad; contra war
Reagan Doctrine, 97–8
religious language in political
discourse, dangers of, 254
Renamo, 89–90, 91, 92, 93–4, 101,
102, 117, 271*n*
Renan, Ernest, 35–6, 45
Rendon Group, 196, 197
Revolutionary Association of the
Women of Afghanistan, 287*n*
Rhodesia, 89, 94
Ricci, Matteo, 28
Rice, Condoleezza, 253
Ritter, Scott, 193
Robelo, José, 108
Robertson, Pat, 47, 109, 110, 245
Robinson, Mary, 204, 205
Rockefeller family, 70, 271*n*
"rollback" policy, 12–13, 95–7,
100, 119–20, 124

"Roots of Muslim Rage, The"
(Lewis), 20, 22
Rose, Edward, 73
Roy, Arundhati, 234, 277*n*
Roy, Olivier, 279*n*
Rubin, Barnett, 145, 156, 158
Rudman, Warren B., 100
Rumsfeld, Donald, 181, 196, 199
Rushdie, Salman, 229
Rusk, Dean, 73
Rwanda, 204–5, 251

Sacramento Union, 93
Sadat, Anwar, 85, 121, 167, 204
Sadiqi, Fatima, 33
Safari Club, 84–7
Said, Edward, 22, 27, 32, 212–13
Saiman, Qays Al, 218
Saladin, 51
Salisbury, Lord, 6
Sarekat-i-Islam, 121
Saudi Arabia, 52, 105, 122, 126,
128, 129, 130, 132, 141, 158,
176; BCCI and, 149; Safari
Club, 84; terrorism in, 140
Savimbi, Jonas, 90
Sayyaf, Abd al-Rabb al-Rasul,
157, 158
Scheer, Robert, 198
Schlafly, Phyllis, 43
Schulze, Reinhard, 46–7, 55, 267*n*
Schwartz, Stephen, 24, 219–20
science, history of, 30–1, 45, 265*n*
Scopes trial, 39–40, 41
Scott, Peter Dale, 113
Second World War, 7, 195, 249–50
Sendero Luminoso, 233
settler colonialism, 242–6; Israeli
settler movement, 222–5,
285–6*n*; in South Africa, 227–8
shah of Iran, 86, 121
sharia law, 60–1, 174–5
Shariati, Ali, 47, 58

Sharon, Ariel, 111–12, 214,
223–4
Sheehan, Neil, 183
Shulsky, Adam, 199
Shultz, George, 98
Siad Barre, Mohamed, 86
Sierra Leone, 209, 233, 244, 250,
251
Sipah-e-Muhammad, 152
Sipah-e-Sahaba, 152
slave trade, 51–2
Smith, William French, 238
Social Justice in Islam (Qutb),
55–6
Society of Muslim Brothers, 48–9,
56, 121, 167
Somalia, 85–6, 204
South Africa, 83, 101, 105, 244;
Angolan civil war, 78, 79–80,
90; Congolese civil wars, 74, 75;
constructive engagement and,
13, 92–5; counterinsurgency in,
232; democratic despotism,
246–7; Mozambican civil war,
89, 93–4; necklacing debate,
225–7; settler/native issue,
227–8; U.S. proxy-war strategy,
87–8
Soviet-U.S. détente, 115
Spaak, Paul-Henri, 73
Spain, unification of, 4–5
Spencer, Herbert, 262*n*
Stahl, Lesley, 190
Stone, Martin, 132
strategic sabotage, 169
Suciou-Foca, Nicole, 216
Sudan, 34–5, 52–3, 131
Suez Crisis, 242
suicide bombings, 219–22, 225,
285*n*, 286–7*n*
Sukarno, 121
Swerdlow, Noel, 30
Sydney S. Baron and Company, 93

Tablighi Jamaat, 134–5
Taliban, 13, 136, 150, 151, 176,
    279*n*, 287*n*; rise to power in
    Afghanistan, 159–63, 176–7
Tambo, Oliver, 226
Taney, Roger, 243
terrorism: Angolan civil war, 90,
    91; civilians as targets of, 88, 91,
    232; Congolese civil wars, 74–5,
    76; contra war, 101–2, 116–18;
    counterinsurgency and, 231–2;
    crime/terrorism distinction,
    229–30; Culture Talk and,
    219–21; genocide and, 11;
    global-local connections, 252;
    guerrilla/terrorist distinction,
    233; Israeli state terrorism,
    212–15, 222–5, 247–8;
    Mozambican civil war, 89, 91;
    necklacing, 225–7; political
    basis of, 61–2, 219, 255–6;
    popular support, need for,
    163–4; proxy wars and, 87, 88;
    routes to, 251. *see also* Islamist
    terror; U.S. embrace of terror;
    war on terror
treaties, U.S. withdrawal from,
    207–8
Tshombe, Moise, 70, 75
Tuhamy, Hassan, 85
Tunisia, 134
Tunney, John, 82, 83
Tunney Amendment, 81–2
Turkey, 48

Uday, Amnar, 198
Uganda, 251
Union for the Total Independence
    of Angola (Unita), 77, 78,
    89–90, 92, 93
Union Minière du Haut-Katanga,
    70
United Nations, 91; Angolan civil
war, 80; International Drug
    Control Program, 143, 153; ICC
    and, 209; Iraq sanctions regime,
    179, 180–1, 185–94; U.S.
    disregard for, 203–7
United States: Afghanistan
    invasion of 2001, 133, 183,
    229–30; al-Qaeda, similarity to,
    257–8; civil-rights movement,
    42, 44, 243; direct war against
    militant nationalism, switch to,
    178–9; genocide of colonial
    period, 6; Gulf War, 167, 179,
    180, 182, 183–4, 194–6, 204;
    intelligence failures regarding
    Iraq, 198–201; international
    rule of law, dispensing with,
    202–11, 256–7; Iraq, alliance
    with, 122, 180, 181–3; Iraq,
    peacetime bombing of, 185; Iraq
    invasion of 2003, 24, 180,
    196–202, 207, 217–18, 258–60;
    Iraq sanctions regime, 187,
    190–1; Israel, special
    relationship with, 240–6;
    Israeli-Palestinian conflict,
    211–12, 213; Middle East, "new
    regional order" policy
    regarding, 201–2; Pakistan,
    relations with, 125–6; political
    Islam, change in attitude
    toward, 120–2; preemptive war,
    policy of, 211; press freedom,
    erosion of, 239–40; propaganda
    programs, 196–201;
    "responsibility for its own
    actions" issue, 250–3, 255;
    settler colonialism, triumph of,
    242–4, 246; Soviet-U.S. détente,
    115; Taliban's rise to power
    and, 159–61; Vietnam War,
    64–5, 68, 231, 235–6, 239, 260;
    weapons of mass destruction

United States (*continued*)
used against Iraq, 194–6; "world domination through absolute military superiority" policy, 210–11. *see also* Cold War; 9/11 terrorist attacks; political Christianity; proxy wars; U.S. embrace of terror; war on terror; *specific administrations and agencies*
University of Nebraska, 137
Unocal company, 160
UPITN, 93
U.S. embrace of terror, 13; Angolan civil war, 90; Casey's role, 87; Congolese civil wars, 76; constructive engagement and, 92; contra war, 101–2, 116–18; cost to United States, 233–8, 255–6; increasing levels of terrorism over time, 118; Iraq-Iran War, 122; low-intensity conflict, 88, 95, 97–100; official condemnations of terrorism, 92; in post-Cold War period, 250–1; terrorism directed at United States, relation to, 255–6; training for proxy forces, 116, 169

Venture of Islam, The (Hodgson), 29
Vidal, Gore, 256
Vietnam, 100
Vietnam War, 64–5, 68, 231, 235–6, 239, 260
violence, 3–4; modernity and, 4–8; native violence, 8–10. *see also* terrorism
Von Sponeck, Hans, 191, 192
Vorster, John, 94

Waghelstein, Col. John D., 95
Wahhab, Muhammad Ibn Abdul, 52
Wahhabism, 24, 52, 220
war on terror, 12, 179; changes needed in United States to win fight against terrorism, 260; Islamist terror, common ground with, 230; as offensive imperial war, 259; rule of law and, 257; self-righteous and punitive conduct of, 230–1
War Powers Act, 81, 82
Washington Times, 93, 110
Watson, Robert, 204, 205–6
weapons of mass destruction, 255; Iraqi program, 181, 182, 184–5, 186, 193–4, 198–201, 206; U.S. use against Iraq, 194–6
Webb, Gary, 236
Weber, Max, 5
"West, the," 28–30
What Went Wrong? (Lewis), 23, 24–5
Wolfowitz, Paul, 199, 201, 210
Wolin, Sheldon, 239
Worden, Gen. Simon, 196
World Trade Center bombing of 1993, 135, 139, 234–5
Wretched of the Earth, The (Fanon), 8, 9–10
Wright, Jim, 113
Wright, Lawrence, 126–7

Yariv, Gen. Aharon, 112
Young, Andrew, 80
Yousef, Ramzi Ahmed, 139, 234
Yusuf, Brig. Muhammad, 138

Zahir Shah, king of Afghanistan, 125, 158–9
Zia ul-Haq, Mohammad, 125, 126, 142, 149–50, 176, 249, 287n

© Eileen Barroso

Mahmood Mamdani, a third-generation East African of Indian descent, grew up in Kampala, Uganda, and received his Ph.D. from Harvard in 1974. Since 1999 he has been the Herbert Lehman Professor of Government in the Departments of Anthropology and International Affairs, and director of the Institute of African Studies, at Columbia University. He taught at the University of Dar-es-Salaam in Tanzania, Makerere University in Kampala, and the University of Cape Town in South Africa before coming to New York. He lives in New York and Kampala with his wife and son.

Printed in the United States
by Baker & Taylor Publisher Services